The poetry of
W. S. GRAHAM

FOR J. H. PRYNNE

The poetry of
W. S. GRAHAM

TONY LOPEZ

EDINBURGH UNIVERSITY PRESS

© Tony Lopez 1989
Edinburgh University Press
22 George Square, Edinburgh

Set in Linotron Palatino
and printed in Great Britain by
Redwood Burn Limited,
Trowbridge, Wilts

British Library Cataloguing
  in Publication Data
Lopez, Anthony
The poetry of W. S. Graham.
1. Poetry in English. Graham,
   W. S. (William Sydney), 1918–1986
I. Title
821'.912

ISBN 0 85224 587 4
ISBN 0 85224 588 2 pbk

Contents

	Acknowledgements	
1	Life and Contacts	1
2	The Early Poems	26
3	The White Threshold	41
4	The Nightfishing	61
5	Malcolm Mooney's Land	80
6	Implements in their Places	100
7	Conclusions	125
	Notes	133
	Bibliography	138
	Index	169

Acknowledgements

My main debt (and also much admiration and affection) is expressed in the dedication. I should also like to thank Edwin Morgan for his advice and Mrs Graham for permission to quote from poems, manuscripts and letters by W. S. Graham and for her patience and help. Robin and Sylvia Skelton not only gave me access to Graham manuscripts but also their extended and very generous hospitality. Nigel Wheale took an early interest in the project as an editor of *Ideas & Production*; Neil Reeve of *Swansea Review* and Peter Kravitz of *Edinburgh Review* have also published early versions of work that appears here.

Mrs Kemp, Librarian of Newbattle Abbey College and Mr Simpson of the manuscript department of the National Library of Scotland have been especially helpful. Alan Clodd, Bill Featherston, John Heath-Stubbs, Richard Kerridge, Sara Lopez, Ralph Maud, Ian Patterson, Peter Riley and Simon Shaw have all helped this project along. The Master and Fellows of Gonville & Caius College, Cambridge, have provided me with research expenses on more than one occasion. My sincere thanks to all those mentioned here and in the notes.

CHAPTER ONE   1

Life and Contacts

William Sydney Graham was born at 11 a.m. on 19 November 1918, at 1 Hope Street, Greenock, Renfrewshire, Scotland, son of Alexander Graham (journeyman engineer) and Margaret Graham (née Mac-Dermid). He attended Greenock High School, where he took the Higher Day School Certificate, before leaving in the third year. His home was a top-floor tenement in a hard-pressed community overlooking the docks and shipyards of the Firth of Clyde. Graham was very keen to continue his studies but 'owing to a collapse in the economic position of his family he could not be sent to University'.[1] At fourteen he was apprenticed as a draughtsman to a Glasgow engineering firm, and for two years he attended part-time classes in structural engineering at Stow College, Glasgow. Then, while still serving as an apprentice, and much to the dismay of his family, he took up evening classes at Glasgow University to study art appreciation and literature. After a five-year apprenticeship he became, like his father, a journeyman engineer.[2] His address at this time was 13 Brisbane Street, Greenock. He was a member of the Association of Engineering and Shipbuilding Draughtsmen (AESD) trade union.

In October 1938 he was awarded a bursary to Newbattle Abbey College, a residential Adult Education College, which had been set up only two years before Graham's time there. The college is a unique institution in Scotland, offering working people the opportunity to return to full-time education, with a special course of study tailored to their needs. Graham joined a group of forty-six students who, like himself, had been working for some time. Many of them had come up through the Trades Union movement, and their studies were either in the Social Sciences or the Humanities. The teaching was conducted as much as possible in the manner of a university, with lectures and discussion groups. Visiting lecturers came from the University of Edinburgh and the standard of teaching appears to have been very good indeed. The Warden was a fervent believer in individual tuition in what he called the 'Oxford' tradition. At the same time he was aware of the difficulty of adapting to long unrelieved bouts of study and instituted a half-hour break for activities such as Scottish dancing, ball-games and running. All the students were expected to do some forestry, gardening or similar work on two afternoons a week. In the session 1938-39 (when Graham was resident) some students worked at turning an old stable into a college theatre.³ Graham was a resident student for one year at the college.

He seems to have been a successful student, both in his studies and in the general life of the college, active in student music and drama. Among the college productions in which Graham took a part was *Riders to the Sea* by J. M. Synge. He could not be said to have fitted in easily, however. He was self-consciously presenting himself in the role of the poet as outsider, and his contemporaries relate various stunts designed to impress on them his oddness and originality. He was regarded, at least by some of them, as a *poseur*. He was, according to his contemporaries, already writing poetry at that time.

The course of study in Literature was broadly historical, beginning with some Anglo-Saxon and working through to modern writers. Major topics in the three terms included Early Scottish Poetry, the Lake Poets and the work of T. S. Eliot.⁴ Graham also attended lectures in Philosophy given by Mr John Mack, assistant warden of the college, that included a term devoted to the Pre-Socratics.⁵ His subsequent and continuing interest in the Pre-Socratics shows up especially in his poems *The Nightfishing* and *Implements In Their Places*.

Among the Newbattle students at that time was Agnes (Nessie) Dunsmuir, who later lived with Graham on and off for some years before they were married in 1954.

In 1939, in order to avoid conscription into the forces, Graham went to Eire, where he worked on a farm in Galway, travelled with a fair in the south, and then worked at the docks in Dublin.⁶ Later he was employed as a precision engineer in a torpedo factory on Clydeside. During the war, Graham also worked briefly in an experimental school in southwest Scotland, whilst Nessie was 'interviewing for the Ministry of Food'.⁷

In 1942 Graham's first book was published by David Archer's Parton Press. Archer had run the Parton Street Bookshop at Red Lion Square, London, which had been *the* meeting place for young writers and artists who came from the provinces to explore the London Literary scene.⁸ Archer, who was independently wealthy and very generous to those whom he considered gifted, would offer visitors somewhere to stay. He first published David Gascoyne, George Barker, Dylan Thomas and W. S. Graham.⁹ In the early days of the war he moved to Glasgow, opened the Scott Street Arts Centre, and gathered another circle round him. Graham's *Cage Without Grievance* was illustrated by Robert Frame and Benjamin Creme, and it was at Creme's invitation that Graham moved into David Archer's flat in Sandyford Place, Sauchiehall Street, Glasgow. There Archer provided free accommodation for the painters Douglas Campbell, Benjamin Creme and Jankel Adler, the sculptor Helen Biggar, and the actress Julian Order (a girlfriend of Graham's). Graham moved in with the resolve to become a full-time poet, something that he kept to for the rest of his life.[10] At the Arts Centre and at Sandyford Place, Graham was in touch with Hugh MacDiarmid, Dylan Thomas, Robert Colquhoun and Robert MacBryde. Archer organised debates, musical and dramatic evenings, while Graham gave poetry performances of his own and traditional works.[11]

The two Roberts (Colquhoun and MacBryde) were a famous gay couple of painters whose outrageous drunken behaviour and fierce Scottish pride became lively features of the Fitzrovia scene in wartime London. The poet David Wright met Graham in company with the two Roberts (and the rest of the Scott Street crowd) in the summer of 1944. They were all staying in Julian Orde's top-floor flat in Highgate, London.[12] The two Roberts were regulars at the *York Minster* known as the 'French Pub' in Soho and Graham, Michael Ayrton and John Minton were also often there. The two Roberts lived in Minton's studio and, when he inherited his family fortune, Minton was a very generous patron to Graham.[13] Graham's second published book *The Seven Journeys* was published in 1944 in the Poetry Scotland series from MacLellan of Glasgow. His daughter was also born in this year.[14]

Late in 1944 Graham and Nessie Dunsmuir went to live in a nest of caravans called the Wheelhouse at Germoe, near Praa Sands, southeast of Marazion in Cornwall.[15] They were visited there by David Wright in August 1946 and he describes meeting Graham's fanatic disciple Jimmy Burns Singer who was at that time living under canvas close by.[16] In 1945 Graham's third book, *2nd Poems*, was published in Tambimuttu's Editions Poetry London series in association with the publishers Nicholson and Watson.

Late in 1946 or early in 1947, Graham and Nessie Dunsmuir moved to a fisherman's cottage at 23 Cliff Street, Mevagissey, in Cornwall. Soon after this they separated for some time and Graham lived for a while with the American academic and critic Vivienne Koch of Columbia University, with whom he went to America. He gave a series of lectures at New York University entitled 'Forces in Contemporary British Literature'. Vivienne Koch also managed to arrange an 'Atlantic Award'. 'The White Threshold' was published in *Sewanee Review* and 'A Note on W. S. Graham' (by Vivienne Koch) appeared in the same issue. The article, if not a collaboration, must at least have had Graham's approval. Vivienne Koch wrote a number of intelligent reviews and articles about Graham's work, certainly the best that had been written at that time. No doubt this helped to bring his work to the notice of a wider audience and it may well have influenced his later career. During this period Nessie Dunsmuir was living in Paris and teaching at the Berlitz school.[17] 'Vivienne' turns up in the late poem 'Private Poem to Norman MacLeod' and Graham's experience in New York is touched on in 'Implements'.

On his return from America in 1948, Graham lived in Mevagissey but stayed there only until 1949, the year in which *The White Threshold* was published by Faber and Faber. Though he was working quite well on his poem 'The Nightfishing', he complained of loneliness and his health was far from good.[18] He suffered from a duodenal ulcer which was the result of heavy drinking while eating very little – presumably both because he was very poor and as a result of his use of benzedrine, which diminishes the appetite. Graham used the drug to help him while writing both *The White Threshold* and *The Nightfishing*. His weight had dropped to just over nine stone, the ulcer caused some vomiting of blood and Graham was advised to drink only milk. He felt that he was progressing well with his work, however, and he saw this in part at least as a result of visiting America with Vivienne Koch and broadening his experience.

Later in 1949 Graham lived for a while in a basement flat on the corner of Grays Inn Road and Guildford Street, London (lent to him by Donald Harwood) and then at 3 Warwick Gardens, London W.18, with Vivienne Koch. She was working on her book *W. B. Yeats: The Tragic Phase*, which was published by Routledge in 1951.

Julian MacLaren-Ross recorded his impressions of Graham in London at this time:

> One of my last memories of Minton was connected also with a poet, W. S. Graham. It is not the most pleasant memory I have of him, but before this happened I had already found that Graham in some way contrived to promote unpleasantness around him. Unpleasant things tended to happen in his vicinity.
>
> Graham himself was not unpleasant, just inordinately prickly. If one entered a club or pub where he happened to be and acknowledged him simply with a nod or smile he would call out 'You didn't say good-afternoon to me,' making out of this an issue which could, unless ruthlessly cut short at the start, last for what was left of the day. If on the other hand you greeted him by saying 'Good-afternoon', he would morosely reply 'What's good about it,' making you feel that you had tactlessly interrupted his meditations on some unfortunate mishap that had overtaken him a few moments earlier.
>
> Or else you had omitted to add his name to the salutation, another terrible offence (if this were done he would affect to believe you were addressing someone else, and glance all round in search of this non-existent other person), or alternatively you had added his surname instead of calling him Sydney as his friends did, thus publicly proclaiming that you'd no wish to be considered a friend of his.
>
> Even if the difficult hurdle of the initial greeting were successfully surmounted, any chance remark could give rise to a fancied

slight, and endless argument would ensue or reproaches if not actual abuse would be heaped upon your head.

Graham was of sturdy build, dressed as a rule in blue-grey tweeds and had light brown curly hair, a snub nose and protuberant grey-blue eyes. My first introduction to his work came through Kitty of Bloomsbury who had a great belief in it and gave me his second volume of verse with the prophecy that he would become another Dylan Thomas; and I see that the above description of him sounds as if he physically resembled Dylan, which was not the case. The total effect was quite other, being predominately Scottish: his lips moreover were a very different shape, always twisted or prehensilely thrust out to accommodate themselves to his accent which was also Scots to a degree.

His expression was that of one stolidly bearing up under constant injustice or undeserved misfortune, and an atmosphere of brooding perpetually surrounded him. He sat over his beer as if reviewing every insult he had ever received with the purpose of devising effectual retorts for the future. In fact nobody insulted him at all and most people had a great respect for his poems.

Sydney Graham was quite the most competitive poet I have ever met: and this in a profession where competitiveness and rivalry by far surpasses any existing among writers of prose . . .

Dylan Thomas might well have had W. S. Graham in mind when declaring that poetry was not a competition.[19]

Graham and Vivienne Koch separated in 1950, and in the same year he was employed as a copywriter by the advertising firm Foote, Cone and Belding Ltd, where he wrote copy for the Shell account.[20] His letters of 1950 are mostly addressed from 'The Office'. There is mention of *The White Threshold* being reviewed in the papers and, perhaps more important to a poet in Graham's position, was the response from T. S. Eliot who (as his publisher) took him out to lunch and discussed his work in detail with him. Eliot praised 'The Nightfishing' especially as a successful long poem.

Later in 1950 Graham was in Paris, reunited with Nessie Dunsmuir. They were married in 1954 and in 1955 (the year in which *The Nightfishing* was published) they moved back to Cornwall, where they lived at the Old Coastguard cottages, Gurnard's Head, near St Ives from March 1956.[21] A visitor remembers the Grahams' household at that time:

> They were living in one of a terrace of abandoned Coastguard cottages which had a leaking roof, no cooking stove, no electricity, an outside toilet and no bathroom. I remember visiting them and taking food with me – but there was nothing to cook it on. On my next visit I took them a primus stove – before this they

were cooking on an open fire, when there was fuel. They used an oil lamp for light and a paraffin stove for heat.[22]

Nancy Wynne-Jones first met the Grahams in 1957 in St Ives and went often to visit them at Gurnard's Head. She describes Graham as 'a gregarious but shy man who was unable to face people without the support of a drink'.[23] She also mentions his close friends among the artists of the St Ives community, his love of music and his beautiful singing voice.

Graham was to subsidise his way of life by the sale of his manuscripts. The first indication of this is in a letter to Professor Robin Skelton in 1958.[24] Graham was in need of money to pay back rent, buy food, and send cash to Mrs Graham who had gone to her birthplace, Blantyre in Scotland, to be with her mother who was seriously ill. Professor Skelton sent money and sent his poems to Graham for comment. On 5 November 1958 Mrs Graham had stopped her seasonal work for a local hotel, and the Grahams were fixing up their house for the winter gales. The Coastguard cottages were of course in a very exposed position on a headland facing the Atlantic. Visitors mentioned include Michael Snow (sculptor and previous husband of Mrs Skelton) and Bryan Wynter, the painter, who brought a welcome bottle of whisky. Graham also mentions an adventure: falling off the roof of a girlfriend's house and breaking his foot as well as damaging a kneecap. This injury was to cause him trouble repeatedly, hence his self-characterising in *Malcolm Mooney's Land*: 'clumping taliped' and 'my impediment' (*Collected Poems*, pp.143 and 150).

In 1962 the Grahams went to stay with Nancy Wynne-Jones and she lent them a house opposite her own in Trevaylor. They lived almost as a family, the Grahams eating dinner at Miss Wynne-Jones's house. Graham is said to have enjoyed taking his turn at the cooking and to have done it well.[25] In 1964 they all travelled to Greece together and this exotic change of scene was later used by Graham in several poems.[26]

In 1968 or thereabouts the Grahams moved into a cottage in Madron owned by Nancy Wynne-Jones, where they lived rent free. They suffered some considerable hardship, none the less. Robin Skelton helped them now and then, and eventually became an important patron.

Skelton set out the terms of his support for Graham in a letter dated 11 June 1972. First there was a gift of £50 enclosed with that letter. Thereafter Graham was to send Skelton all of his working materials, notebooks, manuscripts, typescripts, as and when they were thought to be finished with. In exchange, Skelton paid Graham an allowance of £25 a month. It is clear that had Skelton not made this collection, much of the material might have been scattered in separate sales. Graham estimated his income over a three-year period as £45 a

Life and Contacts 7

month, so the payments from Skelton were the greater part of his income and amounted to much more than his combined royalties from Penguin and Faber, and fees for broadcasts and readings. The fees for publication of Graham's poems in *The Malahat Review* must be added to the amount which Skelton paid Graham, since Skelton was the sole editor of that journal and paid separately for the poems he published. Some of the material was also re-published in British journals, thereby gaining Graham extra fees.

In 1973 Graham visited Canada, where he gave a series of poetry readings at various Universities and Colleges. His letters to Bill Featherston, a lecturer at Calgary School of Art, gave the best picture of Graham's character that I have found:

> Dear Bill, Come on the Boy there! How lovely to hear the old shitgravelling voice. What can I say? How angry I am you thinking that I would not be arranging to see you. Forchristsake I was waiting till everything was fixed which is not even yet. The letters I am writing to various schools in Canada are keeping me busy like a fool and there it is I suppose I really am coming over there to the wampum land at last.
> how lovely to be touched by your irresistible rustironic voice. (Clean the m of your typewriter.) My dear Bill, I took it for granted you would be on the scene when I did my bit there. But I would have been telling you anyhow. Now I answer your letter. Why should November be a lousy month for Alberta? Will it be cold?
> About the class thing. What shall I do? I suppose I am lower working class. Shall I be superior or inferior? How shall I behave? What shall I wear? I'm coming anyhow and I'll have to make the best of it fuckthem. Come my boy. When you say, quote – 'Things have not been exactly rosy for me in the past year' why dont you try to get back here, Bill? Is it all that difficult? Are you still ok with Alan? All that I know nothing about. You think youve got troubles kid! I am hoping to get to Canada before my lower teeth go to pieces. I am breaking up daily.[27]

Graham's uneasiness at what he took to be his rather humble social position explains a good deal about him. Many accounts of his behaviour indicate that he was comfortable only in the company of close friends. His continuing interest in the difficulty of communication, and in language as the subject of his later poetry, was thus by no means the theoretical matter that it is in academic literary studies.

Skelton helped in Graham's dealings with Faber and Faber and applied through the Royal Society of Literature (of which Skelton is a fellow) for support. Graham was eventually granted a Civil List Pension of £500 a year in 1974. It was thus thirty-two years from when Graham made the writing of poetry his sole occupation (on the publication of his first book in 1942) until he gained a kind of basic security with his Civil List pension. Throughout his career he relied on the generosity of patrons and on the hard work of his wife Nessie, and they accepted hardship rather than change their way of life. The 1970s were productive years for Graham, new poems were published regularly and his reputation grew. Both *Malcolm Mooney's Land* (1970) and *Implements In Their Places* (1977) were choices of the Poetry Book Society and Graham was often asked to give readings of his work.

In Canada and elsewhere, Graham's public style at poetry readings was to steady himself with large quantities of whisky, to be directly challenging and often aggressive towards the audience. Graham had the kind of reputation that Dylan Thomas and George Barker had. This public style, whether it did Graham harm or not, was certainly reinforced when he went to live among the St Ives artists. His closest friends (Sven Berlin, Roger Hilton, Bryan Wynter) all had reputations for heavy alcohol and/or drug use. Some idea of the way of life of the younger painters and writers of the St Ives community can be gained from the no doubt unreliable novel *The Dark Monarch* by Sven Berlin.[28] Graham appears in Berlin's book thinly disguised as 'Jamie Greenock', while Nessie is called 'Tessa'. Roger Hilton's life and alcoholism is described in the introduction to his *Night Letters*, and Bryan Wynter's use of mescalin for his work is mentioned in the Hayward Gallery exhibition catalogue, *Bryan Wynter 1915–75*.[29]

St Ives is a resort town in which the remnants of a fishing community co-exist with what has been the most influential separate artistic community in Britain. Fifty years before the School could be thought of as established, artists went to St Ives for the light and the landscape. Early names associated with the place are J. M. W. Turner, Stanhope Forbes, Norman Garstin and James McNeil Whistler.[30]

As it was portrayed more and more by visiting artists, St Ives gained a reputation, and artists began to settle there. The property was very cheap and rents were very low, so that studio space (in sail lofts) was easy to get. The artists who settled there visited London to sell their work and eventually there were regular shows in St Ives before the Royal Academy Summer Exhibition. A train was chartered to take St Ives painters' works to London for the Royal Academy selection competition.

Wartime conditions in London led to many people's wishing to live in the provinces, and the cheap accommodation, together with the by then established artist's community, made St Ives seem very attractive indeed. The important names in the St Ives modern period are Alfred Wallis, Ben Nicholson, Christopher Wood, Barbara Hepworth, Naum Gabo, Bernard Leach, Peter Lanyon, Roger Hilton, Patrick Heron, Bryan Wynter, Alan Lowndes, and Terry Frost. The names are a short history of modernism in British painting. Nicholson and Wood visited St Ives in 1928 and discovered the paintings of the completely self-taught 'primitive' Alfred Wallis (1855–1942), who helped them towards a quite new way of working. Nicholson, Hepworth and Gabo moved to St Ives in 1939. With the potter Bernard Leach, who had imported a fundamental approach to ceramics from his studies in Japan, they formed the beginning of the modern community through the war years.[31]

Graham's work, some of which is based on his own experience as a fisherman, links with the experiments of this community at its inception.[32] Hepworth's idea of a work that breaks the subject-object relation of the artist to the world, is paralleled in Graham's portrayal of a fragmented self, constituted through experience.[33] His continual interest in writing a voyage poem which explores the nature of the self through the experience of language, takes up what he finds in the subjects and methods of Wallis, and then the younger abstract or near abstract painters who brought St Ives to international fame. Graham is in a special sense the poet of the modern St Ives community and what it represents culturally in postwar Britain. He wrote poems for Alfred Wallis: 'The Voyages of Alfred Wallis', Peter Lanyon: 'The Thermal Stair', Sven Berlin: 'The Song of the Tower', Bryan Wynter: 'Wynter and the Grammarsow', 'Dear Bryan Wynter', Roger Hilton: 'Lines on Roger Hilton's Watch', 'Hilton Abstract', Tony O'Malley: 'Master Cat and Master Me' and Alan Lowndes: 'For Valerie and Alan'.[34]

Both in *Malcolm Mooney's Land* and in *Implements In Their Places*, Graham wrote about his life on the western tip of Cornwall. As in a quiet way he became the recorder (and thus a constructor) of the St Ives community, his attention turned also to Scotland, where he found much in common between Cornwall and West Strathclyde. His *Collected Poems 1942–1977* was published in 1979 and it caused some interest in the national press. Graham's blue smock and fierce eyes looked out from a photo-feature in the *Observer Magazine*, where he was allowed to gently mock interviews by interviewing himself.[35]

He was in demand for public readings in the 1980s, and even did a short tour of Scotland organised by *Cencrastus*, reading in Edinburgh for the festival and at the Third Eye Centre in Glasgow. He was often ill, however, and travelling was a strain. He died at home in Madron on 9 January 1986 after a long illness.

With the publication of his *Collected Poems 1942–77*, Graham began to be recognised as a major British poet whose work is quite different from anything else we have – quite independent, that is, from the dominant trend in British poetry since the 1950s. He used a great variety of language and forms and wrote ambitious poems, whether narratives, epistles, ballads, elegies or short lyrics. He extended the range of poetic usage by experiment and helped to conserve traditional forms and vocabulary against the current trend of restriction in the poetic voice.

Graham's recognition was by no means universal. His *Collected Poems* was published with the financial support of the Scottish Arts Council and, like his other books, it was not a best seller. He was a neglected poet whose work turned inwards in certain productive ways that make him now seem central in the development of British and American poetry in the Pound/Eliot tradition. Just how it is that Graham seemed to come from nowhere to this position of being the author of a body of work that is influential among contemporary poets is what I would like to consider here. One useful version of the story is given by Michael Schmidt:

> *The Nightfishing* appeared in the same year as Larkin's *The Less Deceived*. It came out when the Movement was in the ascendant, and despite the impressive novelty of Graham's book, the positive development from his earlier style, it excited little interest. Fifteen years passed before another collection appeared, years of hardship and general neglect.[36]

This account of what Schmidt calls Graham's 'unlucky' career suggests that it was an unfortunate and arbitrary change in taste that affected Graham's position in England. This is far from the case, for the perception of what was good poetry in England in 1955 is something that was carefully constructed by those (the Movement critics and poets) whose interests were best served by a shift in public taste. And we have been served by that same group (and their inheritors) to this day.

But Graham's career did not begin in England. Before anything else Graham is a Scottish poet, and it is in this context that he must first be understood. The histories of Scottish Literature do not make much of him. Duncan Glen in his *Hugh MacDiarmid and the Scottish Renaissance*, is fair to Graham, but writing in 1964 he was not able to say anything about Graham's later work. Alan Bold notices one or two Scots words as evidence of Graham's heritage but finds the poetry 'obscure' and 'essentially private'.[37] Roderick Watson's accounts are positive about Graham's later work but add nothing to what Michael Schmidt has already said.[38]

MacDiarmid's response to Graham's first book was a mixture of high praise and serious reservations and it shows how distant Graham was from a Scottish National Literature as conceived by MacDiarmid and his friends:

> Sydney Graham is a real poet of calibre Scotland has seldom produced in the past five hundred years. Not only so, but he is entirely a new kind of poet for Scotland to produce, since Scotland's trouble all along in developing its literature and other arts

> has been the extraordinarily anti-aesthetic nature of our people (the least artistic of all civilised people) and Graham's poetry is purely aesthetic. Since Graham is a young man, that means, then, that this poetry has been produced under other influences than have usually operated on young Scottish poets, and that those influences are non-Scottish. It remains to be seen to what extent they can be successfully combined with the Scottish tradition and whether finally that combination is desirable or not. In the meantime at least this work would seem to have no root in its native soil . . . I cannot regard Graham's work as in any way answering to the crucial needs and possibilities of our time. It is not responsible work in this sense; it is an adolescent playing with the materials of great poetry . . . [The materials] give out their lovely lights and colours not less bountifully when they are tossed about capriciously by a child's hands than when they are ordered into a work of art by a great poet, and hence it is all too easy to mistake the one activity for the other . . . 'Cage Without Grievance' is a self-convicting title. The poet should be not a contented cage-bird in no matter how ornate a cage, but a great outgoing spirit, with full personal and social responsibility and with complete intellectual adequacy.[39]

What Graham thought of MacDiarmid's project of creating a synthetic literary Scots is clear from the following letter:

> I now consider myself as banished, more or less, from the Scottish Lit scene, which I don't hold with and seems to get more embarrassing with its playing bards and glimmerin lufts keekin wi sna. The final wow was reading an intimation of a ceremonious dinner for presenting the Bard (MacD) with his portrait and it was written in this plastic Scots (which all the bards have a different idea of) and ended by giving the address of some office where tickets could be had and the *telephone* number, and, dodging the leprous word he ends with – 'Farspeak 7638' – I don't know that did it.[40]

Yet Graham and MacDiarmid were friends throughout their careers, and each wrote verse tributes to the other that were well meaning and rang true.[41]

What is clear is that Graham decided that he wished to make his mark through the English Literary scene, though he wished to make it as a Scot. He moved south and connected with the literary scene of his day. He made the best of connections (David Archer, Tambimuttu, T. S. Eliot) for establishing a career in poetry published in London, but he did not (or could not) live for any time or in a settled way in the English capital; his visits there were all sprees. He had not grown up in London and he never took part in literary journalism, which is how almost all recent poets have made their living, unless they had academic careers.

Without building an audience in Scotland in the way, for example, that Edwin Morgan has, and without moving into literary journalism or associated trades (though he did, as we have seen, try his hand at advertising), Graham was not felt as a literary presence beyond his books. Many of our serious writers (especially in the post-1945 era) have kept their names in print and their voices on the air and this has had an important effect on the first reception of their works. Graham went from Greenock to the Land's End peninsula via Glasgow and London. He became very remote from any possible Scottish audience therefore, and he was not on hand in London or in any way established when the Movement took power.

Blake Morrison's *The Movement* provides us with an account of how these poets (D. J. Enright, Kingsley Amis, Robert Conquest, Donald Davie, John Holloway, Elizabeth Jennings, Philip Larkin, John Wain and Thom Gunn) came to prominence.[42] The personnel was announced by various means but finally established by the publication of two anthologies: Enright's *Poets of the 1950s*, and Conquest's *New Lines*.[43] Conquest was important as a propagandist for the Movement; if Davie was the most substantial theorist and critic of the group, Conquest was the populariser and his introduction to *New Lines* established the way in which the Movement would subsequently be seen.

In 'Thrills and Frills' Andrew Crozier has shown how the postwar canon as it is now perceived was founded by the poet-critics of the Movement and how their view of their position in the tradition of British poetry has survived and been extended without fundamental challenge to the present day.[44]

> When we trace the terms by which the canon was defined it becomes apparent that they are also those by which it was validated; controversy never infringed certain agreements, and these largely unexamined positions cover major exclusions of poetic discourse. In terms of the poetic history of the period the present-day reader is ill served indeed.

The canon that Crozier is beginning to question is that given by Blake Morrison in his monograph on Heaney. Crozier shows how Morrison's version of the British poetic tradition 'derives its force more from its air of unassuming conviction than from anything it says about the poets in question' and that 'it functions rather like those systems of radio interference used to jam other signals' (Crozier p. 202). The 'other signals' are those aspects of British writing that have been completely obscured since the Movement was established. The canon as it is now seen (according to Morrison, Larkin-Hughes-Heaney) completely ignores the Modernism of Pound, Eliot and Joyce

Life and Contacts 13

and its subsequent influence on poetry published in Britain. To understand this we must look a little more closely at what 'The Movement' was and how it came about.

From Morrison's survey and from Crozier's account of it, we can be sure that while there was 'no membership, no push or direction, no common programme or general agreement on principles' (Crozier p. 207) there was a common ideology – or at least a set of ideological characteristics. These were: 'Low Church and middle-class origins; the concern with classlessness and upward social mobility; the hostility to the "posh" and the "phoney" and the nostalgia for traditional order, the connection with the provincial universities'.[45] These ideological characteristics meant that they developed, as a group, a rather insular approach to literature and culture in general, although Enright was knowledgeable about German Literature, and Conquest and Davie were interested in Russian poetry. When it came to English literature they all worked for a purer form of the English tradition than that which they had inherited from the Modernists Pound, Eliot and Joyce. That part of English literature that was most influenced by foreign elements was either attacked or marginalised by Movement writers as their rather tentative group identity began to take shape. They began to see a common aim in connecting with the pre-1914 tradition of English poetry, and recovering the traditional values associated with pre-Modernist art.

Larkin's 'MCMXIV' (first published in 1960) is an important poem in this respect, because, as Morrison has shown, it is not only a monument to the youth of 1914 lost in the Great War, but also to a lost pure English poetic tradition that was broken by Modernism. Larkin clarified his position much later in 1973 when interviewed concerning his anthology *The Oxford Book of Twentieth-Century Verse*:

> I had in my mind a notion that there might have been what I'll call, for want of a better phrase, an English tradition coming from the nineteenth century with people like Hardy, which was interrupted partly by the Great War, when many English poets were killed off, and partly by the really tremendous impact of Yeats, whom I think of as Celtic, and Eliot, whom I think of as American.[46]

We can see that the most representative and influential Movement poet thought of Yeats and Eliot as alien to the English tradition. Davie, while he accepted some of Yeats and Eliot, had his own serious reservations:

> *Ash Wednesday* is a poem in the Symbolist tradition. Images are ranged about, and the meaning flowers out of the space between them. Poetry of this sort depends upon the dislocation of ordinary normal syntax, and so it can never be written in a pure

diction. It seems to me that the most enduring work of both W. B. Yeats and T. S. Eliot is that in which they have reached a pure diction.[47]

Davie had a rather complex relationship with the work of Ezra Pound: on the one hand he devoted much space to it in his critical writings; on the other, his conclusions were seldom positive. He accused Pound of 'scrapping the contracts traditionally observed between poet and reader' by failing to provide 'metrical landmarks to assist us'.[48] By other Movement writers, Pound was ignored. Joyce (who had been drastically misread for English readers by Eliot, who suggested that *Ulysses* was importantly a reworking of classical myth, rather than a radical unworking of the English language) was on the whole dismissed impatiently by Movement writers as an eccentric whose work produced no issue.[49] Beckett, an important inheritor of those Modernists who had worked in England and in English, was ignored by almost all the Movement writers. Davie's account of Beckett's poems: 'a mish-mash of Joyce and Eliot', was rather extreme.[50] In each case we can see the 'English' Modernist writers cut off from the tradition to which they belonged and contributed.

Something that the Movement poets had in common was an aversion to the poetry of the previous decade and in particular to Dylan Thomas, whose *Collected Poems* was published in 1952.

> Thomas was identified as the major poetic reputation against whom any new generation of poets would have to react. This suggests, rightly, that some element of strategy was involved in the reaction: in the years 1952–4 the Movement poets were young and not yet properly established, and it was clearly in their interests to claim to be offering a departure from the leading figure of the day. But if the Movement tended to exaggerate their antipathy towards Thomas, the case against him was crucial to the development of their own artistic programme: through resistance to his work, the Movement became more sure of their own aims in writing. (Morrison, p. 146)

Morrison documents adverse comment on Thomas by Wain, Amis, Enright and Davie. He also shows how Amis's play *That Uncertain Feeling* parodied both Thomas's play *Under Milk Wood* and his poetry. Enright's poem 'On the Death of a Child' is a kind of 'revision' of Thomas's 'A Refusal to Mourn, the Death by Fire, of a Child in London' and Larkin's poem 'I Remember, I Remember' and Donald Davie's poem 'A Baptist Childhood' both 'revise' Thomas's 'Fern Hill'.[51] The Movement clearly had a debt to Thomas in that he was the established poet against whom they made their protest. He stood for the whole Neo-Romantic tendency because of his popularity and his position in the imagination of his generation.

Linda M. Shires has recorded the Movement's reaction to the poetry of the forties in this way:

> Looking back from the vantage point of the 1950s, the poets and critics of the Movement saw only an imagination gone wild ... The labels and paradigms they applied to the decade behind them were convenient but incorrect ... Desiring to restore a native poetry marked by restraint, logical argument and a realistic adherence to common life, the poets of the fifties insisted that the forties was a decade of punch-drunk apocalyptic writers, a time of irrational excess, a poetry solely of myth and dream. They dismissed the period as drowning in the illogical unconscious storms of such poets as Henry Treece, J. F. Hendry, and Dylan Thomas ... By associating this new subjectivity exclusively with the group known as the Apocalypse (headed by Hendry and Treece) and by choosing Dylan Thomas as the chief exponent of such excessive tendencies, the Movement critics falsified the period on several major counts ... As the most recent and best organised group of poets the forties had to offer, the romantic New Apocalypse offered a recognisable target. Yet by making the group stand for the decade, the Movement poets and later critics blurred important distinctions. They failed to separate the Apocalyptics from forerunners such as the Surrealists ... The Movement poets and propagandists ignored the central fact that the Apocalyptics originated in 1938 and probably rose to the peak of their influence in 1941 with their second group anthology rather than exercising an important influence throughout the 1940s.[52]

Her point is that the Movement critics took one tendency and made it stand for the decade, that they did not look into that one tendency carefully, and misrepresented it. They largely ignored the best of the war poets (such as Alun Lewis, Sidney Keyes and Keith Douglas), calling all the rest 'Apocalyptics'.

That the Movement poet-critics did to a greater or lesser extent misrepresent the writing of the previous decade is therefore agreed by Blake Morrison, Linda Shires and Andrew Crozier. These three are the only commentators with any kind of detachment from the issues and personalities involved.

The principal critic of this group who created a false view of the forties was Donald Davie. The best of his critical writing is so perceptive and so well reasoned that he has been very influential indeed. Michael Schmidt's retrospective view is quite likely to be coloured by his close association with Davie in more recent times. Graham the 'unlucky poet' who suffered from 'bad timing' was reviewed by Davie in just the terms that Shires describes.[53]

Davie's piece is a review of books by George Barker, Graham, and

Sheila Wingfield. He begins by attacking Barker and the forties in general:

> It is hard to be fair to Mr. George Barker. One sees him as the laureate of the Forties, that dire decade when the English poetic tradition came near to foundering altogether. The war aroused a temporary and wrong-headed enthusiasm for poetry, and on the swell of this enthusiasm rode in a generation of poets who had adopted from their revolutionary predecessors all the licences those masters had permitted themselves, while ignoring altogether the untraditional but equally stringent disciplines that Eliot and Yeats and Pound had submitted to. The only principle of poetic structure was the pun, the unit of poetic composition was the line that struck the reader in the midriff, imagery was either erotic or else thrown out trustfully on to the lap of the collective unconscious, and rhythms however shambling could always be excused as 'expressive'. Yet with all this slovenliness, the poet was never more arrogant; wrapping his singing-robe around him, he solemnly hectored and harangued his reader. This was intolerable but also ludicrous.

Graham is compared quite favourably with Barker:

> Mr. W. S. Graham ... is actually and potentially a much better poet. The worst of the mannerisms in his case is the hieratic solemnity with which he takes his own poetic vocation. For he is one of those poets who make the writing of poetry into the subject of the poems they write. The commonsense view is that this drastically limits the importance and the interest of what they write; and I think this is true. Yet if once we admit, as Mr. Graham seems to require, that a poem is an artefact, not a communique, it is difficult to complain about the materials that go into it – it is the making that counts, not what it is made of. And Mr. Graham's quality is apparent at once, when we see that instead of improvising line by line, he has obviously planned his long poem, 'The Nightfishing,' precisely as an artefact, as one thing whole in itself. This is to speak of what he planned, what he intended; whether he is wholly successful is another matter. On the literal level his poem is an account of a night's fishing in the open sea; allegorically it is an account of what it means to write a poem; on another level still it hints at the nature of all spiritual and devotional experience ... But 'The Nightfishing' remains a very impressive experiment. My misgivings have to do with the unvarying solemnity of the tone, the use of words such as 'ambitioned' and 'illusioned,' and (most of all) the rhythms.

Then Sheila Wingfield is mildly praised for her 'unpretentious' and 'provincial' writing:

Sheila Wingfield's 'A Kite's Dinner' is entitled 'Poems 1938–54.' Thus much of this volume too is the product of the Forties. But this poet, by virtue perhaps of a fortunate provincialism seems to have escaped the vogues and habits of the period. I am glad to report that she shows no signs of having read either Dylan Thomas or Sidney Keyes . . . this poet attempts nothing so closely integrated as 'The Nightfishing' . . . Of a meditation in verse one expects at best only a loose unity; and Sheila Wingfield's chief trouble is to prevent her poem dissolving into a sequence of separate pieces on related topics. She guards against this, paradoxically but with success, by skillfully varying metre, tone and vocabulary from one section to the next, inside of each of the four parts of her poem . . . It says a good deal for 'Women in Love' that it can be read aloud without embarrassment. This is more than can be said for 'The Nightfishing' though that poem supplies fitfully an excitement beyond the scope of Sheila Wingfield's mild and honest talent. In the ordinary way, to call a book of poems 'unpretentious' is to damn with faint praise; but when pretentiousness is so rife . . . it is, or is meant to be, quite high praise.

The comparison to Barker would seem at first to be of benefit to Graham in Davie's argument, but that with Sheila Wingfield has the opposite effect. None of the poets mentioned here is done a service by Davie, and the reader is misled in important ways. Our final assessment of Graham (if we follow Davie) is that he is not quite so bad as Barker but not so good as a very minor and 'provincial' poet. Notice also that Wingfield is praised (in contrast to Graham) for her 'honest' talent and for 'skillfully varying metre, tone and vocabulary from one section to the next'. Graham's work is criticised for 'unvarying solemnity of tone'. This is inaccurate. 'The Nightfishing' is a poem in seven sections of greatly varying metre, tone and vocabulary. Davie fails to notice this and turns his attention only to the third section which is in the form he describes and quotes from.

Davie objects, further, to the use of words such as 'ambitioned' and 'illusioned'. If, as he says, effective communication is his criterion here, there will be no difficulty; there is no doubt, I take it, as to the meaning of Graham's words.

Whether or not we consider 'The Nightfishing' to be important, we can hardly progress in our understanding of what constitutes viable poetic language by disallowing small details of a scheme we have largely ignored. Davie recognised what he took to be symptoms of self-expressive excess in Graham's language use, and this stopped him going further to see what this work had to offer at more extended or subtle levels.

This poem is an examination of what constitutes being-in-the-world (in the Heideggerian sense); there is no presiding self who relates to us a narrative, whether of a voyage, a poem, or a 'devotional experience'. Graham's reversals of normal syntactic relations create an ambiguity in our habitual perceptions of cause and effect. Words like 'ambitioned' and 'illusioned' are minor developments compared to the suspension of attribution in pronouns, the location of perception in activity, and the notion of a reflexive actively-constituted self known only in retrospect. Davie engages with none of this, because he too rigidly applied the notion of pure language-use as developed in his critical work *Purity of Diction in English Verse*.

At a later stage in his career, Davie gives us some self-critical insight into what the Movement poet-critics were up to and what they were blind to:

> What we all shared to begin with was a hatred for writing considered as self-expression; but all we put in its place was writing as self-adjustment, a getting on right terms with our reader (that is, with our society), a hitting on the right tone and attitude towards him. And in fact, this was the only alternative to exhibitionism, to 'self-expression', which our education and the climate of ideas presented us with. It's still true that literary criticism in Britain cannot conceive of anything else. Just consider how much of an okay word 'tone' is, and has been ever since I. A. Richards put it into general currency; and how difficult we find it to conceive of or approve any 'tone' that isn't ironical, and ironical in a limited way, defensive and deprecating, a way of looking at ourselves and our pretensions, not a way of looking at the world. Hardly ever did we seem to write our poems out of an idea of poetry as a way of knowing the world we were in, apprehending it, learning it; instead we conceived of it as an act of private and public therapy, the poet resolving his conflicts by expressing them and proffering them to the reader so that vicariously he should do the same. The most obvious register of this is the striking absence from 'Movement' poetry of outward and non-human things apprehended crisply for their own sakes.[54]

In criticising Graham's 'solemnity of tone' Davie was using the terminology of I. A. Richards to disallow something beyond the range of the Movement's self-deprecating ironies, and it was precisely that dimension that the later Davie missed in the work of the Movement which Graham provided: 'poetry as a way of knowing the world we were in, apprehending it, learning it'. Graham's poetry, which marginalises the self, was beyond the range of Movement interests. It was also deliberately obscured by them. As Schmidt points out, there was no new book after *The Nightfishing* for fifteen years 'of hardship and neglect' – that is, until the influence of the Movement had been brought somewhat (but less than altogether) into scale.

The next question is what exactly was obscured by the simplification of poetic history that the propagandists of the Movement brought about.

From its outset the Neo-Romantic revival (of which the New Apocalypse was a part) was two things: a reaction against the work of Auden and his followers, and the way in which diverse strands of the non-rational or anti-rational impulse were accommodated within British literary culture.

Auden and his followers had been the mainstream of British poetry of the thirties. With the threat of war and the fear of a complete collapse of western civilisation there were new conditions which made writers impatient with the recent past. The reaction to Auden was no doubt heightened by what was seen by many as his defection in time of crisis. Political commitment seemed suspect and, facing what they thought would be the end of culture, rational progress seemed absurd. Like the Movement, the Neo-Romantics took what was established and reacted against it to make something new.

There was a mixture of non-rational elements that came into British culture at this time. Influential from the recent past in England was the Modernism of Yeats, Joyce, Pound and Eliot, which many today will argue was characteristic of a late phase of Romanticism in that it showed an obsession with myth and individual self-determining endeavour. The work of Lawrence, especially his *Apocalypse*, which was quoted in the second Apocalyptic anthology, was of prime importance.[55] The interest in the unconscious and in extreme psychological states is something that the Neo-Romantics took up from Lawrence and from Graves. Freud, Marx and Jung were widely read at the time and their works interpreted in a new and so-called 'anti-mechanistic' way by the theorists of the Apocalypse.[56] Religion and the survival of religious feeling in some of the works of the Modernists was very important when taken together with the general sense of civilisation being under threat of destruction.

The work of Gerard Manley Hopkins became available to a much wider audience than had previously been the case on the publication of Charles Williams's edition in 1930. The technical novelty of his work was accepted in a way that it had not been when it was first introduced in 1910 by the apologetic and circumspect Robert Bridges. This committed Christian poetry was an important touchstone for the critical writing of the Apocalyptics; Henry Treece, for instance, made much of Hopkins when accounting for the language use of Dylan Thomas.[57]

The most significant material to be adapted by the Apocalyptics was Surrealism. In 1935 David Gascoyne published *A Short Survey of Surrealism*, his historical account of the movement. In 1936 his own Surrealist poems, *Man's Life in this Meat*, followed along with a translation of Breton's *What is Surrealism?* Eluard's poems were published in *Thorns of Thunder* (edited by George Reavey), and Herbert Read's

Surrealism was also published at this time. The first international Surrealist exhibition opened in London also in 1936 and there was a great deal of interest in this strange new work.[58]

Pure Surrealism had not caught and did not really catch on – perhaps, as John Heath-Stubbs has suggested, because England had no need to augment her own native element of the fantastic. 'She had her own "Kubla Khan" and rich stores of dream poetry to draw upon.'[59] While Surrealism may have produced work of lasting interest in the English visual arts, the English literary version is not, as one would expect, shocking or even surprising. It is quite tame and dull. There is nothing quite so flat and dull as a Gascoyne Surrealist poem; his 'Cubical Domes' makes the point clearly enough:

> Indeed indeed it is growing very sultry
> The Indian feather pots are scrambling out of the room
> The slow voice of the tobacconist is like a circle
> Drawn on the floor in chalk and containing ants
> And indeed there is a show upon the table
> And indeed it is as regular as clockwork
> Demonstrating the variability of the weather
> Or denying the existence of man altogether
> For after all why should love resemble a cushion . . .

What is missing here is energy and control. Add those to the anti-rational progress of so called 'unconscious' or 'dream' imagery and something of more substance is possible. The Apocalyptics saw themselves as incorporating elements of Surrealism. Henry Treece made the distinction through the work of Dylan Thomas in the first anthology of the Apocalypse:

> The images of Dylan Thomas . . . may come as spontaneously as those of Breton or Perét or Gascoyne, but while these poets, because of their artistic beliefs, make no attempt to select, or to write critically, he, as he tells us himself, applies to his images what intellectual and critical forces he possesses, allowing them to exist only within certain organic, formal limits.[60]

Dylan Thomas was already established as a poet with his own reputation when the idea of a new movement called the Apocalypse came about, he was a standard by which Apocalyptics could define themselves. But while Dylan Thomas accepted fees and publication, he nevertheless refused to sign the manifesto produced by Hendry and Treece:

> Answering your first letter: I won't sign, with or without argument, the Apocalyptic manifesto. I wouldn't sign any manifesto

Life and Contacts 21

unless I had written every word of it, and then I might be too ashamed. I agree with it and like much of it, and some of it, I think, is manifestly absurd.[61]

Thomas's feelings about the Apocalypse may be best shown by the following extract from his satire 'How to be a Poet':

> If Cedric were writing in the forties, he would, perhaps, be engulfed so that he could not see the wool for the Treece, in a kind of 'apocalyptic' batter, and his first volume might be entitled *Plangent Macrocosm* or *Heliogobalus in Pentecost*. Cedric can mix his metaphor, bog his cliché, and soak his stolen symbols in stale ass's milk as glibly and as glueily as the best of them.
>
> Next, London and the reviewing.[62]

The Apocalyptics needed Thomas as a reputable poet to add weight to their anthology.

The origins of the Apocalyptic movement are documented in T. H. Helmstadter's dissertation and followed closely in Shires.[63] The term was first applied in this context by John Goodland in a letter to Henry Treece written from King's College, Cambridge, 15 October 1938.[64] Hendry edited the anthology *The New Apocalypse* (1940); and Hendry and Treece edited *The White Horseman* (1941); *The Crown and the Sickle* (1944). The writers included in the first volume were Dorian Cooke, J. F. Hendry, Robert Melville, Nicholas Moore, Philip O'Connor, Dylan Thomas and Henry Treece. The second added G. S. Fraser, Tom Scott and Vernon Watkins. The third also included Terence White, Alex Comfort, F. J. Brown, Fred Marnau, Peter Wells, Gervase Stewart, Leslie Phillips, Robert Herring, Robert Graecen, Wrey Gardiner, Ian Bancroft, John Gallen, Maurice Lindsay, Sean Jennet, Stefan Schimanski, Terence White and D. V. Baker.

It is quite a large list and by the time that the third anthology was published any sense of a coherent group was quite lost. Graham was not published in any of the anthologies, so he cannot (at least in this sense) be thought of as an Apocalyptic at all.

> ... the Apocalyptics do seem to have been in tune with the times ... certainly they carried out a remarkable *putsch* against the literary establishment. *New Writing* held out, *Horizon* stopped short at Dylan Thomas, George Barker, W. S. Graham and Norman Nicholson (these were Connolly's chosen 'new romantics', not Apocalyptics), but *Poetry (London), Kingdom Come, Now, Adelphi*, and *Life and Letters Today* all fell under the neo-romantic spell. (Hewison, pp.112–13)

Among the most influential of these new writers a high proportion were Celts: Hendry, MacCaig, Scott, Lindsay, Fraser, and Graham were all published in the 'Scottish Renaissance' anthology edited by

Lindsay.⁶⁵ Dylan Thomas and Vernon Watkins were of course Welsh. The fact that these writers found a place in the Neo-Romantic revival affects the way that it was perceived by the Movement, whose idea of the poetic tradition was very definitely English – and the Englishness of a quite narrow social group was where their interest lay.

Shires has stressed the importance of religion in the poetry of the 1940s. Surely the most important British poem published at this time was Eliot's *Four Quartets*. It is all too easy to imagine that because Auden and his followers had come on to the scene since Eliot that Eliot's importance had waned. This was not the case. Eliot's work had continued to be influential; his place as editor in charge of poetry at Faber and Faber was also a position of great power. The progress in his writings from what seems a kind of agnosticism which retains spiritual and mysterious feeling in *The Waste Land* to the deliberate Christian and Anglican writing of his later years is, I take it, what the elder Eliot would have seen as his great theme. Though the progression is not the same, any account of Yeats, Lawrence, Joyce, or Beckett would seem to require the same kind of attention. Religious feeling, even if expressed through blasphemy or parody, is an important part of Modernism's later modulations.

Dylan Thomas had no doubts about claiming a religious purpose in his work, even if he did so in an irreverent way.

> I read somewhere of a shepherd who, when asked why he made, from within fairy rings, ritual observances to the moon to protect his flocks, replied: 'I'd be a damn' fool if I didn't!' These poems, with all their crudities, doubts, and confusions, are written for the love of Man and in praise of God, and I'd be a damn' fool if they weren't.⁶⁶

He used biblical language and imagery steadily throughout his career. Whilst others, like Graham, may not have shared Thomas's certainties they nevertheless explored so-called 'unconscious' and 'dream' imagery which is often biblical in origin. In this sense the importance of religion and religious feeling is structurally related to the attraction of Surrealism, because they are both manifestations of anti-rationalism.

When the Movement reacted so strongly against Dylan Thomas they were reacting against a number of things at once. They saw a kind of undisciplined drift in British poetry since the Modernists. They recognised that the Modernists, while working in the English language at the apex of the culture, were not, for the most part, English. Pound and Eliot were American, Yeats, Joyce and Beckett were Irish. The culture had been seized, in effect, by provincials.

Those provincials were bringing in a mélange of European standards of thought. They were heavily influenced by European poets and philosophers. According to one's point of view they were either breaking down the isolation or contaminating the sturdy independence of *English* culture that stems ultimately from Chaucer, Dryden, Fielding, Austen, Arnold and Hardy and more deeply perhaps from the establishment of the Church of England. The later phases of Modernism, moreover, began to attack the rationality that was the very root of tradition since the Augustans. For a relatively chauvinistic group such as the Movement, this was the high point of British culture, before the excesses of Romanticism.

The subjective nature of late manifestations of Romanticism or Neo-Romanticism (that which showed the influence of Continental *expressionism*) was what the Movement critic-poets abhorred. They attempted to portray this work as an isolated aberration in British poetry. We are closer to the truth if we notice that any history of twentieth-century poetry in English will require acknowledgement of a constant pull between a very public poetry made of an urbane version of simple speech which upholds a view of eighteenth century standards as a model; and that opposite (expressionist) impulse which is a passionate turning inward, seeking to express what in another time would have been called religious feeling. Lawrence obviously looms over the latter impulse – and his work connects with a tradition of English writing that goes back to Christopher Smart and William Blake. Whilst we may not think much of the Apocalypse as a movement now, the Neo-Romantic tendency included some fine poets (G. S. Fraser, Nicholas Moore, J. F. Hendry, Dylan Thomas, and the early Graham) and it is ill informed and polemical to suggest that it was an isolated or even sudden event.

John Heath-Stubbs was first introduced to Graham's poetry at a reading given by Dylan Thomas in Oxford in the 1940s. Thomas, according to Heath-Stubbs, was promoting the work of what he described as a very promising new poet. That Thomas and Graham knew each other is clear from MacDiarmid's account of his time with Graham in Glasgow. That Graham was influenced by Thomas is not in dispute, but at a later stage I will show how the early 'influence' was a matter of common sources as much as it was direct. Graham's later poems also show residual Thomas-like phrasing, and the matter of coined composite words (which is what Davie noticed) is important throughout Graham's career. Typical of Thomas, it is also found with great frequency in Gerard Manley Hopkins, who had in any case been a profound influence on Graham. For Graham the main early enthusiasm was Rimbaud, whom he read in translation.

Graham did not consider himself to be a religious poet – he was never a member of any religious group or sect.[67] He said, furthermore, that he would prefer his poem 'The Nightfishing' (the most likely poem to be read as religious) to be considered in philosophical terms as a philosophical poem.[68] Readers will not find a poetry of religious statement in Graham's work, but there is (except in the later work) a great deal of Christian language. The survival of religious feeling in secular and specifically elemental experience is one of the main characteristics of his early and mid-career, leading up to and including 'The Nightfishing'.

That Graham's suppressed early sequence *The Seven Journeys* may be read as a poem which shows the kind of adaptation of Surrealism which I have described above, shows that he should be thought of as a Neo-Romantic at least in his early career. His later work, however, is in a manner quite different from the Neo-Romantics and his achievement is finally of another kind. Graham's ambitions for his poetry were long-term and his major work was conceived on a larger scale than anything else which came out of the Apocalyptic or Neo-Romantic movements.

Though he was disenchanted with the 1920–1945 Scottish Renaissance movement *as such*, he by no means lost sight of the Scotland of his hard childhood and early years, nor of a Scottish identity that is maintained and developed through its literature. He furthermore brought the influence of that identity to bear upon English poetry (or more properly poetry in English) and he enriched it by re-opening certain areas of subject matter and technique which had been lost, making them relevant to our time and tongue in a way that is quite his own. His Scottish identity is defined by his use of Scottish speech habits and vocabulary. Later he began to take the forms and subjects of the border ballads into his work until he reached a point, quite late on in his career, when he was able to write a deliberate and seemingly effortless *Scottish* poetry, with the sense of history and community that that term implies.

The main theme of Graham's work is a voyage of self-discovery. Graham's first written book *The Seven Journeys*, contains the germ of the major poems of his whole career. Carefully and patiently worked out from *The White Threshold*, through *The Nightfishing* and *Malcolm Mooney's Land* to *Implements In Their Places*, Graham used the figure of various kinds of voyaging and exploration to turn his poetry in on itself, dramatising the relationship between writer and reader, and bringing language more and more firmly into the subject matter of the poems.

Recognising from quite early on the special importance of the work on language in philosophical debate in our time, Graham's poetry presents language as the medium in which we move, dwell, and know the world. But unlike that tendency which seeks to explain literature and the world by means of the application of the language model and the methodology of linguistics (what we have come to call Formalism and Structuralism), Graham's work produces a living, animate, and mocking 'language' that resists codification, and seems at least as complex as what it has been made to represent.

All this seems programmatic in the extreme, and it is true that

Graham's work is single-minded to a surprising degree. But we fail to understand it and do justice to it if the project is applied too rigidly in an account of the poetry. Some of Graham's finest work (the narratives in *The White Threshold*, 'The Dark Dialogues', the elegies for various friends that are also tributes to them as artists, and single lyric works such as 'I Leave This at Your Ear' and 'To My Wife at Midnight') is aside of the main thrust of his extraordinary development. When insights from that process are applied to other occasions (as we might expect) a great facility is brought to bear upon what we hold in common.

However much Graham's work is writing about writing, it never strays far from the basic needs and drives that constitute family and community; the sexual drive and the intimacy of belonging one to another. A good deal of his later work was about growing old in love, learning to face death, and the awkwardness of outliving friends. In these poems he speaks with a disarming directness and hard-won simplicity as a Scot who has made himself heard above the babble, and as a member of the St Ives community of artists, a community which his work above all helped to define.

The Early Poems

When it was first published in wartime Glasgow, *Cage Without Grievance* (1942) must have seemed a strange and exotic production with its uncompromising, difficult text, and its Piccassoesque illustrations by Robert Frame and Benjamin Creme. The imagery of the drawings (bullfights, semi-nudes, warm climate interiors) is by no means native Scottish but rather South European, and they show a hesitant and partial absorption of Cubism which they use not as an organising principle but as a decorative effect.

The poems do have Scottish elements. There is a scatter of Scots and Gaelic derived words: 'gowan', 'burn', 'Calder', 'firth', 'law' (meaning hill), 'whinfire', 'hoodiecrow', Cruachen', 'ptarmigan', 'blaeberries', 'kirkyard', 'cairn', and 'glen'. But this vocabulary is not the first quality that one would notice on reading the poems; though it is an important aspect of the rather sumptuous mix of language, which, together with the suspension of narrative argument, makes up the impression of exotic strangeness that they have.

The poems are difficult – but not so difficult as they have been made to seem by those who have opened the way to an assessment of Graham's achievement.[1] There has been an impatience with the early work among these critics, the poems are seen as written under the influence of Dylan Thomas, and as a set of rather exuberant experiments.

> Over the apparatus of the Spring is drawn
> A constructed festival of pulleys from sky.
> A dormouse swindled from numbers into wisdom
> Trades truth with bluebells. The result unknown
> Fades in the sandy beetle-song that martyrs hear
> Who longingly for violetcells prospect the meads.
>
> 'Over the Apparatus'

> Of the resonant rumour of sun, impulse of summer
> My bride is born. Love finds not here ambition.
> I am the dunce of sacrifice yet at the sun's table
> With vein after vein unmaking the cadence of blood

The Early Poems

> My hope is wildly heaven's, certain of conflict.
> Who, with a heart bound to his writing battle
> Would sign humanity and index legendary bliss?
> 'Of the Resonant'

The passages quoted above are the first stanzas of the first two poems in the book. Both of them have seasonal references early on; the first developing a kind of conventional and artificial landscape, and the second more explicitly working up key words for a love-lyric: 'bride', 'love', 'hope', 'heart', 'bliss'.

It is not simply nature imagery that makes up the first piece. The 'apparatus' and 'constructed festival of pulleys' show either the works of man or the works of nature seen as if made by man's industry. This kind of imagery is used throughout the poem which has 'A derrick in flower' and 'Birches erect / The ephemeral mechanism of welcoming'. We have shifting points of view, implicit comparisons and most of all the sense that this thing, this poem, is made or patterned for us.

The second piece is clearer in its sexual content – 'the cadence of blood', 'blood builds its platform', 'Love cascades', 'the hovering ram', 'lust in a palace', 'hoist a sign of veins' – because the natural imagery is closer to the body. If the first piece seemed to declare itself as an artefact, the second is more explicit: 'Who, with a heart bound to his writing battle / Would sign humanity and index legendary bliss?' The self consciousness is underlined for us by the word battle being an inversion (a kind of rhyme equivalent) of 'table' from line 3 so that 'writing table' is suggested in the sixth line.

The poems are love-gifts whose crafted surface is a display of skill and effort as a measure of ardour. The work is as non-functional as a Welsh love-spoon or as fine embroidery. Like the Elizabethan lyric, the work is about its surface, about the play in a highly conventional landscape of love, where parts of the lover are compared to aspects of nature: sun, stars, moon, running brooks and so on.

Graham's early work stands quite apart, in some ways, from what he wrote later in his career. Despite his re-using of material, the manner of the early work is so different as to appear written by someone else. That person (Graham's early self as a writer) is *not*, as has been maintained by Bedient and Schmidt, a kind of substitute Dylan Thomas, though Thomas is a tangible presence, part of the voice.

The way in which a poem like 'Of the Resonant Rumour of Sun, Impulse of Summer' is organised, with a repetitive syntactic structure to tie up each stanza, is very much like Thomas. The last two lines in each stanza of the poem read (my emphases):

> *Who, with a* heart bound to his writing battle
> *Would* sign *humanity and index* legendary bliss?

> *Who, with a* nettle fore*finger* sparking covenants
> *Will* sting *humanity and* point the docken ground?
>
> *Who, with a* map of picnics primed for April
> *Could probe humanity and* hoist a sign of veins?
>
> 'Of the Resonant'

Compare the structure of the Graham sentences with these from Thomas's 'The Force that through the Green Fuse Drives the Flower':

> *And I am dumb to tell* the crooked rose
> My youth is bent by the same wintry fever.
>
> *And I am dumb to* mouth unto my veins
> *How at* the mountain spring the same mouth sucks.
>
> *And I am dumb to tell* the hanging man
> *How* of my clay is made the hangman's lime.
>
> *And I am dumb to tell* a weather's wind
> *How* time has tricked a heaven round the stars.
>
> *And I am dumb to tell* the lover's tomb
> *How* at my sheet goes the same crooked worm.

In both cases it is from the repeated elements of the sentence structure that the lines derive their sense of inevitability and declarative power. In Graham, however, the usage is somewhat more homely or home-made. 'Map of picnics' would seem to work against the grand tone of 'sign humanity'. There is also, clearly, a common source: 'Who, with a nettle forefinger sparking covenants / Will sting humanity and point the docken ground?' is as much like Blake's 'The Garden of Love': 'Binding with briars my joys and desires' as Thomas's poem with its 'crooked rose' and 'crooked worm' is to 'The Sick Rose', also in Blake's *Songs of Experience*.

Another presence strongly felt in these early poems of Graham's is the Rimbaud of *Illuminations* whom Graham read in translation. It was the first time he had seen industrial imagery used in combination with that of the natural world and the experience was liberating. In the Rootham translation of Rimbaud was language such as: 'A hare paused in the clover and shaking bell-flowers' (p. 53), 'erect in the wallflower rampart' (p. 63) and 'among the apparatus . . . on this fugitive shipboard' (p. 72). The latinate vocabulary of construction (parapets, rampart, apparatus, viaducts, apexes, canopy) was some-

The Early Poems

thing that Graham took up. The peculiar combination of shipbuilding superstructure (cranes, derricks, pulleys and scaffolding) with the surrounding natural features (the Renfrew hills, Loch Thom, the southern highlands in view just across the Clyde) also became the matter of Graham's poetry in response to Rimbaud as well as to the primary experience of living in that place.

In *Dylan Thomas: Dog among the Fairies*, Henry Treece shows that Gerard Manley Hopkins's language-use greatly influenced that of Dylan Thomas. Treece's argument is based on the preponderance of compound words such as 'hornlight', 'owl-light', 'womb-life' and 'womb-eyed' in the writings of both poets. He lays out a table of compound words in Hopkins and Thomas that makes a very convincing case indeed. If Graham's work is applied to the table, the comparison between Hopkins and Graham works somewhat better than that between Hopkins and Thomas.

Using the mechanism of compound word occurrence (which might well be seen as proof of Graham's debt to Thomas), it is therefore apparent that Hopkins is a common source of material to Graham and to Thomas. Graham's later work was more closely based upon that of Hopkins. Graham's 'The White Threshold' and 'The Nightfishing' (poems with an ambition on a scale not found in Dylan Thomas) have a common ancestor in Hopkins's *Wreck of the Deutschland*.

A good example of the quality of Graham's best early lyrics is 'O Gentle Queen of the Afternoon' from *Cage Without Grievance*:

> O gentle queen of the afternoon
> Wave the last orient of tears.
> No daylight comet ever breaks
> On so sweet an archipelago
> As love on love.
>
> The fundamental negress built
> In a cloudy descant of the stars
> Surveys no sorrow, invents no limits
> Till laughter the watcher of accident
> Sways off to God.
>
> O gentle queen of the afternoon
> The dawn is rescued dead and risen.
> Promise, O bush of blushing joy,
> No daylight comet ever breaks
> On so sweet an archipelago
> As love on love.

Whilst it is clear that the poem is a love-lyric (and almost, retrospectively from the afternoon, an aubade) there seems to be no argument as such so that we are directed by this difficulty towards other kinds of meaning in order to proceed with the poem. The sound-structuring of the piece is intricate; the relation between lines 1 and 4, for instance, is quite seductively almost a reversal of vowel sounds: single 'o', 'e', double 'e', 'o':

> O gentle queen of the afternoon (1)
> On so sweet an archipelago (4)

lines 2 and 3 end in assonance: 'tears / breaks' and 3 and 4 begin with the reversal 'No / On'. The vowel pattern of the fifth line 'As love on love', is almost exactly echoed in the pattern of the next end-of-stanza line: 'Sways off to God' (10). This association without rhyme is on one level the logic of the piece (as in stanza 2 we pick up the sequence: fundament / invent / accident) and is made to marry the overall structure, with no two stanzas similar in shape or statement – though there is a good deal of repetition and near repetition of lines.

> The fundamental negress built
> In a cloudy descant of the stars

The dimension of these first two lines of the second stanza is very quickly laid out with 'fundament, cloud, stars'. We have already 'seen' an expanse of day and night sky from the words 'daylight comet' (line 3), and sea studded with islands from 'archipelago' (line 4).

The image of a full female form, seen in a dark cloud bank, floating, conceals a tacit privacy, and yet by its striking prominence (almost impudence), asks to be fathomed, decoded: breaking taboos of privacy. The 'wave' of the opening is both a farewell to receding dawn-ecstasy and also the lap of salt surf upon the inlets and outlands of these recumbent forms.

The images of female sexuality such as 'Promise, O bush of blushing joy' (line 13) are complemented by the lines 'The dawn is rescued dead and risen' and 'No daylight comet ever breaks' with their load of masculine meaning. The phrases 'dead and risen' and 'O bush of blushing joy' give their Christian connotations (crucifixion, resurrection, the burning bush) a sexual resonance, as is frequent in Graham's work. The control of the essentially private subject matter, by placing it in an image complex that is strong but not quite explicit displays Graham's assurance and his mastery of the lyric form.

The poetry displays exactly the qualities that we find in Hart Crane's early poems. *White Buildings* (1926), contains a sequence called 'voyages' that is clearly a source for Graham.

The Early Poems

> And onward, as bells off San Salvador
> Salute the crocus lustres of the stars,
> In these poinsettia meadows of her tides, –
> Adagios of islands, O my prodigal,
> Complete the dark confessions her veins spell.
>   (Hart Crane, *Complete Poems*, p. 55)

In it the landscape is figured as a lover to the poet-onlooker, and it is precisely the play of surf upon what Crane describes as 'Adagios of islands' ('adagio' a substitute for 'archipelago', one of Graham's key words), that releases the latent sexual energy into the poet's scheme. Notice also how similar are 'Salute the crocus lustres of the stars' and 'In a cloudy descant of the stars' and that both poems have a dark female character (Graham's negress, Crane's Carib). The sequence 'Voyages' is clearly an ancestor of Graham's *The Seven Journeys* also.

What should be plain from the examples of Blake, Rimbaud, Hopkins and Crane, is that though Thomas was an influence on Graham's early work, he was by no means a dominating influence. What was common to Thomas and Graham was used differently by each author and they developed as writers in different ways.

The Seven Journeys (1944) was published in the 'Poetry Scotland' series by William MacLellan who was the key publisher of the Scottish Renaissance (1920–45). Books and periodicals published by MacLellan form the greatest part of *Modern Scottish Poetry* (1946) Maurice Lindsay's anthology of the movement, where Graham appears in the company of Ruthven Todd, J. F. Hendry, G. S. Fraser and Tom Scott, all of whom were involved with the Apocalyptic movement in British poetry. This was the nearest that Graham came to them, since he was not represented in any of the Apocalypse anthologies.

In the poetry / rare books collection of the State University of New York at Buffalo, there is a copy of Graham's book *The Seven Journeys* which belonged to Vivienne Koch.[2] It is inscribed to her in Graham's hand thus:

> Vivienne Koch
> W. S. Graham
> 1947

The title page is inscribed, in the same hand: 'Poems 1941–42'. This, together with a letter from Agnes MacLellan (wife of the publisher) suggests that *The Seven Journeys* was Graham's first book.[3] It contains eight poems entitled: 'The Narrator', 'The First Journey', 'The Second Journey' and so on to 'The Seventh Journey'. 'The Narrator', which is dated December 1941, is the only item that Graham collected, firstly into *2nd Poems* and then into *Collected Poems 1942–1977* where it was included as one of the poems from *2nd Poems*. No mention of *The Seven Journeys* is made in the *Collected Poems*. It could be said, therefore, that

Graham suppressed this work from his personal canon. This explains the title *2nd Poems*, Graham's second book if we count from *Cage Without Grievance* and ignore *The Seven Journeys*. I intend *not* to ignore this book, however, as it is very important in the sequence of Graham's career.

The view of Graham's development that we get from the *Collected Poems* is that of a poet who began by writing short occasional lyrics, which were all he published until the sequence of more extended works began with *The White Threshold*. *The Seven Journeys* alters this impression. Graham may have decided to omit *The Seven Journeys* because he thought the work immature and preliminary – or he may have been trying to avoid too much thematic repetition. Nevertheless, the collection contains in embryo almost all the subjects of his major works. Graham's development and ambition was prefigured at the outset of his writing therefore, and was not something that occurred to him after getting clear of youthful influences. The introduction is of interest in terms of Graham's development, it is written by the Scottish Renaissance poet William Montgomerie:

> What does it mean?
>
> If by being dissuaded from asking this question, the reader is persuaded to approach these poems from another angle from which meaning is not primary, but secondary, something will have been done to adjust his mind to this book.
>
> Without attacking the assumption in our minds, that in prose meaning is primary, W. S. Graham by *making* his poems out of words, as a Cathedral is built out of squared stone, has assumed that we will ultimately approach his poems in a frame of mind from which meaning is not so much a practical question, as a metaphysical question, as we might say, what is the meaning of St Mark's in Venice?

The terms of the argument, which we may reasonably assume had Graham's approval (and perhaps active participation) are from the beginning completely uncompromising. The poem does not 'mean' in the sense of prose meaning. Like Montgomerie's own poems in the Scottish Renaissance anthology, Graham's work resists paraphrase by offering no direct argument. It thus demands the development of new reading procedures and the suspension of some old ones.

Notice also the thematic description: 'The First Journey is Scottish . . . The Third Journey . . . aspects of water. The Fourth Journey is through ice and snow, the Fifth suggests sex, the Sixth the sea. Graham's notes for Vivienne Koch in the Buffalo copy largely agree with these descriptions. On 'The First Journey' he notes : 'Young exuberant poem / Landscape – Hebredian – Islands'. 'The Second Journey' has no note of theme (as in Montgomerie's introduction). 'The Third Journey' is described as 'a journey of rivers and seas'; 'The

The Early Poems

Fourth Journey' as a 'journey in arctic ice – northern – hardness – intellect – Rimbaudian'. 'The Fifth Journey' is described as a 'journey in sex'. 'The Sixth' has no note. 'The Seventh Journey' is described as 'a grand journey'.

This thematic outline of *The Seven Journeys* links up in a surprisingly programmatic way with the main stages in Graham's career. His sequence of voyage poems follows the sequence of themes in *The Seven Journeys*: rivers and seas (no. 3) 'The White Threshold', 'The Nightfishing'; arctic ice (no. 4) 'Malcolm Mooney's Land'; sex (no. 5) 'Implements In Their Places'; sea (no. 6) 'The Nightfishing'; a 'grand journey' (no. 7) all the voyage poems. It would seem, therefore, that *The Seven Journeys* became a kind of source book for Graham's later writings, that its themes were enlarged and adapted throughout his career. The comparison works more closely in terms of the vocabulary and the sound patterns of the respective poems (my emphasis throughout):

> That whorls my ruddering heaven in grammars of tide.
> That swims on the foam of your *whale* in a gland of *blood*.
> Still I pass *fathom-voyaged* in a volted thread
> Rigged with a spray of *justice* devised in fables
> 'The Third Journey'

> Wear me my words. The nettling brine
> Stings through the word.
> For heart and *whales* in covenant
> The caaing thresher in his splendid *blood*
> Up *famous fathoms* well *over* strongly
> The *pacing* whitehaired kingdoms of the sea
> 'The White Threshold'

> There are *no certain miles* in ice-invented vales
> Yet look where my saint's value *pads* in *snow* turrets
> That *veer* on infant-levered *winds* over pale ranges.
> Answering the *abstract* annals of unhero'd *floes*
> 'The Fourth Journey'

> Today, Tuesday, I decided to move on
> Although the *wind* was *veering*. Better to move
> Than have them at *my heels, poor friends*
> I buried earlier under the printed snow
> The real un*abstract snow*
> 'Malcolm Mooney's Land'

Graham seems to have adapted and re-used certain key-words and sounds in much later work, as for example 'Elizabethan turtled air'

('The Fourth Journey'), 'a fen of swerving queens' ('The Fifth Journey') and 'Elizabeth, my furry / Pelted queen' ('Malcolm Mooney's Land').

The journey was the most important theme or subject for writers of the 1930s. Many of them turned directly to travel writing but their travels often became interior journeys and parables of their times. When war broke out the metaphor of the voyage continued in a modified form, holding back from ultimate success to present a more gloomy prospect. Journeying on water through hallucinatory and unreal surroundings was a development that in a way captured the mood of those early years of the second world war. A broad description of the change in writing from the 1930s to the 1940s (which might be found in Samuel Hynes, *The Auden Generation* and Linda M. Shires, *British Poetry of the Second World War*) could be summed up as a move from public and political concerns to a more private world of intuition and metaphysics. The shift accompanies a loss of faith in the political process and an increasing pessimism as a response to world war.

Now Graham was not in any sense of the phrase a 'war poet' as we have seen. He actively avoided conscription into the forces and war did not become a major theme in his work until *The White Threshold* (1949). He did pick up major themes that other writers were working on and make them his own.

The Seven Journeys, while they include recognisable bits of Scottish landscape, also include what was for Graham exotic and imaginary. Thus in 'The First Journey' we get 'Sgurr nan Gillian' which Graham glosses in the Buffalo copy as 'mountain on Skye – means – the hill of the young man' as well as:

> Becoming a dhow from the reign of a finial phallus
> My deity bouyed on the lake of a basin of bone
> Unreefs a windy code across the gruff season
> And twines a linen language on tilting acres.
> The lame girl pegged on the daughter's bitter sheet
> Marks out in Sanskrit her love-broke bible
>
> (*The Seven Journeys*, p. 31)

lines which Graham notes as 'Asiatic'. Already in this work, Graham is moving in 'language' as much as any real landscape. The journeys are not real journeys in which one gets tired, bored, lost or hurt; or, arrives. 'The Fourth Journey', which is in 'arctic – ice – northern – hardness – intellect – Rimbaudian', has the note 'strange northern hardness against English softness' by the second stanza and 'surrealist feeling' by the third. The landscape is imaginary, a literary construct whose sources we can trace. From Graham's notes it would seem to be an imaginative extension of what it is to be a northerner,

The Early Poems

firstly a Scot, but with links to other peoples of the north – and with Rimbaud because he is perceived as an imaginative voyager.

Like 'Malcolm Mooney's Land', it must be based on Graham's reading of Fridjof Nansen's *Farthest North* and mixes the ideas of moving in landscape, language and altered consciousness which is represented fearfully in 'Malcolm Mooney's Land' as a terrain of madness.

> There are no sheer frontiers of bliss in astral prisms
> The crystal pastures unsure with spectral foals
> The stallions stamping rainbows on unbridged graves.
> And under icy garments of the waves and plains
> The barriers lay a maze athwart exchanging battles.
>
> (*The Seven Journeys*, p. 27)

Graham was right to label this section of the work as 'surrealist feeling' – for like the poems of a Surrealist such as Gascoyne, it delivers a sequence of images *without* an argument. There is a fundamental difference, however. A basic characteristic of Surrealist writing (and for that matter all Surrealist art-forms) is the juxtaposition of contrasting and / or contradictory images, so as to break up and controvert any implicit or latent tendency to connected narrative, or even to actively prevent any such tendency forming. Graham's use of an apparently Surrealistic *surface* lies over a connected and developing process of latent themes and related images which represents as primary (imaginative) narrative precisely what many of the Surrealists suppressed completely. The effects which had a shock value in their time do not last – and this is especially true of Surrealist writing.

In the passage quoted above, Graham develops a description of a place, albeit imaginary, which we can picture quite clearly. We can see a frozen landscape with either horses and foals or, more likely, the shapes that suggest them in the snow and ice. The poem is a definition of self in terms of a contrast or conflict between North and South, and this conflict is sexualised:

> Let me from a Celtic *sex* with granite my costume
> *Rise* like a bangled Messiah in a Saga's beak
> And break the Arctic girl with no *seal's barrier*
> And set her madrigals round my flint wrists
>
> (*The Seven Journeys*, p. 27, my emphasis)

'Seal here refers to *Phoca vitulina* and to hymen. Both of these passages are densely patterned sound structures:

> Th*ere are* no sh*eer* front*iers* of bl*iss* *in* astral pr*is*ms
> The crys*tal* pas*tures* un*sure* with spec*tral* foals

> The *st*allions *st*amping *r*ain*b*ows on un*b*ridged *g*raves
> (*The Seven Journeys*, p. 27, my emphasis)

The combination of 'rainbows', 'bridge' and 'stallions', together with the reference to 'Saga' (above), suggests that Graham had been reading *The Poetic Edda*, and was deliberately manipulating Icelandic and Norse imagery.[4] While it may not have the control of Graham's later work, the descriptive, thematic, and musical elements all add up to a much stronger and different control than a Surrealist would wish for. Without creating an easily paraphrased meaning, Graham's poems in *The Seven Journeys* show a sophisticated handling of latent themes and evidence of the very large ambition for the work that he developed later in his career.

It is interesting to see just how much Graham glossed for his friend Vivienne Koch, pointing out lines which he thinks are good or 'striking' for one reason or another. But he is more often concerned to give definitions of words which he feels are specialised in some way. Some of the words are Scots or Gaelic, and some of them are connected with trades or science.

> Sgurr nan Gillian: Mountain on Skye – means 'The hill of the young man'
> creel: crab and lobster pot
> sprit: 1 bowsprit of ship, 2 watersprite, 3 Male symbol
> minch: channel
> skerry: low small island
> milt: fish eggs, roe
> gaelic kilns: in which they burn the seaweed kelp to make iodine
> lyns: small cascade
> whinstone: special kind of sandstone

As a Scotsman, Graham is aware that his language use might not always be clear to an American. Whether or not we feel that the glosses are necessary, the notes make Graham's sense of his origins quite plain.

If Graham's first book was the outcome of a particular cultural group in Glasgow and his second came from the key publisher for Scottish Renaissance poetry, the third book was a product of 'Fitzrovia' – the wartime literary and artistic community who met in the pubs of Soho and nearby. The scene is described by Derek Stanford (*Inside the Forties*), Julian MacLaren-Ross (*Memoir of the Forties*), and Robert Hewison (*Under Siege*).

The poems of *2nd Poems* (1945) are different in kind from those of the previous two volumes; they are neither quite separate lyrics, nor do they have the close thematic unity of *The Seven Journeys*. There are

The Early Poems

connections between the poems but Graham does not seem to be trying for sequential meaning as he does in later works. We have an insight into the way that Graham himself saw these poems, and the way in which he thought they ought to be read, from a set of notes that he prepared for a friend who was to give a reading of Graham's work:

> Read once through in a businesslike BBC announcer's style, a little cloyness of the lecture room. Then go through it with them slowly. Title in the style of a headline.
> 'Perceived by lyrical action' lecture style and other phrases such as 'chiefly by accident' and end ending with the style of a professor setting a theme for the class to do.
>
> (Note to 'Remarkable Report by some Poetical Agents', dated Glasgow 1943)[5]

Graham's directions for reading show that the kind of performance and the voice that the poem demands is something that he was writing towards.

The poem begins: 'There was from March 3rd to April 3rd the appearance of reality.' A very unusual opening for a poem. It looks like rather strange topical information from a news report. When Graham's note mentions a 'professor setting a theme', he must be referring to the lines: 'Relate by means of grief / Your own fled court to its once pleasant country.' The note makes it certain that Graham was deliberately trying to set these voices (contemporary authority figures) in his poetry. The idea of 'Poetical Agents' suggests Auden's *The Orators*, where the narrator is working in enemy territory. Voices are set in *The Orators* by the titles of sections (The 'Address for a Prize Day', for example, which is certainly close to what Graham wants in his note). Auden's work looks into the pathology of his characters, is interested in psychological damage, and it creates a modern hero from the airman. 'The Prologue' to *The Orators* includes the lines, 'With the finest of mapping pens he fondly traces / All the family names on the familiar places', and this is a theme that Graham takes up in his poem 'Explanation of a Map' which uses the conceit of a map compared with reality as a metaphor for writing compared with reality. The title, again, is something like a school exercise but the writing which follows complicates rather than clarifies. Graham includes what could not possibly be seen on a map: the sound of a dog barking, the way a walker sees a place, the sense of a place as a neighbourhood, the way a place might be spoken of, how it might be known by a hunter.

'The Serving Inhabiters' has a similar guiding conceit which the verses explore and develop. The person is like a house with many selves inhabiting it: the spectator self, the hooligan self, the shepherd self (better self, guide), the lizard self (cold blooded). It connects with the previous poem in the couplet: 'Can blood admit a people's map / Together district to a common shape?'

The map and radically shifting points of view (seeing from the land and from the air) are important in *The Orators*, and the same is true in these poems by Graham.

The heroic figure that Auden creates is approximated in another of Graham's notes:

> Title from a phrase which seemed to me to occur so significantly and frequently in northern exploration accounts.
> Again like 'O Gentle Queen' it evokes that strange barbaric female figure, here, 'that furry queen', even a little comic. (Note to 'His Companions Buried Him')[6]

Here it is the hero of Graham's later works, Nansen, who is suggested by 'northern exploration' though the name is not given here; Nansen's exploration writings were important source material for Graham. The 'furry queen' is a kind of muse-figure (or fairy queen) who turns up again in *Malcolm Mooney's Land*, where Nansen is named.

Northern exploration and the poem as letter are brought together in Auden's work *Letters From Iceland* (written with Louis MacNeice, 1937). Graham uses the title 'letter' for many of his poems – this might not in itself be significant – but taken together with the interest in northern exploration, and another instance in which Graham quotes from Auden (in 'Clusters Travelling Out' in *Malcolm Mooney's Land*, which quotes Auden's 'Letter to a Wound', also from *The Orators*), and the extended theme of the journey, it shows that we can certainly count Auden as another presence behind Graham's early work.

What is new in the *2nd Poems* volume is a radical experimentation with abstraction. 'Remarkable Report', 'Explanation of a Map', and 'His Companions' are attempts to extend what can be accomplished with lyric poetry. Another poem 'Allow Silk Birds That See', seems to me to be an attempt to parallel in language the kind of new developments occurring in the visual arts at that time.

> Allow the local morning make fire.
> Silk bars the road, a spider rope.
> Birds trail the slippery harbourer
> That steers from what eye builds its blinder deep.
>
> See light on man devise the best collision.
> See man on word devise the best collision.
>
> Now call the newt with river eyes.
> Call brook and girl, the bower sunshine.
> And call each drop. The early boys

The Early Poems

See word on God devise the best collision.
'Allow Silk Birds That See'

Graham provides us with a varying refrain line: 'See light on man . . . See man on word . . . See word on God' that alludes to St John ('In the beginning was the word') and thus has a kind of inevitable cadence. Against this there is an acrostic title (see the first words of lines 1–5) which is a balancing structure to the varying refrain. The usual reason for acrostics is a personal dedication, using a code derived from a friend's or lover's name. This kind of private meaning cannot be deduced from Graham's title (though its possibility is implied by the very deployment of acrostics). Lines 5 and 6 both begin with 'See', and the stanza which follows has initial words that make a kind of sense: 'Now Call And See' (as much as the lines that the words come from). Though any coded meaning seems unlikely, we have been encouraged to look for one and to read the lines vertically as well as from left to right.

We are directed to the patterns which emerge from reading the poem, the line endings, for instance: 'spider rope / blinder deep', 'river eyes / early boys'. Half-rhymes are used in combination with repetitions or chimes. The patterning of the writing is attempting a pleasure-equivalent of what is mentioned in the poem. It is an early morning scene on a country road, crisscrossed with spider's gossamer threads. Birds are hunting for snails hidden in the foliage. We construct a fiction to contain the elements in the first stanza and have to guess again to whom it is that the instructions which follow ('Now call' etc.) are addressed. 'Call brook and girl' suggests that it is not a lover, who would hardly call up a rival. It could be a reader, it could be the poet's (or a fictional narrator's) memory.

It would also seem to be an account of primal creation: the allow / see / call sequence modelled on the let / saw / called sequence of Genesis, I. The man is thus (latently) Adam, and perhaps the early boys the disciples.

The acrostic title is a set of reading instructions addressed quite clearly to the reader. It is at the same time an arbitrary phrase picked out of what turned up in writing the first five lines. This highly abstract language-game is full of creature names, it rhymes with them, or plays at nearly rhyming with them. The game is very similar to what is required in 'Remarkable Report'. There the tones of authority from the newscast and lecture-room are used to extend the lyric voice. Phrases like 'Man is a third class road' are thus to be delivered in a neutral matter-of-fact voice as if they were self-evident rather than inscrutable. In 'Allow Silk Birds That See', we have a poem that forces us to invent a scene in the world and then delivers no more or less than the naming of its creatures. Working out a method of abstraction in writing, the poems nevertheless seek a notation and poetics for their own time (heavy industry, the voices of the new technical experts, maps and spies).

Graham's early poetry attempts to transmit something of European artistic and literary endeavour into Scotland. In this sense Graham is to be understood as a Scottish writer and as a European who retains a strong sense of Scotland in his choice of subject, imagery and vocabulary. Unlike MacDiarmid and his followers, Graham chose to write in English, while resisting the standard form of the language by retaining Scottish words and usage. His poetry was therefore much closer to the speech of his region of Scotland than synthetic Scots.

Right from the beginning, Graham numbered painters among his circle of close friends. The move towards non-representation in the artistic community is something that he consistently developed in his own work. The early poetry has a special value because it is *not* explicit. It requires us to develop new reading methods and refuses to let us pass beyond the impression of a patterned object made of words. As the modern European painters were holding back their audience from projecting into the picture-plane by breaking up the image (cubism) or using false or synthetic colour (fauvism), so Graham's work, in its very resistance, has something particular to say.

CHAPTER THREE

The White Threshold

The White Threshold (1949), the first of Graham's books to be published by Faber and Faber, was accepted for publication by T. S. Eliot, who was the poetry editor at that time. Graham wrote the book when he was quite unsettled domestically and in considerable financial difficulty, just before his year in New York as a visiting lecturer.

Sewanee Review first published 'The White Threshold' in 1948, together with 'A Note on W. S. Graham' by Vivienne Koch. She presumably had his cooperation when writing her article and we may assume that it tells us how Graham wished his work to be read. Notes that Graham made on the Buffalo copy of *The Seven Journeys* are incorporated here, and her description of the book as 'his first little-known collection' reveals Koch's inside knowledge, as it was not the first to be published, though the first to be written. Her parallel of Graham and Rimbaud picks up his own suggestion.

Koch's article is an early attempt to show the development of Graham's work – and it is wholly alive to the way in which his poetic character is to be understood in terms of his language use:

> Graham's 'Scottishness' is a matter of syntax, the heard cadences of spoken language, and the selective use of a vocabulary which is the common possession of the people who speak it, as did his parents....
>
> Poetry is language, and just how the Scots components participate in Graham's special language deserves a brief exposition. First, it is well to remember that some of the older language words (Old Norse, Gaelic, Anglo-Saxon, and even Norman) have stayed alive in Scotland in actual colloquial usage and thus their employment implies neither nostalgia nor archaism. For example, in 'The White Threshold,' printed in this issue, 'brae' meaning hill is in common use and is Old Norse is origin; when combined with an Anglo-Saxon word like 'sea' it makes a powerful new-minted noun. 'Caaing' from 'to caa,' meaning to drive, is again from Old Norse and is in daily use. Here Graham speaks of the 'caaing thresher,' a type of whale which Melville (whom Graham admires) mentions as 'The Caaing Whale.' 'Rhinns,'

perhaps a more exotic word, is Gaelic and is in use among the islanders of the Hebrides to mean rocky headlands. 'Venust,' from the Latin, represents a slight archaism although it stems directly from Scottish ballad where it customarily means delightful, pleasing; 'waly,' meaning alas, is also encountered frequently in old ballads which are sung by the people. A common colloquial turn of syntax is seen in the position of 'fairly,' meaning well, in the line 'An infant fairly twigged on heartoak'. (Koch, p. 666)

We can sense Graham's presence in the passage in that judgement on 'caaing', that it is 'in daily use', as well as in the bracketed detail 'whom Graham admires'. We also get some insight into how we might usefully approach Graham's larger themes:

> ... a profoundly serious search for a fresh morality, but one sought for in poetic rather than in philosophic terms. For Graham's morality is a morality of the antimoral in the sense that the poet is questioning an ethic of self-sacrifice, of human saviourdom. (Koch, p. 668)

> Almost all of Graham's poetry beginning with *2nd Poems* shows an increasing purposive drawing on sea-imagery. This imagery is successful because its resources for ambiguity are grounded in an authentic knowledge of the sea itself. But to think of Graham as a sea poet in the descriptive, literary sense is to falsify his greater achievement ... the realistic documentation of the sea's activity is put in the service of a philosophic inquiry which compares physical death by drowning with spiritual salvation, which is seen as a drowning of the past self. The 'exchanging sea' is like a bridge between two aspects of the self, the most recent self which drowns in the arrival of the new. That is, the self, as a movement toward a perfection, moves toward another death. (Koch, p. 669)

The place-names of *The White Threshold* are the Scottish names of the area in which Graham grew up: Dechmont, Greenock, Lanark, Shian, Gigha, Clyde, Ben Narnain, Ben Cruachen. This is the simplest kind of location we find in the poems. What makes these names resound in the work is the use of little words like 'tig', 'linty', 'mavis', 'airts', 'bing', 'gowan', 'makar', 'brae', 'burn', 'lythe', 'kern' and 'kyle'. Graham's usage is not Lallans, but the effect of conserving the little Scots words in the English may be more telling than inventing a language. English readers are sent to the dictionary, unless they are prepared to read on in uncertainty.

In 'The Children of Greenock', the picture of a pregnant woman in a high tenement room is set against the Clydeside docklands, foundries, streets full of children, and a threatening government. In

The White Threshold

'Listen, Put on Morning' a Black Maria searches the street where corner boys loiter. 'The search by a Town' lights up slag heaps and furnaces; 'The Children of Lanarkshire' links this heavy industry with bombed streets, 'immense warfare' and again, threatening authority. This effect is made forcefully across the poems, through phrases that turn up consistently through the book: 'petition of fears', 'suiciding principle', 'caged cry of prisoners', 'a pillar of war', 'sown outcome of always war', 'barefoot on authority's alphabet', 'one empire', 'scaffold of the times', 'bomb . . . in its idiot bed', 'our wrecks of rage', and 'surrounded by the dead'. Clydeside's Greenock, Lanarkshire's Bothwell and Blantyre, are thus set for us culturally, as subject in life and work to a warring industrial power.

There is no political statement and no ideology in the poems. Graham, a Faber poet whose early work is difficult, is not a likely candidate to be read politically. Yet his work has a political dimension that is obvious as soon as we begin to read across from one poem to another. The language resists a remote standardising authority, and the same authority is implicated in the suffering that comes from warfare, to which the region's industry is harnessed. A view of this warfare is available in, for instance, the phrase 'suiciding principle', which is far from neutral and offers comment and judgement on the remote authority that polices the town.

Structure in this work is given the appearance of growing out of the location, but there is a deliberate principle bending the shape of the book to the place. It is worked up first of all through the high tenement above the street and the hills Dechmont, Cruachen, and Narnain. The space diagram is filled in with shipyard superstructure, derricks rising over the docks, and the church towers high above the crowd. Greenock exists in the shadow of the hills, and the works of the townspeople echo this relation. When the sea comes into the book, the town can be seen to be interposed between two kinds of hostile environment. The poet locates himself by discriminating these distances and relationships. Thus he places himself at the outset on Ben Narnain, quite separate, from where point of view can be carefully manipulated to illumine memory and topography, aligning them on the same scale. The edge of the sea is the most important location in the poems of *The White Threshold*. It is there in poems in which it is not the main subject, as well as those in which its presence is very strong.

> Since all my steps taken
> Are audience of my last
> With hobnail on Ben Narnain
> Or mind on the word's crest
> I'll walk the kyleside shingle
> With scarcely a hark back

> To the step dying from my heel
> Or the creak of the rucksack.
>
> 'Since all my steps taken'

How quietly the sea enters the book through that Scots word 'kyle' when the 'k' pattern is being audited in the verse. See how it changes, stretches, the word 'crest', which is already loaded with the ambiguity 'word / world'. The sea is there and not there, mentioned but outside the present time of the first three poems in *The White Threshold*. This binds the common shape of the poems; they form a metrical group, the first two setting a three-stress line pattern that is the standard for the two-and-a-half to three deviation in the third. The repeat endings are also common, and the shift to a four-stressed, four-line stanza for the next set of three poems is felt quite acutely.

The sea is always there in the town poems, there as a measure, a backdrop that is felt spatially as well as emotionally. It is in 'Shian Bay' and 'Gigha' that the sea comes into the foreground, with the people of the town and their works cleared away. Calvin Bedient chooses these poems as the only 'syntactic successes' of the volume.[1] They do have a stillness and simplicity that is absent elsewhere. It is as if Graham is creating a neutral space, an emptying, before the major works which confront the sea head on.

The play of surf at the water's edge, an ever shifting and erotic boundary from which Venus-Aphrodite is brought forth, is the location of the major group of poems, which seek to link death on a personal scale (Graham's family is addressed in 'Three Letters') with our universal expectation, through the figure of the breaking wave.

The narrative poems of *The White Threshold* are Graham's most successful work up to 1949 and they stand with anything he wrote. In 'The Children of Greenock' the four-line stanzas with three-stress lines seem effortlessly composed, with rhymes and half-rhymes, and some lines unrhymed. It looks as if the poet is unwilling to acknowledge straining to find a rhyme where one does not come easily. The verse feels taut without any striving, therefore, and it has great authority because of this ease. The subject of 'The Children of Greenock' is how the world appears to a woman (presumably modelled on Graham's mother) in her tenement above the docks. Below, children are playing in the streets, and the sights and sounds of industry, 'winches and steel giants', press upon her high enclosure. She cries alone in the room, she stays awake through the night:

> She leaned at the bright mantle brass
> Fairly a mirror of surrounding sorrows,
> The sown outcome of always war
> Against the wordperfect, public tear.

The White Threshold

This gentle description of grieving for members of the family, lost in war, whose remains are their pictures on the mantelpiece, is framed by a view of the community. The sun comes to her through the window, it is already high over the children playing outside. She is pregnant:

> It watched the blind unborn
> Copy book after book of sudden
>
> Elements within the morning of her
> Own man-locked womb. It saw the neighbour
> Fear them housed in her walls of blood.
> It saw two towns, but a common brood.

'It' here is 'her window' – in other words no one is watching her, no one is there to share her concerns and her fears. The poet presents her at a slight distance by attributing a sort of general gaze (the day, the light, us the readers) who might see through the window. Later the window assimilates her viewpoint:

> Her window watched the shipyards sail
> Their men away. The sparrow sill
> Bent grey over the struck town clocks
> Striking two towns, and fed its flocks.

There is a kind of economy in the transforming of unexpected nouns into adjectives: 'The sparrow sill' which is obviously the window sill where sparrows come for crumbs. It is exactly the kind of word arrangement one would expect from Dylan Thomas, but here it is used without crammed lines and without a sense of haste. These lines are easy and efficient, they have a sense of regular pace and spaciousness, like those of an early lyric such as 'O Gentle Queen of the Afternoon'.

The companion piece 'The Children of Lanarkshire' opens with pastoral:

> To put it springtime the green shepherd
> Sheepdogging my fertile heel to word
> Plants this birthplace with one rebellion
> As one place flourished with flute and whin
>
> And royal occurrence of this one empire.

The pastoral theme befits a love poem, but there is a political theme too: a rebellion happened here, the music of the rebellion survives ('flute') within the United Kingdom. In 'Greenock' the effects of the

Second World War (and the first also in the photographs) is felt in the community, in its industry, in 'authority's alphabet' in the street. In the second poem the inland industry is an equivalent: 'immense warfare', 'Bomb sent home to die', 'the tapped furnaces'. It is a picture of the county with its industry based on the Calder and Clyde. The foundries make the hardware for war and the visible evidence of this ('Lanarkshire's flowers rebelling fly / The smelter's furnace in the sky') is brought into uneasy relation with the mood of pastoral. The sparks and fumes are like flowers but are not flowers and will 'bloom' again as bombs.

'The Lost Other' mentions Lanarkshire, Dechmont, Blantyre, Bothwell and Calder river – but also America and New York: 'And New York turns Dechmont in sleep', 'Nor I'll (by Blantyre and Bothwell go) / Doubt my house cages America'. It suggests from stanza two, by the use of 'dove', 'ark', 'sprig' and 'feather', the notion of a voyage for peace (cf. 'Flood' p. 63). This journey, from the mention of 'America' and 'New York' would appear to be a *projected* voyage to the United States:

> Am I to start, as sound a Bacchus
> In travellers' myrtle, citizen of lochs
> Day by deep day under Ben Cruachen.
> So strike me now, her companies again,
>
> Strike deadly through my piling justices,
> Roof of my grave, sky of my histories.
> Strike day by diving on the sea,
> The brine of sailing to The One Liberty.

It is 'projected' because the poet questions 'Am I to start' and suggests he is talking about the future: 'For prophecy I begin with The One Liberty'. 'The One Liberty' might well therefore be the Statue of Liberty in New York, standing visibly for escape and also exile. As well as the narrator of the poem we have a female character, unnamed, the 'Lost Other' of the title:

> Or come in hark this fair spring morning
> Of her lost cry never herself losing
> Even in this place. I'm out within
> The walls I endlessly shoulder down.

This female character is, at least in part, a 'child of Lanark' (Nessie Dunsmuir) from the previous poem. The details of mining: 'Lanarkshire's wheels / Unwind men underground' are reminders of what we know of Nessie Dunsmuir's family from her own poems.[2]

The voyage to America is characterised as escape:

> Content with true promise of Indies
> Worth every while I'll cool my cries
> On runaway waters white and blue
> Out of the shell of the pleasant sky.

And the woman appears therefore to be the one left behind: 'One time she's to stop by my journey / So gentle with a lost answer to my cry'.

This kind of paraphrase is possible with the narrative poems of *The White Threshold* in a way that it is not with the earlier poems, but paraphrase does not give a satisfactory account of them. The male and female identities in 'The Lost Other' are not strictly adhered to. Graham is writing more generally about men who journey and women who are left behind. The 'Kings of the air' would appear to be pilots from the Second World War, but the warriors who appear further on in the same poem are clearly from another war, the Scottish rebellion.

> my dead and gentle brothers.
>
> At hand only a Flood away,
> At war only an ignorance away.
>
> *They rise up* through those elements,
> So gentle a battle in my encampments.
> A thousand fantails over the Calder
> *Darken the royal scale of this empire.*
>
> And becomes a *furious* difference
> To each man in his *rebelling distance*.
>   (my emphasis)

'So gentle a battle in my encampments', especially in the light of this image as used in 'To My Wife at Midnight', would seem to be love-making seen as warfare, since it is a 'gentle' battle and occurs 'in' and not outside or near an encampment. Notice also that 'Flood' is the flood of the Bible and of Noah's ark (as in the opening image of the poem) and also a flood of warriors. We are referred back, therefore, to re-read the earlier flood-ark-dove imagery as standing closer in relation to a theme of war.

The flares of wrecked machinery and / or aircraft, and the flares of industry with men walking in among and rising out of them as 'kings of the air' are brought into combination in the image of 'Daniel of Fire'. The man who walks in the flames must have taken on a new relevance to those who had lived through incendiary bombs in the blitz. Graham's adaptation of the ark and Daniel in this poem is very like T. S. Eliot's 'dark dove with the flickering tongue' (the image gaining power because, as in Graham, the emblem of peace is perverted, here 'dove' is a warplane) in 'Little Gidding'.

Gerard Manley Hopkins's first mature work was the poem 'The Wreck of the Deutschland', which, according to Elizabeth W. Schneider, is 'stated baldly ... an ode on conversion, conversion to the Catholic church'.[3] The occasion of the poem was the disaster involving the liner *Deutschland* which ran aground on sandbanks off the Kent coast in the mouth of the Thames. Five Franciscan nuns, exiled from Germany by the Falck laws, were drowned.[4] When the *Deutschland* was lost, Hopkins's mother sent him newspaper clippings of the event. The wreck was an important event for the English because their maritime reputation was compromised by the events which followed the natural disaster. *The Times* editorial 'was concerned with the "painful surprise" and "shame" with which the nation learned "that a wreck should be stranded off the English coast, appealing to English sailors for aid, and for thirty hours should be left without aid"' (Schneider p. 17). The liner was looted, but the passengers were left to die, among them the five nuns who had been emigrating to America because of Bismark's repressive measures against the Catholic church. Hopkins's poem took this material (the facts of the case *and* the national sense of guilt and shame) and worked it into the framework of an ode on the conversion of the nation to Catholicism. In the first part he describes his own conversion, and in the second he relates the narrative of the wreck as the prelude to a miracle in which Christ appears (walking on the water) to one of the nuns, and takes her and her sisters to heaven.

Hopkins then calls on the saintly nun to intercede on behalf of the nation in his hope and prayer for the conversion of 'rare-dear Britain'. At the centre of the poem, then, is the idea of a supernatural occurrence (the miracle) which is an attempt to heal a national sense of guilt that was about the response to this disaster at sea.

All of this is deeply relevant to Graham's voyage poems which, though foreshadowed in *The Seven Journeys*, properly begin with the poems in *The White Threshold*.

'The Lost Other', like 'The Wreck of the Deutschland', begins with ark and dove imagery and considers a voyage to America. In it there is a saintly female figure who is associated with wrecks and miracles:

> But not touches Saint Other of the Athanor,
> More valuable floored with fountains or
> Our wrecks of rage and custom house,
> Daniel of fire and Kingdom of Agonies.
>
> This better morning she times my search.
> She chimes in ships the flowering bleach

The White Threshold

Of the dead on the bitter wreckageside.

It also mentions prophecy: 'for prophecy I begin with the One Liberty'. Hopkins's poem has 'but you were dovewinged' (stanza 3), the saintly female figure (the Franciscan nun) who is 'A prophetess' and heroine of the wreck. The construction of the sentences in Graham's poem is also similar to Hopkins in the preponderance of reversals of expected forms producing a reflexive mode:

> This fair spring morning she may be found
> By how I call her. The sea makes land.
> Shepherds make by and by their sheep.
> And New York turns Dechmont in sleep.

which is often highly compressed (my emphasis):

> *H*ope *h*olds me *h*igh. All my days tell.
> All palmed my Mays have rambled full.
> I'll shout that ferrysong over water.
> *Th*e *C*alder *h*old *h*er. *Th*is *h*ill *call h*er.

> Question makes measure of the true answer.

In Hopkins's poem we have (my emphasis):

> On Saturday sailed from Bremen
>   American-outward-bound,
> *T*ake *s*ettler and *sea*men, *t*ell *men* with wo*men*
>   Two hundred souls in the round –

and:

> Into the snows she sweeps,
>   Hurling the *h*aven be*h*ind,
> The Deutschland, on Sunday; and so the sky keeps,

which have similar reflexive structures, compression, and alliterative patterning.

'The White Threshold' is a mimetic and meditative poem on the sea which opens (in high alliterative style) with drowning, storms, and crying maidens. In the second section there is a wrecked plane (either from Germany or used to attack potential German invaders) and a

'Watermaster'. Elements of pastoral and martyrdom come together with a modified image of Christ-Phoebus in the last section. Hopkins's 'The Wreck of the Deutschland' has 'A master, her master and mine!' (stanza 19), 'Martyr-master' (stanza 21), 'the master, / *Ipse*' (stanza 28), and Christian pastoral imagery in stanzas 24 and 31.

Hopkins's characterisation of Christ, 'Thou art lightning and love', suggests at least a continuity (given that Hopkins wrote an explicitly Heraclitean poem) between the Greek god Zeus (conventionally invoked by lightning and thunderbolt) and the Christian god of love.

Drowning is a theme developed in several of the poems in *The White Threshold*. In 'Three Poems of Drowning', there are connections with the title-poem: poem number one includes the lines 'Far over early / This morning's wide sea you speak at the white threshold'; the second poem has 'Now endured sea-martyrdom crucified by the soldier sea'; the third poem has 'Now in these seas, my task of the foam-holy voyages / Charted in a bead of blood, I work'. The ideas 'white threshold', 'matyrdom' and the voyage as a writing project are tried out here.

'The Voyages of Alfred Wallis' is a tribute to the so-called primitive St Ives painter (1855–1942), who was the subject of a book *Alfred Wallis-Primitive*, by Graham's friend Sven Berlin. Wallis went to sea as a boy and worked on fishing ships between Penzance and Newfoundland. He moved to St Ives in the 1890s, gave up fishing and became a marine scrap merchant. His wife died in 1922, and soon after he began to paint to relieve his loneliness. He used materials that he scrounged: hardboard from boxes given to him by a grocer, paint from near-empty tins that the boatyard workers had thrown out. His painting was discovered by Ben Nicholson and Christopher Wood in 1928.[5]

Graham was in touch with Sven Berlin when he was writing the book on Wallis and read sections of the work before publication. Wallis painted ships and lighthouses, small harbours and ports of Cornwall. Like childrens' paintings his works are not bothered by a sense of scale or perspective. His letters to H. S. Ede of Kettle's yard show that he was uneducated and almost illiterate.[6] He died in complete poverty in the Madron poorhouse.

That his work appealed to men like Sven Berlin and Graham, who themselves lived in poverty, is not surprising. They valued a man who, without the benefits of an education, had made himself into an artist of international fame. Graham's education had been rough and ready and Berlin had had a similar career. Neither of them achieved financial security, and Graham's circumstances were eased only when he was awarded a pension from the Civil List. When Graham writes 'His poor house blessed by very poverty's religious / Breakwater, his past house hung in foreign galleries' he is describing Wallis's career; the 'poor house' is that of Madron and 'past house' refers to the ships in Wallis's paintings that were hung in galleries

The White Threshold

when he became posthumously famous. The linking with Herman Melville is absolutely right:

> The ship of land with birds on seven trees
> Calls out farewell like Melville talking down on
> Nightfall's devoted barque and the parable whale.

Melville was another man who went to sea and came back to make an art of his experience, a manifestly self-educated writer, whose use of Shakespeare in *Moby-Dick*, for instance, shows the enthusiasm of only half-digested influence, and speaks of a great effort of self-improvement. Melville wrote masterpieces which were formally uncouth, and they have a special kind of vitality because he did not allow himself to be contained in the genres known in his time. Wallis's painting is similar in this way, and Graham claims them both as ancestors in this poem of tribute.

'The Voyages of Alfred Wallis' is the first of Graham's tributes to artists, a genre in which he was to excel later in his career. Graham became the poet of the St Ives community, mourning its dead while bringing a particular view of the place and its artists to life. In this early example Graham celebrates Wallis's seafaring life, but the line 'Oils overcome and keep his inward voyage' shows that even here, Graham is using the tribute-poem to say things about his writing-project, while still fulfilling the first function of mourning.

The pair of poems 'Shian Bay' and 'Gigha' commemorate those drowned at sea. The poems are both named for places to the west of the Clyde. 'Shian Bay' is located on the west coast of Jura and 'Gigha' is a small island between Kintyre and Islay.

> That firewood pale with salt and burning green
> Outfloats its men who waved with a sound of drowning
> Their saltcut hands over mazes of this rough bay.
>
> Quietly this morning beside the subsided herds
> Of water I walk. The children wade the shallows.
> The sun with long legs wades into the sea.
>
> 'Gigha'

We see the 'rough bay' after a storm which has killed and which has coincidentally brought in firewood to be cast up on the beach. The salt which encrusts the wood has cut into the sailors' hands. The onlooker walks by the water's edge and notices children playing there. He compares them with the sun which also 'wades' in. The human fact of generations succeeding each other in their growth and mortality is framed by the untamed and elemental presence of the sea. The 'saltcut hands' reminds us of Jesus's hands pierced by nails, and the variants of walking on water ('beside the ... water I walk', 'the children wade', 'the sun ... wades') while perhaps suggesting connection and elaboration through 'firewood' and 'herds' of the wood of the cross and a hint of pastoral, does not finally contain what is at issue here. The sea takes the men to itself in drowning and their offspring are seen playing at the edge, sometime later to move into the unstable medium that will both support and take them.

'Shian Bay' is again located at the shore's edge:

> Gulls set the long shore printed
> With arrow steps over this morning's
> Sands clean of a man's footprint

The traces are readable (compare 'the printed snow' etc. in 'Malcolm Mooney's Land'). Where the sea has erased the traces of men, gulls have re-written their presence.

> Last gale washed five into the bay's stretched arms,
> Four drowned men and a boy drowned into shelter.
> The stones roll out to shelter in the sea.

The disaster is taken into the context of human relations: 'into the bay's stretched arms' suggests caring, as does 'drowned into shelter'. The absolute impersonality of the last line 'The stones roll out to shelter in the sea', worries the idea of shelter and the difference between human and inhuman. In this remote community whose economy is sea-based, the people's livelihood is the sea's produce. The movement of the stones is a response to the tidal rhythm which is what erases the patterns of footprints on the sand and allows, therefore, a new pattern to be written. Writing in nature (the gull's footprints) and the writing of man are used to compare life and its extinction. That which comes from the sea is erased by it, as in the 'clean sand' after the tide.

'The White Threshold' is the first of Graham's truly extensive poems to appear in *Collected Poems 1942–1977*. It contains various kinds of language use that are returned to and developed in the later poems.

> Let me all ways from the deep heart
>
> Always the welcome-roaring threshold
>
> Let me all ways from these seas
>
> Always the saving seadoors well

The White Threshold

> Let me all ways from the deep heart
>
> Always these all sea families felled

The first section has a structure of phrases put in opposition that open each stanza block. 'Let me all ways' and 'Always the' is a chime that creates a rising rhythm in a section that is clearly intended to be loud and intense. Against this pattern there are single lines placed so that they have an extra rhetorical weight: 'I walk towards you and you may not walk away', 'I rise up loving and you may not move away'. They look as if they should be declared as climaxes against the rising rhythm that is being established. The chime is made by splitting the word 'always' into two parts, something that Graham does consistently in his later work in a more complex and interesting way.

> Let me all ways from the deep heart
> Drowned under behind my brow so ever
> Stormed with other wandering, speak
> Up famous fathoms well over strongly
> The pacing whitehaired kingdoms of the sea.

Hopkins's poems are the precedent for this word order, which is so far from normal speech. Unlike Graham's later poetry, there is a surplus here, the passage is bursting with stuff. It is patterned internally: 'Drowned under ... so ever / Stormed ... other wander / fathoms well over / kingdoms of the'. 'Under', 'ever', 'other', 'over', 'of the', gives us a continuity of sound that is broken up with surprises made of extra words. 'Under behind', 'ever / Stormed', 'famous fathoms' are points at which we feel the sentence is crammed, we cannot be sure which way the movement is going. Again, this is something that Graham takes up and uses in his later work, where there is often an ambiguity from the odd placing of words combined with line ends. He does it, for instance, in 'Imagine a Forest' with:

> In that deep ballad very not
> A dream and the fire noisily
> Kindling up and breaking its sticks.
> Do not imagine I put you there
> For nothing. I put you through it
> There in that holt of words between

'Deep' is unexpected perhaps, 'very not' is strange enough to make the pace of reading uncertain and hesitant. 'I put you there / ... I put you through it' is developed for the comparison that makes us read 'I put you through it' as a phrasal unit and halt again, stumbling before we continue with the next line 'There in that holt of words between' (where 'holt' begs to be read also as halt). The uncertainty in the pace and the stumbling are a kind of fine control related to the subject of 'Imagine a Forest', where the reader is imagining a difficult, stumbling, progress through undergrowth. Such control in Graham's late work has its antecedents. Graham was using unexpected word orders, overloading of adjectives and adverbs, sound echoes, alliteration and delay in his early work.

The main force of this first section of 'The White Threshold' appears to be acting on the build-up to strong lines which are another form of surplus, of overload. This is something Dylan Thomas always did; the line is there for its own sake, just as much as for what it contributes. Graham's 'The pacing whitehaired kingdoms of the sea', 'The caaing thresher in his splendid blood' could almost have been written by Thomas. But Graham has a passage in this section that could almost be from 'The Nightfishing' (and is therefore quite beyond the range of anything that Thomas did):

> Always these all sea families felled
> In diving burial hammocks or toppled
> Felled elm back into the waving woods,
> Wear me my words. The nettling brine
> Stings through the word. The Morven maiden cries.
>
> Section 1

Using the word 'felled' for alliteration, Graham is seeing the mast and the high branches of a wood moving like the sea 'the waving woods'. He is also compressing the felling of a family with the 'felled elm' or coffin timber, and playing on 'hammock' which is slung between trees, or on deck; or (here) used for burial at sea. The 'nettling brine' tells us that the saltwater stings, but 'nettling' is based on 'nettle' which is another reminder of woodland. The next couple of phrases 'wear me my words. The nettling brine / Stings through the word' are ideas that we find repeated in 'The Nightfishing': 'The keel in its amorous furrow / Goes through each word'. The control of language is again stronger in the later piece where 'word' is a substitution for 'wave', so that we are brought to the recognition of the poem as object *without* damage to the narrative continuity, as we read 'wave' and 'word' at the same time.

The first section of 'The White Threshold' is a special kind of language performance. The groups of words in the stanzas denote too much to speak to us in the way we expect speech to work. This is what I have called 'the surplus'. It happens in each stanza. The writing is written to be and sound strong. The rising rhythm against which the strong lines are sounded is a language pattern made to re-enact the waves breaking against land. The imagery of the section is sexual, all

The White Threshold

of it (unlike Hopkins, where this is more deeply sublimated) regarding the force of the sea, equating it to passion and the beginning and end of life. Through the spray we discern a wild northern Aphrodite:

> I rise up loving and you may not move away
>
> The caaing thresher in his splendid blood
>
> maiden- / Headed foamthatch

The second section of 'The White Threshold' seems more immediately approachable than the first. There is a recognisable activity that has a sense of clear movement. The poet, walking at the sea's edge and calling himself 'Watermaster' (which reminds us of 'Master of the tides' in Hopkins's 'Wreck of the Deutschland'), describes what he sees. From line four:

> Wrecked aluminium (what trinket gone
> Down out of hounded air to the drowned?)
> Bound kerns of spray, loud sweeps of foam
> And sea-trapdoors.

What he sees is a crashed aeroplane. Again the image is sexualised, this time by the suggestion that the plane is a 'trinket' for the goddess who is invoked by 'bound kerns', 'foam', 'sea-trapdoor'. The watching 'Watermaster' stance is taken up at a clifftop:

>   Five fathoms up
> Into nightair I emerge safe.
> I see shorefire and needfire burn
> Buried far out in island air
> So near fanned into answer venust
> Or black wind blow their courage out.
> Shelled and fabled flying sprayricks
> Over the hosters of the lythed water

From here he sees fires burning, and it is not clear whether the fires are crops, wreckage, alarm flares, or bomb damage. The words made by rough joining are dense in this passage: 'nightair', 'shorefire', 'needfire', sprayricks'. We cannot be quite sure how the word 'shelled' is being used, but we can be sure that the use is deliberately ambiguous.

Further on in the second section we get a picture of the moon's light on the water, and the light is a 'waif': a person uncared for, a neglected child, but also a nautical term for a flag used as a signal. All this reminds Graham of the drowned. Then we have the idea of swimming out towards an island, and a call for the goddess to guide the boat out on the water. So thought, youthful aspiration (swimming), and sexual longing ('goddess-enamoured oar') are tried one after another as a response to the 'one faint waif, the whipend moon'. After the roaring and overbearing first section, we get a relatively clear set of responses to the prospect of the sea at night, reflexive and retrospective: 'my lifesaved youngest', 'fleetly / Older stranger by changing stranger'.

Those phrases are typical of Graham's later work. The idea of the younger or past self as separate, seen as quite another person, is something that is used again and again in *The Nightfishing*. ('He drowns, who but ill / Resembled me'; 'Only / Myself I died from into / These present words that move'), and is developed into the sustained ambiguity of say 'The Dark Dialogues' in *Malcolm Mooney's Land* ('And this is no other / Place than where I am. / Here turning between . . . And you, whoever you are. / That I am other to'). The goddess, incidentally, appears in 'Implement 51': 'Brigit of early shallows', and the same name occurs, together with 'wrack and shingle on the Long Loch' in 'Clusters Travelling Out'.

The third section uses clearly recognisable autobiographical material such as we find in 'The Dark Dialogues' in *Malcolm Mooney's Land*. It is divided into three blocks, and these, like 'The Dark Dialogues', represent three viewpoints that come towards the speaker: 'For him her heart she wore'; 'For her his heart he wore'; 'They walk towards me kindly as I hold'. It is the poet looking back at his own and his wife's youth.

> For him her heart she wore.
> Veinhaired kingdoms of the heart.
> And as a child on Dechmont side
> She looked down her loud seasons
> Down on pits and wheels
> Unwinding in diving cages
> Young kings mad under meadows,
> An infant unwound into her own heartbreak
> Hearing the beechtop cradles noisily
> Below on the burning season's side.
> A woman folkhomed by red Lanarkshire's slag
> Held in her foster heart
> She endured the furnace in the sky
> And with her looking young lifetime
> Suffered the high perched season.

This section of 'The White Threshold' is based closely upon 'Raith Pit' a poem by Nessie Dunmuir first published in 1946, which has the same matter ('pit-wheels whirr . . . descending cage . . . coalface rumble . . . blinding shaft of the sun') present also in Graham's poem 'The Lost Other'.

The second block of this third section does for Graham's youth what the former did for Dunsmuir's. The Clydeside tenement which becomes familiar through Graham's *Collected Poems* is the matter of it, the shipyard with cradles, arclights and derricks. The mining machinery is brought into comparison with that of shipbuilding and the docks. The tenement's height above the street and the firth is measured against the depth of the mines. Both of these give scale to the birth / sex image that ends the second passage:

> He fell down his steep life
> And with his bloodline in his hand
> Followed the fox in his fables.

So who is the 'I' voice in the third block of this section? We cannot quite identify him with the male figure of the second part. He is looking back at a former self, feeling distant from that self by a change in circumstances.

> They walk towards me kindly as I hold
> Well into memory drowned in the crowded seanight.
> Drowned in my crowded head and singled out
> I walk the midnight waters of the heart.
> They walk towards me too well suffered from,
> Bright opposites in imagination's room,
> Voiced on my seachanged lifetime from their home.
> These two are other, with my likeness enhungered
> And meet me shared in the bed of the listening world.
> But I'm cried out loud on the breath of the dead.

'Shared in the bed of the listening world' is a quiet, passionate line. The distance between 'he' and 'I' in this section is self-consciousness, that is what shifts us into the present. The section has gone back over personal history to establish the voice of the first section, with its loose-seeming pronouns (who is speaking to whom?). The piece ends with a typical Graham construction in the *passive* voice: 'But I'm cried out loud on the breath of the dead' which sets up a symmetry between his imaginary figures (the lovers), himself in the present, and 'the dead'. The consciousness of this section is a constructed thing.

> These two are other, with my likeness enhungered
> And meet me shared in the bed of the listening world.
> But I'm cried out loud on the breath of the dead.

It is difficult to stabilise the opening phrase of section four: 'All this night are answered', because we have read the 'always / all ways' pattern earlier. The meaning is established by reading *back* and relocating the stress. We need a little more on the word 'all' to make sense, and it slows the pace, which is slowed more with this new line-length that is to become Graham's standard metre. And when he says 'We've met when on a time' (line 6), 'I've met you across a look' (line 20) and 'I move towards you across' (line 24) it seems clear that the 'you' is the reader, addressed directly as in so much of the later work. The settings: walking home at night, drinking bouts in bars, the sea, the wind on a hillside; these are typical. A song 'The foggy, foggy, dew' is there, and the name 'Kevin', which does not yield anything except that he is talking about a particular memory or set of memories. Greenock, I take it, is 'the whisky town' – it has six distilleries nearby, and Greenock is the point at which Highland and Lowland malts divide.

The pace and the phraseology of this section locate it with the later work:

> I've met you across a look
> In a quick room cropped up
> Out of the law I break.
>
> This night the hill bothies
> On the windbreak of Kintyre
> Hear the downbearing sea
> Break on the seashelled door.

'Across a look' and 'a quick room cropped up' are the kinds of phrase that we associate with Graham's later poems. They are made out of delay, are a function of the three stress line. The 'hearing' attributed to the 'bothies' is typical also, as is the way the line break makes the word 'bothies' look as if it is being used as a verb. The pause and the human attribute that is suggested by this verbal equivocation makes the near pun on 'bodies'. The language is being used in a way that is not quite possible in the surplus state at the beginning of the poem. The other new note in this section of the poem is the Christian reference: 'This night I make my haul / From the twelve-discipled seas'. Graham uses this kind of matter in *The Nightfishing*, but in a different way. 'I make my haul' puts the poet, as fisher, in the position of Christ – but it does not tell us much else. It is in the next section that the Christian matter comes thick and fast.

The last section of the poem goes back to the style of utterance that was used in the first section, and the Christian matter is quite dense: 'that other wandered seawalker', the 'Phoebus' crucifixion image, 'your sacrifice', 'the martyr', 'churches, error', 'The bush I burn', 'angelic bread', 'cleft cathedrals in the furnaced city', 'My daily dead' (a mute echo of 'my daily bread'). As in the first section, the very obvious division of material into stanzas beginning with a similar phrase gives us a symmetry: 'Good not', 'Good Phoebus', 'Good now', 'Good voice'.

Another pattern is set up, giving us a line and a half before the sentence-break in stanzas one and three. Stanza two has another break at the end of line one, but this still fits into the form. The last two have two-and-a-half lines before each break. The arbitrary pattern of line pause and sense pause gives us an extra structure to hold to. Like the opening of the poem, we have here a set of equivalent units of sound which begin with repeats.

At all points in the section we have a mix of Christian imagery with warfare, burning and drowning imagery. The connection is made clear in lines 13–15:

> I'll hold you off your sacrifice even for
> The martyr in burning cities brother sister
> All of the elemental founded churches' error.

According to Vivienne Koch: 'Graham's morality is a morality of the anti-moral in the sense that the poet is questioning an ethic of self-sacrifice, of human saviourdom' (p. 668). If we assume Graham's co-operation in Koch's essay, then we should be clear that he wanted 'The White Threshold' to be read in this way.

The 'churches' error' is therefore the philosophy of sacrifice, which is established by the praise of martyrdom. Sacrifice of the self for state is the logic of warfare, it creates 'burning cities brother sister': The hellfire that the church used to keep the people in fear, has broken out in twentieth-century cities with air raids. Graham enforces the point with 'cleft cathedrals' – not broken, bombed, or smashed cathedrals. We think of cleft foot, cloven foot, devil. The Christian cathedral is supposed to be a diagram of unity: one god, body of Christ, body of the church, one congregation. Graham is subverting this in his description of war damage. His description of the Christ figure 'Good Phoebus youth nailed on the bleeding branches' steals the young man who suffers torture from the church and what is seen here as the churches' misuse of that imagery. By identifying Christ with Phoebus, the poet is pre-empting the claims of the church. Ultimately the target is the Christian state, which brings us to warfare through Christianity.

If the poem is meant to be against self-sacrifice, which is seen as something that the Christian church and therefore state upholds in time of war, it is also concerned with another kind of sacrifice, and it questions the stability of the individual self.

The seductive imagery of the 'watermaster' section suggests that the prospect of making a voyage is, in some sense at least, seen as a sexual adventure. The special regard for a past relationship that is shown in the next section, would seem to be a process of putting the past straight, of self-justification. There is a firm link between the matter of, 'The Lost Other', 'The Children of Greenock', 'The Children of Lanark' and the title poem. In all cases the poet is putting the past in order and considering a voyage. Drowning is a necessary hazard, in real terms, for those who venture on the sea. It is also a figure for radical alteration to the self and for a self retrospectively constituted through experience, as in say a swimmer's perception being reconstructed by the resistance of his or her medium, the sea. This accounts for a great deal of obscurity in the poems, and for the reflexive formulae: 'His story invents his following eye'; 'I'm cried out loud on the breath of the dead'.

The Nightfishing

'The Nightfishing' is an ambitious poem, a large and varied structure, which must be regarded as among the poet's major works. It is a narrative poem that has at its core a voyage that is also a night's fishing after herring; going out in a boat, setting the nets, bringing in the catch, returning home. These events occur in the poem but they do not sum its action because another kind of voyage and voyaging is at stake, and the events narrated have a significance which, while it does not fail to carry us on a particular fishing trip, connects with a more fundamental questioning of our common experience in work, in knowledge, and in what we might call the inner life.

Beyond even the smallish social world of a fishing community, and deep in the quiet and strangeness of the night, a fisherman goes out to sea in a boat. The description of his progress is intercut with other material, a sense of himself watched from without and a kind of heightened self-awareness. Memories of birth and other early perceptions also feed in, so that we read this journey as on a scale with a whole life and not just one night's fishing.

The necessary hazard and the hard labour of the venture are recorded in the central section of the poem. But beyond this narrative function, these events take the reader to a special place outside the comforts and limitations of the social world. The fisherman (and here we should note that details of the presence and activities of his companions are suppressed) is at the mercy of the sea, and in a special relationship with it since he is anxious to get his catch safely home.

The reversal in the expected agency of the verbs, the consistent use of reflexive sentence forms creates a strong sense of passivity in the protagonist. 'These words take place' (p. 97, *Collected Poems*), 'So I have been called by my name and / it was not sound' (p. 97) – these are examples of the impression that the reader gains of the fisherman put into existence by his activity, through the resistance of the elements (and one of these elements is language).

The experience of fishing, in a way wishing to be true to itself, is brought into a language-space on which (or in which) the reader moves. The fisherman exists as one of the things and beings encountered in this progress, not privileged in his perceptions, and not identical with the voice that we give to the poem by reading it. Thus the shifting levels of the water and the lack of fixity in the course of the boat's progress (reading weather-signs, animal-signs, and star-signs) moving towards an unknown end (the catch) is paralleled in the withholding of a guiding narrative voice. Throughout the poem there is a shifting between the voyage and its literary manifestation, and these levels are never quite separated and thus not allegorised.

The model of reality that informs the poem is that view of the world expressed by Heraclitus: 'All is flux, nothing is stationary'.[1] It is part of the great strength and originality of this work that the ideas associated with the Pre-Socratics are not tacked on to the poem but account for the way it is made:

> We're well hinted herring plenty for the taking,
> About as certain as all those signs falling
> Through their appearance.   (p. 96)

'Signs' and 'appearance' are thoughts not only concerning poetical and philosophical language, but also the natural orders of weather-signs and animal-signs that speak through appearance. These 'signs' are 'the best / Fishmarks the gannets' (p. 96), and the metaphysics is thus an outgrowth of precision of observation and recording in and from the natural world, as well as an accuracy of language use that dovetails these meanings together.

G. S. Fraser's early response to the poem was the only contemporary criticism which began to take its measure as an ambitious and important work. According to Fraser, Graham's 'central theme' in 'The Nightfishing' is:

> That of Plato's *Theaetetus* as interpreted by Cornford – the theme of the tension between conceptual order and sensational flux. The sea for him [Graham] is a symbol for everything in human experience that seems to evade our attempt to impose order on it, and the word, the poet's word, is a symbol for the struggle to impose or discover order which, nevertheless, we persist in . . . what is our or anything's identity within the flux? Language is the boat with which we ride the flux, a flux which, like the sea, is in some sense our source and at once threatens us and feeds us.[2]

The language of description is subject to the same flux as the perceptions it seeks to record. Fraser sees Graham as 'a man struggling concretely with the problem of identity-in-change'.

This notion of speaking 'concretely' from a fluid identity is a main theme or precondition of much of Graham's work. Sometimes (as in the early poem 'The Serving Inhabiters') it is the explicit subject, but more often it accounts for the way in which the writing proceeds. In 'The Nightfishing' it is both and this is the fundamental difficulty of the poem. The matter of 'The Nightfishing': the narrative of the voyage, the biography of the speaker, elements of Christian and pre-Christian allegory, and the business of writing, is presented in such a way that events are scattered, refracted and transposed. The fishing sequence is in the expected order but it has (by the time we get there) been prefaced and intercut with other material which maintains uncertainty.

Edwin Morgan has noted that Graham's 'use of words like "innocence" and "grace" and "perfection" is likely to be counter-productive, making the reader restless, by their withdrawing of imaginative sympathy'.[3] What is at stake here (and what Edwin Morgan and others have responded to in this way) is the loading of the language with significances beyond the descriptive task of recording a fishing-trip. We cannot accept the speaker in the poem as a fisherman-character, though he is plainly informed by practical knowledge. The evasion of a coherent self, the refusal to be located behind any particular instance of speaking, might be said to characterise the voice in the poem. This is explicit through the opening section and it is the logic of the sense of suspension that is developed in the piece.

The voyage, while it remains an experience that is presented as work, of getting food, a matter of physical survival, is also a voyage into the kind of territory that we know from Coleridge's *The Rime of the Ancient Mariner* which operates in the area we think of as the spiritual, the sacred and the unconscious. The symbolic ordering of Coleridge's narrative: the wounding of the bird, the isolation of the protagonist, the journeying beyond the real and the final not quite Christian redemption of the mariner, informs the reality that Graham presents in 'The Nightfishing'.

> When writing The Nightfishing I knew I had read Pound's translation of the Seafarer, and other voyages literature. Nansen helped me to steer.[4]

The tradition that Graham's poem enters is that which begins with Homer, and which is extended by many works whose basis is a voyage or quest into the unknown, where trials are suffered, and where the resolution of the narrative involves changes in the perception of the protagonist, whose new self finally comes home. There is a kind of mythic identity between Odysseus lashed to the mast in the Sirens episode of Homer, and later Christian versions of the hero mariner, which grow out of the story of Christ the fisherman who makes his disciples fishers of men; who walks on the water, and is later crucified. In the transmission of the story, lashing to the mast becomes nailing to the cross. The Christian version of this tradition is developed in full in Hugo Rahner's *Greek Myths and Christian Mystery* (1963):

> Odysseus, the homeward-faring wanderer has successfully overcome all perils, but only because he has been bound to the mast. The Christian version of this has been given us by Clement: 'Bound to the wood of the cross, thou art freed from all danger of destruction. God's Logos will steer thy ship and the Holy Pnuema will give thee a safe return to heaven's harbour'.
>
> (p. xxi)

The identity of cross and mast is made plain in section 7 of Rahner's book, 'Odysseus at the Mast':

> If in the course of time Christians regarded the mast to which the immortal seafarer was bound, as a symbol of the cross, they were by no means guilty of any forced or arbitrary association of ideas, nor would their pagan predecessors or contemporaries who sailed the same Mediterranean waters in the same kind of ships, ever have accused them of that. The giant mast, crossed at right angles by the yard, of itself suggests the cross to which rightless or foreign criminals were nailed or tied. (pp. 371–72)

This traditional transformation of imagery is clearly at issue in Coleridge's *The Rime of the Ancient Mariner*, as it is in Hopkins's 'Wreck of the Deutschland'.

Graham's more immediate ancestors in this work are Nansen and Pound. Nansen's name is used for its heroic import in Dylan Thomas's poem 'Once Below a Time':

> On the old seas from stories, thrashing my wings,
> Combing with antlers, Columbus on fire,
> I was pierced by the idol tailor's eyes,
> Glowed through shark mast and navigating head,
> Cold Nansen's beak on a boat full of gongs,
>
> To the boy of common thread,
> The bright pretender, the ridiculous sea dandy
> With dry flesh and earth for adorning and bed.

Nansen was a Norwegian explorer who went on his ship *Fram* to the far north, and then trekked towards the North Pole over the arctic ice, farther north than any man had been before. Graham's use of Nansen and his writings is more extended than the mention of the name by Thomas. Graham's work follows the course of Nansen's great expedition. 'The Nightfishing' may be seen as following Nansen's voyage, while 'Malcolm Mooney's Land' goes beyond into the ice-bound north. We shall be considering Nansen's career and writings in detail as they relate to *Malcolm Mooney's Land* below.

The Nightfishing

In Pound's poem 'The Seafarer' (which advertises itself as 'from the early Anglo-Saxon text'), a mariner looks back over the hardship of his life at sea. We have seen how Graham's early work *The Seven Journeys* established a distinct northern identity, with material from *The Poetic Edda*, and how this was developed in 'The White Threshold' with its special vocabulary of Scottish, Old Norse and Anglo-Saxon origin. Pound's 'The Seafarer' attempts to portray the mariner's persona by making it reside in a carefully chosen northern (Anglo-Saxon, Norse) vocabulary, as well as a version of the standard Anglo-Saxon metre in which a four-stress line has alliteration (or initial rhyme) on three of the four stressed syllables.

> Bitter breast-cares have I abided,
> Known on my keel many a care's hold,
> And dire sea-surge, and there I oft spent
> Narrow nightwatch nigh the ship's head
> While she tossed close to cliffs, coldly afflicted,

Graham's poem (and all his later work) is built of a metre that is related. His shift from a three- to a four-stressed line in the poems of *The White Threshold* and in 'The Nightfishing' sections one and two, is related to Pound's practice, as is the alliterative structure of 'The Nightfishing', section three. The later sections of 'The Nightfishing' move towards the three-stress line which is Graham's standard metre (Graham has made the iambic trimeter very much his own) in his later work. The mariner in Pound's poem is, though remote in time, not elevated socially. He is a hard-worked and sometimes hard-pressed seaman, who is supposed to be the author of his tale of hardship. This was perhaps the most significant detail (apart from the language) for Graham. A character who knows the sea through experience and work, who speaks out of that experience, must have seemed powerful to Graham who had himself worked on fishing boats in Scotland and in Cornwall.[5]

The first section of 'The Nightfishing' is a series of instances of calling. From the first event in the poem there is doubt about cause and continuity, which comes from the unexpected word order and the significant suppression of narrative detail. Add to this the deliberate ambiguities of Graham's lineation (the feeling that lines are often placed uneasily between fulfilling the sense of what they follow and beginning anew) and we have something like the texture of the verse.

> Very gently struck
> The quay night bell.

> Now within the dead
> Of night and the dead
> Of my life I hear
> My name called from far out.
> I'm come to this place
> (Come to this place)
> Which I'll not pass
> Though one shall pass
> Wearing seemingly
> This look I move as. (p. 91)

We do not discover who strikes the bell and we experience the event in the passive form as happening to the bell (or in the ear of one who hears it). The placing of the words is unusual since 'bell' has two adjectives preceding it: 'quay' and 'night'.

The stress pattern in the first two lines is arranged so that the strong beats in each line sound on the hard 'c' (here spelt as 'ck', 'qu') so that we might hear the strike in the words pronounced. The sense of suspension comes both from the absence of any named person who strikes the bell, and from the first line's speed being slowed by the three stresses together (without intervening unstressed syllables) in the second line.

The rest of the quoted passage has its primary form through repetition: lines 3 and 4 end in 'dead', 4 and 5 begin in 'of', 7 and 8 end in 'place', 9 and 10 in 'pass'. Line 11 is tied to itself by the internal 'wearing-seeming' and line 12 rhymes back to 10 with 'as'. The pauses at the line ends are quite strong therefore, and this pattern pulls against our sureness of the continuity of the piece. Pronouncing the word 'dead', one is torn between 'within the dead' and 'within the dead of night'. This ambiguity between the lines as discrete units and the sense which runs across them is a function of the very short three-stress line which is unlikely to complete a thought in itself. The poet notices and makes clear a resistance or interference in language from the little words that will not quite hold still in their meaning or agency.

The use of brackets in line 8, which as in *The Waste Land* (I, line 26) '(Come in under the shadow of this red rock)' makes the voice seem more intimate and directed to one reader, occurs at the point where the identity of the speaker is for the first time sidestepped:

> I'll come to this place
> (Come to this place)
> Which I'll not pass
> Though one shall pass
> Wearing seemingly
> This look I move as. (p. 91)

The Nightfishing 67

We are by now in doubt as to who struck the bell and who is speaking. The sound of the bell is taken up and magnified. Owls and gulls call, there is a wind 'honing the roof', coming from a distant gale. The dead speak and the sea itself calls to the speaker. There is a powerful sense of otherness in this calling which is not at all in line with the beginning of a fishing trip.

> I bent to the lamp. I cupped
> My hand to the glass chimney.
> Yet it was a stranger's breath
> From out of my mouth that
> Shed the light.   (p. 92)

The 'stranger's breath' is another shift which makes the persona uneasy and another point at which we feel more is at stake, though we have not yet learnt enough to attribute what or whom is at stake.

The whole section is like the Telemachus chapters of Joyce's *Ulysses*, in that both have instances of calling to a voyage and static images left behind. Joyce's usurper seal, dappled light on Nestor's shoulders, and the three masted ship, are like the bell, the house and the harbour left behind in Graham's poem. The significant factor in the rendering of Stephen's consciousness in *Ulysses* appears to be just this inability to be immersed in his experience (to accept it as contingent and continuous) since he formalises everything into static and reductive images to be read against his past life as evidence of his 'calling' (calling to be a poet). The 'stranger's breath' in Graham's poem is just the same kind of self-consciousness, and that Joyce's book is in some part a late Homeric voyage-text, is very much to the point.

The passive constructions, the metre, and the self-conscious instances of calling all contribute to locate the opening section outside normal reality, in that space into which Coleridge's *The Rime of the Ancient Mariner* voyages.

Graham once introduced the second section of 'The Nightfishing' in this way: 'The second section is short. It could be a song. The phrase "a set-in bed" means a bed set into the thickness of the wall, a kind of square cave.'[6] Section two gives us facts about the poet's biography – but see how they are arranged to correspond with the movement elsewhere. The whole play on birth and death gives a measure to what happens throughout the poem. The movement of birth is likened to the boat leaving the harbour, waking from dream, coming out of the cave. That it is Plato's cave in part is underlined by the presence of the midwife:

> When I fell down into this place
> My father drew his whole day's pay,

> My mother lay in a set-in bed,
> The midwife threw my bundle away. (p. 93)

> SOCRATES: My art of midwifery is in general like theirs; the only difference is that my patients are men, not women, and my concern is not with the body but with the soul that is in travail of birth. And the highest point of my art is the power to prove by every test whether the offspring of a young man's thought is a false phantom or instinct with life and truth. I am so far like the midwife that I cannot myself give birth to wisdom.[7]

Further, the line 'My eyes let light in on this dark', typical of Graham's technique of reversing the expected agency of the verb, echoes Plato's theory of perception, as does 'the harbour oil/Looks at the sky through seven colours':

> A stream of visual light flows out from the eye to meet a stream of light whose structure corresponds in such a way that the two streams can interpenetrate each other and coalesce. The marriage of these two motions generates seeing and colour. Physically, 'the eye becomes filled with vision' ... The external thing 'becomes white'; its surface is 'saturated with whiteness' (Cornford p. 50).

This one birth, placed in section two, connects with the repeated instances of death-rebirth through the poem, where the unstable 'I' is many times 'clad anew'. The fisherman's clothes are emblems of death, the boots inlaid with fish scales, the jersey a web of nerves meshed like the net.

The sophistication of the rhythm in this section is remarkable. The move from the three-stress (section 1) to the five-stress (section 3), is graduated in section 2. The opening stanza is held together by repetition of words and vowel sounds as in section 1. In these lines the four-stress unit is at first broken by full-stop pauses, so that there is an approach to the new line. The second (refrain) stanza is end-stopped and part-rhymed. The third is half-rhymed and the fourth carries the same part-rhymes as number 2.

Graham describes it as song, by which he indicates the easy-seeming rhythm, in which each thought or each stage in the process of thought, is located in a line. The regular four-stress helps to build the variety of patterning in the poem, denser here because of the split into refrain/non-refrain. A further function of the refrain is to speak in the right tone of 'mother' and 'father', and the hard-won simplicity is close to nursery-rhyme. It is precisely this lack of inhibition, combined with serious intentions and manifest technical ability, that sets Graham's poetry apart from the other writing of his time.

The third and longest section of 'The Nightfishing' narrates a voy-

The Nightfishing

age that is a night-long trip in a drifter after herring. It is a long way from a factual account. Various strategies are employed to indicate further meaning in what is narrated, but these indications are held back from delivering a separable 'message' in the poem. The narrator is the man who was called in section 1, and about whom we have learnt something in section 2. He is not alone but he does not describe his companions, which is unexpected because there is a special relationship within the crew of the boat – a relationship on which their lives depend. There would be nine of them including the speaker, who, since he appears to take a part in the hauling of nets, is not the captain.[8]

The point of this, beyond the sense that the voyage is one of self-discovery, is that when the narrator speaks of 'us' in the poem there should be some doubt whether he means himself and the rest of the crew or himself and his readers. That he addresses his readers as 'you' and uses the 'us' soon afterwards in the same stanza (p. 94, second stanza) helps this fictional device along. Graham, as Edwin Morgan notes, makes the reader 'a companion, a co-voyager ... who will feel that he has seen and brought back his catch'. The reader might be thought therefore to penetrate the text.

The third section is written in such a way that it continually declares a local interest in the shapes and sounds of language and the patterning that is developed through alliteration, a fairly rigid stanza shape, and a highly variable length between pauses of punctuation. It has been made to look like the rhythms that build up and collapse in a swell at sea.

> I, in Time's grace, the grace of change, sail surely   1
> Moved off the land and the skilled keel sails
> The darkness burning under where I go.
> Landvoices and the lights ebb away
> Raising the night round us. Unwinding whitely,   5
> My changing motive pays me slowly out.
> The sea sails in. The quay opens wide its arms
> And waves us loose.
>
> So I would have it, waved from home to out
> After that, the continual other offer,   10
> Intellect sung in a garment of innocence.
> Here, formal and struck into a dead stillness,
> The voyage sails you no more than your own.
> And on its wrought epitaph fathers itself
> This sea as metaphor of the sea. The boat   15
> Rides in its fires.
>   (pp. 93–94)

The narration is complex, the movement is cut into, deflected, overlaid. 'Time's grace, the grace of change' (line 1), deflects us from these events to view them at a distance. 'Unwinding whitely' (line 5) is curious because it is not quite clear to what it refers. The next line 'My changing motive pays me slowly out' (line 6), makes 'motive' the point, but whether the 'motive' is that of writing or fishing is not clear. The first stanza has the word 'sail' in it three times, yet this is not a sailing-boat at all. See, for instance: 'we dropped to the single motor' (p. 95), 'cut the motor' (p. 96), 'screws spinning' (p. 101), 'screws spun steadier' (p. 102), 'cut the motor quiet' (p. 103). Sailing boats may have auxiliary motors, but they do not drop 'to the single motor' from several. It may well be that the fishing boat carries sails as a reserve, but this progress is definitely motorised. 'Unwinding whitely' does not refer to a sail therefore, and I cannot see what rope would be unwinding at this point of the trip, as the boat leaves the quay. It must be the wake that unwinds from the screw and that the boat leaves behind.

The self here is again passive in relation to events and this reversal is extended in 'The sea sails in. The quay opens wide its arms' (line 7). Of course as the ends of the quay come nearer to those on the boat they can see more through them, their field of view being restricted less and less as they come level with the exit from the harbour.

The action doesn't progress in the second stanza. Line 9 would seem to be an echo of Eliot's 'La Figlia che Piange' ('So I would have had him leave / So I would have had her stand and grieve,') and the language 'Intellect sung in a garment of innocence' (line 11) is not right for a fisherman. This was Edwin Morgan's objection.

The effect is that just as the fishing-trip gets underway, we are reading a legend of it 'formal and struck into a dead stillness' (line 12), 'the sea as metaphor of the sea' (line 15). Here is one aspect at least of the pleasure of the poem, since having become familiar with its frame of seven sections, the work sings of itself, repeats and varies its own language. Thus 'The quay opens wide its arms' (line 7) near repeats 'The present opens wide its arms' (section 1) and the reprise 'And the quay opened its arms' (section 3). 'Formal and struck into a dead stillness' (line 12) points to 'the place fastened still with movement' (section 5, p. 104) as well as the still centre of section 3 itself (pp. 97–98).

Repetition with variation and inversion is used across the poem to quite a large extent. Perhaps the best example is the opening couplet which is reset many times:

> Very gently struck
> The quay night bell.
>
> Gently the quay bell
> Strikes the held air.

The Nightfishing

> Far out faintly calls
> The continual sea.
>
> Far out, faintly rocked,
> Struck the sea bell.
>
> Very gently the keel
> Walks its waters again.
>
> Far out faintly calls
> The mingling sea.

It is made from material we recognise so that the words approach the condition of music, having meaning within the system that has been established, and thus conveying a new kind of information to the reader. It is in this way that the more than descriptive passages of section 3 should be read. We are not intended to be simply located with the crew of the boat.

The narrative proceeds with events in the world, their version in memory, in a metaphorical artwork (as in 'the rigged ship in its walls of glass', the only sailing-boat I find in the poem), and the artwork which records a version of all the others, the poem.

> The keel in its amorous furrow
> Goes through each word. He drowns, who but ill
> Resembled me.   (section 3, p. 94)

Close to the beginning of the section we come across these lines where the self-consciousness of the voice becomes extreme. The description of the boat's movement has taken on a sexual meaning ('amorous furrow') and there is the substitution of 'word' for 'wave'. 'Wave', were it present, would mean a play between the salutation or farewell, and the rythmic flux of the sea's swell in which 'words break' (p. 103) and reform. Substituting 'word' for this play is not simply to refer to the process of making the poem, but to enhance the shifting sense of language and bring in a suggestion of the meanings: word / Word. 'Word' spelt with a capital contrasts with its meaning as a simple sign because it suggests that which organises and controls, ultimately the word of God. This suggestion that is evident in the substitution begs the question of just how much 'The Nightfishing' is a Christian or religious poem.

Fishing, as it is used in the poem, signifies more than a net full of herring. Just after the quiet and the dark and stillness at the centre of the poem comes this passage: 'We haul and hold and haul/Well the bright chirpers home,' (p. 99), and the 'chirp' gives the fishes a voice as they come into the boat (also, we note, as they die). The factual basis for the description is given by Graham: 'On certain parts of the coast, herring are sometimes called "chirpers" because they emit a slight chirp as their airsac collapses when they come in on the net.'[9] The herring is anatomically distinguished, according to Burns Singer, 'by a two-lobed non-functional lung, slung across its back and used as an air-bladder'.[10] But the choice of name is too resonant to be explained completely by Graham's anatomical accuracy. The catch of 'The Nightfishing' is words, *because* the fish make a noise. The language brought back from the voyage is the 'fruitful share' that is made up into the poem. It can hardly be read without considering Christ the fisherman, in the parable where he makes his disciples into fishers of men (Matthew, 4, 18–22), and this is because we allow (in both the parable and the poem) that the fish have another meaning. For the Christian it is the immortal soul or spirit for which the disciples 'fish'. Graham's readers will find 'spirit' in the breath that makes the fishes 'chirp'.

The Christian imagery is a steady feature of the poem: 'Time's grace, the grace of change' (p. 93); 'The cross-tree light' (p. 95); 'all those signs falling / Through their appearance', 'the sea still; Holding its fires' (p. 96); 'to trace all grace', 'Cross in the air', 'A script of light' (p. 97); 'Masters me' (cf. Hopkins, p. 98), 'The whole memory of light, and will not cease / Contributing its exiled quality' (cf. Eliot, p. 98), 'Mingles its dead' (p. 98); 'that white grace' (p. 99); 'All words change in acknowledgement of the last', 'cross on a ball of wool' (p. 104); 'Walks its waters again' (p. 106); 'Words died and awoke' (p. 107).

Now 'cross on a ball of wool' (for instance) may not seem very significant in itself, but the repeated instances add up to more than they mean separately. 'Cross-tree light' and 'Cross in the air', moreover, pick up on the transformed mast image as developed in Rahner's account of the Christian use of Homeric symbolism (see above); and this sets the fishing-trip in the Christian tradition of a voyage home, passing through the cares and temptations of the world to reach heaven and union with God. Some of the instances above would seem also to be allusive to Christian poems (by Hopkins and Eliot) and Graham's language does have a kind of remote thematic glitter that depends upon the use of this matter, not quite brought into explicit focus, as if it is there as a reserved intimation of seriousness rather than a statement of faith. 'Grace', 'light' and 'dead' become, in the context of this poem, words which have a glamour cast back on them from a religious meaning that can no longer be confidently managed.

Graham's poem is not a statement of faith, and I am not clear that such a statement *could* be made from the position of a reserved, dispersed and attenuated self. The very reflexivity of the consciousness (lodged in language as a passivity that reflects the separated

The Nightfishing

actions of material body and energy of person) which is the main feature of the narration is, however, connected with a Christian idea. 'He drowns, who but ill / Resembled me' (p. 94) is a kind of resurrection image, since we know that the self who is speaking is risen again. Taken together with the scattered Christian imagery, we have in the poem a metaphysic of the soul released towards its true and non-material home (Plato), cast into the language of Christian belief as the only current dialect for this experience, but not allowed to converge into fable or allegory. In the stillness from which the 'fruitful share' (p. 103) is taken, we have a survival of the idea of the sacred, which cannot survive completely outside a Christian framework, and thus its elements are signalled in a scattered way. The value of these materials is similar to the imagery of Eliot's *Ash Wednesday*, which also relies on Christian language, but is closer in its forms to Christian liturgy.

The phrase 'He drowns, who but ill / Resembled me' is the nub of the problem, since the 'he' of the speaking subject is constantly slipping because it is being slipped away from, by a reserved (withheld) principle of control which seems stationed personally but anonymously, and which is surrendered but not lost.

> our boat keeps its nets and men and
> Engraves its wake. Our bow heaves hung on a likely
> Bearing for fish. The Mor Light flashes astern
> Dead on its second.   (p. 94)

A strong charge is given to the word 'dead' because it occurs after a line-end pause and because it is noticed as part of a phrasal unit that we use habitually ('dead on time'). This is strengthened by the puns on 'en-grave' and 'wake', by our memory of 'He drowns, who but ill / Resembled me', together with the continual reference to momentary death through the poem. There is a withheld authority in the poem that is unified with the speaker only in *coming home*: 'I am / My fruitful share'.

The third section of the poem is divided about that period of the narrative where the nets are put out for herring. The journey is thereby structured into three parts each with its own distinctive interest. The voyage out is involved with signs of the herring, reading the weather, seabirds and stars. Casting the nets involves the drift-fishing equipment, which completely alters the aspect of the boat as it is described. According to Burns Singer, there would be 'two miles of netting, and every inch might be worth a couple of hundred fish' (*Living Silver*, p. 209). The water is gathered round it and the narrator watches and is watched in quite another way, reflective, highly conscious of the surrounding space, put there by the fishing. The return is a fight with the elements to get the catch safely home, a trial of the crew and the boat through which they win back the familiar and welcoming coast. The movement across the section is therefore simple, tidal, and a satisfying frame for the complexities of the narrative surface.

'The present opens its arms' (p. 92); 'The keel in its amorous furrow' (p. 94); 'So we shoot out slowly the diving nets / Like sowing grain' (p. 96); 'O the land lay / Just as we knew it ... / And lay / Like a mother' (p. 102); 'The quay opened its arms' (p. 103): the movement is sexual, though again the signals are scattered through the text. They account for the power of the fourth section with its refrain (and variants): 'O my love, keep the day / Leaned at rest, leaned at rest' (p. 103) which sets the poem as a love-lyric, coming home, bringing the 'fruitful share' as a love-gift. Sections 4, 5 and 6 each re-set the poem in some way. The fifth section locates us in the town by the sea, thinking on the voyage retrospectively. The sixth takes up the process of writing it out, seated in a room at a table. The inset five stanzas (p. 105) are themselves framed in this section by three before and three after. In the last section elements from number one are reset beyond the time of the first attempt, as a music which sounds upon the rest of the text. The special quality of these sections is an attempt at extension without information, for meaning here is a function of position, to mirror memory reproducing the form of events.

The poem takes us through the work of fishermen into the elemental experience that constitutes modern society. Voyaging on the sea in search of food created the need for the technologies of ship-building and navigation which are still our primary areas of development, albeit (in the space age) in another form. The voyage goes beyond the conflict with nature in which man is present as a voyager and reader of signs, into an extreme place of stillness and silence, from which meaning (food, knowledge and language) is brought back on the voyage home.

The place is a *sacred* place, apart from normal life, and if it can no longer be confidently described in the language of Christianity, it is however signalled by that area of language-use in a scattered way, because that is recognised as the only vocabulary available to show what is at stake. This is a final difference between Graham's poem and Coleridge's *The Rime of the Ancient Mariner*, for though there is allegory in Graham's poem, it does not take us into a mythical unconscious as such. The point of extremity that Graham's fisherman reaches is a kind of metaphysical place, not a place of redemption but a place in which language arises out of the interaction of man and world. The taking of the fish (as food but also as shining fragments of new language) is a peaceful act and one which is dedicated (brought back to loved ones and safe ground). The speaking self is continually lost and re-asserted during the voyage – but is known only in retrospect and as the purpose behind each evasion of the speaking self. The self is constituted through the experience of work therefore, whether that work be fishing or writing (acts of memory and consciousness as mediated by a crypto-reflexive language) or any other kind. With a purpose, perception is always from a position and always constitutive of the world, though seldom only directly so. This poem is made so that perceptions feed back into constituting the self indivisible from position / occupation.

> These words take place.   (p. 97)

> So I have been called by my name and
> It was not sound. It is me named upon
> The space which I continually move across   (p. 97)

> I am / My fruitful share   (p. 103)

Its aims seem to be those of phenomenological description: that is one free of presuppositions, recognising language as the medium in which we live and move.

The 'Seven Letters' carry on the momentum of 'The Nightfishing' and the kind of meaning that has been established towards the end of that poem. Ideas and elements that make up 'The Nightfishing' are inverted and rephrased here in a new context and so meaning is once again a function of position. The relationship between the reader and writer begins to develop in a new way. The voice in 'Letter I', for instance, becomes simpler and more confident in its direct address:

> Dear you who walk
>
> Your solitude on these
> Words, walk their silences   (p. 109)

The 'I' in the poems is unstable because it is escaped from by shifts in the position of the speaking self which is sometimes behind what is being said in direct address, and sometimes looking back at a younger self. The 'you' who is addressed is similarly unstable. Sometimes he or she is talked to with somewhat more intimacy than would normally be assumed by a writer. The opening of 'Letter II' begins with a very general tone, but by the time we get down to lines 13, 14, and 15, it looks as if someone much closer might be being addressed:

> Lie in the world's room,
> My dear, and contribute
> Here where all dialogues write.   (p. 110)

The second stanza of 'Letter II' (line 16 onwards), begins to introduce another view by the change of tense. Yet we know that Graham is talking about his own past ('shipyards', 'lathes', 'welding', 'poetry', p. 110) so it is just a shift into a retrospective voice, and this slight instability is recognised and incorporated into the verse with:

> What's he to me? Only
> Myself I died from into
> These present words that move. (p. 110)

There is no doubt who is speaking. The voice is always Graham's, but his position shifts in relation to his material. The person to whom he is speaking (the reader, a close friend, a lover) is always unstable:

> Tonight in sadly need
> Of you I move inhuman
> Across this space of dread
> And silence in my mind. (p. 111)

The poem goes back deeper into the past as a response to this uneasiness and need, to childhood which is presented by a children's play rhyme:

> Water water wallflower
> Growing up so high
> We are all children
> We all must die.
> Except Willie Graham
> The fairest of them all.
> He can dance and he can sing
> And he can turn his face to the wall.
> Fie, fie, fie for shame
> Turn your face to the wall again. (p. 111)

The uneasiness is in this passage dramatised by the poet's imagined childhood companions calling his name out loud as 'fairest of them all' and by the lines 'Fie, fie, fie for shame / Turn your face to the wall again'. The reader is brought into a special intimacy by this verse – and so the unstable address is kept open. If the poet's intimacy had previously made us doubt whether the reader is intended to be addressed, this passage makes it possible and likely that the reader is being drawn in as at least a trusted friend. The sort of play which the 'Water water wallflower' verse comes from is about finding a place in the community. As the children take turns they learn to accept being singled out, embarrassed, laughed at, loved and relied on. This is the first and fundamental social experience outside of immediate family for most children. It is what builds the adult identity – and it is no accident that Graham includes the rhyme here with himself 'called' in it.

The progress of the poem is circular, the poet grows up:

> To write him to his death
> And to that great breath
> Taking of the sea,
> The graith of Poetry.   (p. 112)

'Graith' is a Scottish word meaning equipment or apparatus. 'Letter II' is thus about becoming ready to write poetry, and Graham locates that matter (which has traditionally been the subject of its own mythology) directly in his home community. Signals of the name of his major poem: 'the nightshipping', 'the nightshifting', rise out of the characteristics of Greenock. The stealing of fire from Prometheus is presented in an individual setting: 'Then in a welding flash / He found his poetry arm'. The 'call' comes from a children's street game and the muse is present in 'My musing love lie down / Within his arms'. The shifts in tone between the writer and reader are all about establishing a relationship of trust and the possibility of communication on this level where the ties of family and community are made.

> Yet the bow climbs back
> Shearing the amorous foam
> And flourishes in this word   ('Letter IV')

>   And quick,
> Take hold, the quick foam blooms
> And combs to our side.   ('Letter V')

> You first rendered the sash
> Of foam your father wore.
> May she be musing there
> Tonight.   ('Letter VII')

Each of these poems (though some more than others) are love poems addressed to the muse. The presence of foam in the poems is always a reference to lovemaking and a discreet invocation of Venus-Aphrodite, whether that foam be the edge of a breaking wave or the head of a glass of beer. The harp emblem from Guinness is used in the same way to characterise 'Old Calum' ('Letter IV') as a kind of modern Homer:

> He'll not see, that poor
> Harper, bat blind, stone-daft
> (That cough was aconite).

> Let him go on. His harp's
> Some strung breastbone but sweet.

'As Mooney's calls Time' sets us in a pub where working men drink hard and talk and sing a language figured with sexual innuendo. It is also an echo of Eliot's *The Waste Land* (Section II, 'A Game of Chess').

The sea has become, in these poems, the store of imagery for this richness of double-speech, and the salt thirst of the seaman has its ally in the eloquence that comes from having drink taken and being among trusted friends:

> Then what a fine upstander
> I was for the cause of Love . . .
>
> . . . holds us in the hull
> That slides between the waving
> Gates and the bow drives
> Headlong through the salt
> Thicket of the maiden sea.   ('Letter IV')

'Letter IV' is similarly presented as early amorous adventure: 'I put my childhood out / Into a cocked hat'. The landscape is perceived as it relates to the sexual theme: 'The Clyde sleeved in its firth' and the poem has hidden referents: 'I heard the moor / Curling its cries' (which is a curlew), also 'the crushed smell of the moor', and 'on the high moor', which both relate to the name Dunsmuir (which is 'high moor' in Scots).

The poems are strong in their handling of sexual imagery, and they have a complex mode of address that draws the reader into a kind of intimacy that is rare in modern British verse. This intimate address and drawing in of the reader, together with the highly physical figuring of the language, suggests that Graham's model is much older. His language use has the vitality we associate with that of Shakespeare's tragedies and *Sonnets*.

The Nightfishing ends with two ballads, 'The Broad Close' and 'Baldy Bane' which both use the persona of a combative drinking man with highly figurative coarse talk:

> Well, I'm jackeasy if I slip
>   The muse a length for she
> Appreciates the starkest man
>   Her length and breadth to be.
>   'The Broad Close'

The muse is a woman called Meg who appears in both poems as a drunken and unruly lover / wife. An old and a young man fight for her favours; in 'The Broad Close' the action is told from the young man's point of view, and in 'Baldy Bane' it is told from that of the older man. The poems depend upon the tradition of the border ballad, both in terms of form and subject. Both have a strong regular rhythm and 'Baldy Bane' uses a refrain couplet that is reminiscent of 'Get Up and Bar the Door'. 'The Broad Close' uses an only part-allegorised swordplay 'I took my weapons up and went' to represent sexual rivalry in the manner of 'The Bonny Earl of Murray'. The poems are unlike traditional ballads in their self-consciousness with repeated reference to the making of verse. Yet their strength, which relies upon variation of colloquial usage (both known and plausibly invented), to make an authentic drunken and sexy wordplay is a convincing extension of the form; especially given the understated but ever-present fear of death: 'Cry me Baldy Bane but cry / The hoodie off the gate'. It is typical of Graham's feel for the form that he should use a hooded crow (closely related to the carrion crow, present in the borders and to the north) as his emblem of death. Graham's interest in the ballad was developed in later poems like 'Imagine a Forest', 'The Gobbled Child', 'The Lost Miss Conn' and 'The Murdered Drinker'. His characterisation of the muse is important also in his later work.

Malcolm Mooney's Land

Malcolm Mooney's Land, which was published in 1970, was Graham's next book after *The Nightfishing* of 1955. Though there are connections between the two works (notably 'Your's Truly' which answers 'Letter IV' and the recurrence of 'Mooney' from the 'Seven Letters'), *Malcolm Mooney's Land* is a very different kind of project and the poetry has undergone an extreme change, both in manner and subject, from what Graham had written before. Though there were instances in *The White Threshold* (1949) where the poet attained simplicity – 'Shian Bay' and 'Gigha', for example – there was not the directness of address to the reader that for the most part characterises the stance of *Malcolm Mooney's Land*.

The book holds together as a unified and interlocking work because of the creation of a fictional territory from which the poems speak. Malcolm Mooney's Land is a kind of floating conception of place to which we add dimension and substance as we come to know the volume better. Graham, in building towards this kind of structure, has moved on from the modified epic programme of 'The Nightfishing' to a sequential meaning, where each individual poem, be it an extended narrative or an occasion lyric, adds to the meaning of the sequence as a whole.

Malcolm Mooney's Land is in many senses a particular place with its own natural history and its own community of strange inhabitants. The full description does not occur in any one place, but reading across the poems we pick up a consistent level of reference which builds a territory outside but linked with normal reality. It is a place of terror and madness, inhabited by monsters, beasts and gods. The title poem's empty and frozen landscape extends into a place of physical, emotional and psychological extremity. The landscape, furthermore, is always as conventional and artificial as Sidney's *Arcadia*, declaring itself an art-place made of language: 'Words drifting on words. / The real unabstract snow', whilst studded with the place-names of Graham's Cornish and Scottish homes. There is a deal of resistant Scottish and outlandish vocabulary. There are reminders of Ireland, 'the changed Mooney's mirrors / Of what is left of Ireland', and the Irish Gaelic dedication to the painter Tony O'Malley. One place that it certainly is *not* is the power centre of Britain that generates standard English. There are, however, frequent references to royalty which are teasing and peculiar, since they are combined with a care for a special regional vocabulary and no clear political subject (the hint about Ireland, above, is not developed). In this work we are inside language as a special terrain, and the idea of exploration that is built into the title poem works on this ground.

In *Malcolm Mooney's Land* there is the continued projection of a fictional author-figure who pretends to speak directly to us about the difficulties of language and the writer-reader relationship. He thus draws us into the paradox that he is trustworthy and reliable, and that his interest is to remove the barriers to direct communication, whereas the whole process of dramatising his isolation through a series of metaphors is what makes that isolation seem so extreme. For however much it speaks of its maker and his strategies, the artwork constitutes the barrier between artist and audience, confirming by its existence the separation of the two roles. This distance is compounded each time we read of a parallel activity, discipline, or enthusiasm that turns our attention back to the writing as an object made and printed for us. In the title poem the activity is exploration. The same kind of parallel is developed in other poems: for a musician, 'Johann Joachim Quantz's First Lesson'; climber, 'The Don Browne Route'; gambler, 'Press Button to Hold Desired Symbol'; kite-flyer, 'Dear Who I Mean'; glider and painter, 'The Thermal Stair'; painter: 'Wynter and the Grammarsow'; madman, 'Five Visitors to Madron'; madman and prisoner, 'Clusters Travelling Out'.

The fictional author, poet, and explorer in language, is a construct very close to the man W. S. Graham. We do not need to know all that much about Graham himself to understand it – and he is careful to give us just enough so that the sense is highly personal. The most constant sense of his presence is the local word-play, together with the choice and management of subject that refers us back to writing. This is writing about the self but not confessional writing, since it is concerned with the writer's position in that relationship which he examines and fictionalises.

One characteristic of Graham's later poetry which is established in *Malcolm Mooney's Land* is the presence in the poems of monsters, beasts and gods. It is a signal that we are outside normal reality in a world like that of the ballads, for instance, where the supernatural is a constituent of experience. Graham's use of this material is often very sophisticated, juggling with different orders of reality and feeling, whilst keeping the tone playful.

The creatures will typically be introduced through wordplay as in the 'wrecked dragon' (a kite with a dragon painted or printed on it, but also *Milvus milvus*) and 'the quick brown pouncing god' (a dog) in 'Dear Who I Mean'. The 'quick brown pouncing god' reminds us of the 'quick brown fox' in typing exercises (and therefore of errors that crop up in poems written on typewriters), as well as Eliot's 'strong brown god' of 'The Dry Salvages' section of *Four Quartets*. The names of the kite and the dog in the poem are suppressed. There is a 'bitch' in 'The Lying Dear', a poem about sex and jealousy, 'cranes' and 'calves' (again, only as puns) in the title-poem, and foxes, grammarsows, black wobblers, unblubbered monsters, monkeys, bats, northern beasts, ravens, urchins, cat and mouse, gulls, moths, owls, buzzards and a walrus. The 'caught habits of language', 'the living animal language', a poem that is described as 'a creature in its abstract cage asleep' and another poem called 'The Beast In The Space', begin to add up to a deliberate characterisation of language as itself animate (and therefore more than just the site of this habitation).

This is no happy fairy-land with funny creatures, however; the gods are present in the terrain and their presence is a symptom of madness. The fear is physical: 'Now it comes and laps my meaning up' is, I take it, felt sexually and fearfully at once. 'The Lying Dear' with its 'At entrance', 'belly sledge', 'mounting', 'high verge', plays with private sexy talk but does not hold control because it is about jealousy. The confrontations with the muse and the fear of madness in 'Five Visitors to Madron' and 'Clusters Travelling Out' explore the same emotional area. David Punter, in his article 'Constructing A White Space', suggests a link between 'The Beast In The Space' and Aleister Crowley 'The Great Beast', who 'tries to convey that magic has to do with the mastery and manipulation of linguistic and quasi-linguistic codes'.[1] Graham is certainly not writing about magic in anything like the way that Crowley does, but the fear of losing a grip on sanity and slipping into the supernatural world is very strong in these poems.

Monsters, beasts and gods have always lived in poems: literature is where these mythic creatures have their being. In the world of *Malcolm Mooney's Land*, a limited sense of 'real life' is not available. Like some recent novelists, Graham takes the elements of fantasy into his version of the world (though in Graham's case it is fantasy with a tradition). One might expect that this work which stresses its own artificiality would produce a heightened sense of language as an arbitrary and conventional code, whereas the opposite is true. We do not doubt that the movement of the language has been fashioned for us, but Graham's activity is presented as a process of revealing a meaning that is latently there. The 'animal language' with its 'caught habits' speaks back with puns, word splittings and substitutions which seem (in this framework) organic. In Graham's work, 'language' is an active force.

The poem 'Approaches To How They Behave' seems to take off from a passage in the *Four Quartets*:

> Words strain
> Crack and sometimes break, under the burden,
> Under the tension, slip, slide, perish,
> Decay with imprecision, will not stay in place
> Will not stay still.
>
> ('Burnt Norton', V)

To Eliot the imperfection of language is a reflection of the fallen state of nature (hence his use of 'decay' here). Ambiguity and loss of currency are a measure of our distance from God. Now and then Eliot's work directs us to these kinds of insight about language and languages. Graham's post-modernism begins from that point and becomes ever more explicitly interested in the language and in the writer-reader relationship. His words are presented as alive in a quite independent way, like mischievous children. 'How They Behave' (in the title of the poem) refers to the words.

Ambiguity is for Graham useful, sexy, funny, awe-inspiring or fearful. Meaning, as in Wittgenstein, is not stated but shown:

> The poem is not a string of knots
> Tied for a meaning of another time
> And country, unreadable, found
> By chance. The poem is not a henge
> Or Easter Island emerged Longnose
> Or a tally used by early unknown
> Peoples. The words we breathe and puff
> Are our utensils down the dream
> Into the manhole. Replace the cover.
>
> 'Approaches to How they Behave'

The poem tells us what it is not and teaches us that we shall die. Yet that opening play on 'not / knot' shows us that *this* poem *is* a string of nots. The negatives are what the poem is made of and what makes the string of examples possible. Since the application of the language model as a system of thought in what we have come to call formalism and structuralism, wordplay of the kind that Graham uses takes on a particular relevance. Clearly Graham's work, by making these issues explicit in another way, demonstrates that philosophical problems are not wound up by restating them as language problems. He also seems independently to be able to come up with formulations that might rest comfortably in post-structuralist theory: 'What is the language using us for?' (p. 191), 'Because always language / Is where the people are' (p. 159).

The title-poem of the book is about a journey of exploration into a boundless frozen wasteland of isolation and loneliness, where heroism and psychological extremity are explored. The emotional basis of the poem is a comparison between the work of a poet reaching into the unknown self through his struggle with language, and that of a national hero and explorer such as Captain Scott or Fridtjof Nansen, who travels far beyond the domestic to confront nature and try the limits of the self, for what are ostensibly patriotic reasons.

Malcolm Mooney combines both aspects and yet he is a not-quite-realised character or persona (at least in this poem). The name comes from a chain of bars owned by Guinness and it has a particular meaning for English literary life since the Oxford Street bar was a meeting place for writers.[2] Namesakes of Mooney's are mentioned on ten occasions in Joyce's *Ulysses* and the name has a literary history beyond the suggestion of lunacy and the resonance of those other places like Van Duren's Land and Franz Joseph Land so-named in the far north.

The form of the work is almost a diary; it has sections which begin with the names of days, and it looks like the quite indirect thoughts and musings on its narrator's circumstances. It is, however, written in a condensed verse form and there are not the connecting passages between incidents that might be present in a real diary. It is presented to be puzzled over, to create the conditions of the reader discovering a diary, and wondering about the identity of its author.

Graham has always produced work to look like this, hence 'Seven Journeys', 'Three Letters', 'Seven Letters' – and it is also clear that something like this was intended in the early poem 'His Companions Buried Him', which is also an exploration poem that mentions the 'furry queen'. The journeys and the letters do not read as journeys and letters exactly, though the idea of a letter is canvassed, as the diary is in 'Malcolm Mooney's Land'. Graham does not seem to have the kind of imagination required for an extended fiction – it is not part of his project. What happens is that the voice shifts. In 'Malcolm Mooney's Land' it shifts very quickly from a narrative to thoughts about the status of the narrative, telling us what is going on here in the poem: 'Wherever I speak from or in what particular/ Voice, this is always a record of me in you.' This is the point at which the switch in voice becomes statement, but it moves several times and therefore becomes indeterminate, shifting between an imagined explorer and the poet-narrator who is telling us about the writing. We get the diary of the poem's progress as a kind of overlay to the imagined exploration diary: 'Have I not been trying to use the obstacle/ Of language well? It freezes round us all.' There is no way a simple narrative view can survive through these contortions. The status of the poem is therefore provisional; it corresponds to and with the discovered diary it speaks of, so that the reader is in the same relation to the poem as the poet to his sources.

The nostalgic-elegiac note is signalled in that early title 'His Com-

Malcolm Mooney's Land

panions Buried Him' – these are the surviving documents of heroism. We think of the blank pages at the end of the Scott diaries, of Oates's famous understatement: 'I am just going outside and may be some time', and the figure walking off into the snow. At the outset the voice is moving with a power derived from this emotional complex. The following poem, by Dr Edward A. Wilson of Scott's scientific exploration party was printed in *Scott's Last Expedition* (volume 2, p. xviii):

> The stone was deep with a breath like sleep
>   As our sledge runners slid on the snow,
> And the fate-full fall of our fur-clad feet
>   Struck mute like a silent blow
> On a questioning 'Hush?' as the settling crust
>   Shrank shivering over the floe.
> And the sledge in its track sent a whisper back
>   Which was lost in a white fog-bow.
>
> And this was the thought that the Silence wrought,
>   As it scorched and froze us through,
> For the secrets hidden are all forbidden
>   Till God means man to know
> We might be the men God meant should know
>   The heart of the barrier snow,
> In the heart of the sun, and the glow
>   And the glare from the floe,
> As it scorched and froze us through and through
>   With the bite of the drifting snow.
>   'The Barrier Silence'

Graham's poems have echoes of Wilson's: the personification of Silence, Graham's use of 'The Art barrier of ice' and even more firmly with 'Words drifting on words. / The real unabstract snow'.

The Scott expedition, like Hilary's ascent of Everest, creates the lordly spectacle of planting the flag in foreign and inhospitable territory. Eliot had used Shackleton's account in 'What the Thunder Said' (see his notes to *The Waste Land*), and this may well have pointed Graham towards a clearer exploration poem than the *Seven Journeys* or 'His Companions Buried Him', based on literary sources. Graham's primary source for 'Malcolm Mooney's Land' is mentioned in the text, it is Nansen. Significantly for Graham, Nansen's most famous work was entitled *Farthest North*. Published in serial form and later collected into two volumes (1897), it was a very popular work and Nansen had a special place in the public imagination, besides providing stirring tales for generations of schoolchildren. For while Nansen's explorations were of serious scientific intention and achievement, he was a heroic figure, a champion skier turned scientist whose methods were daring and unorthodox.

Though he began by using material from the whole of Nansen's book, Graham finally adapted only passages from Nansen's second volume in the finished poem.[3]

> When we got into our sleeping-bag in the evening, our clothes began to thaw slowly . . . we packed ourselves tight into the bag and lay with our teeth chattering for an hour and a half, before we became aware of the warmth in our bodies which we so sorely needed. At last our clothes became wet and pliant, only to freeze again a few minutes after we had turned out of the bag in the morning. (*Farthest North*, vol. 2, p. 7)

> From the rimed bag of sleep, Wednesday,
> My words crackle in the early air.
> Thistles of ice about my chin,
> My dreams, my breath a ruff of crystals. (p. 143)

Characteristically, he made the writing speak of itself – thus the speaker puns on 'rimed' – and it is his (g)ruff words rather than his breath which freezes in the cold air.

> A fox was here last night (Maybe Nansen's,
> Reading my instruments.) the prints
> All round the tent and not a sound. (p. 144)

We are sure to distinguish between Nansen and the narrator of the poem once Nansen is named. This is like the mysterious other person in *The Waste Land*, except that the other person is named and here the narrator is the mystery. We learn about him through the poem in the same way that Graham imagines Nansen (and the other explorers) through his sources. Nansen was trying to reach Franz Joseph Land and his supplies in his trek across the ice. Malcolm Mooney's Land corresponds with it for Graham, who is adrift in a literary version of the shifting ice; the white pages printed with his tracks and the tracks of his beasts. There is a sense of local play in the language use, together with a more serious description of an extreme emotional state.

> Today, Tuesday, I decided to move on
> Although the wind was veering. Better to move
> Than have them at my heels, poor friends
> I buried earlier under the printed snow.

Malcolm Mooney's Land

> From wherever it is I urge these words
> To find their subtle vents, the northern dazzle
> Of silence cranes to watch. Footprint on foot
> Print, word on word and each on a fool's errand
>
> (p. 143)

It is the line break between 'foot / Print' that decides for us that 'printed snow' is as much the page as any real snow out in the world. He is moving to get away from buried friends, from the dead, from reminders of his own death and the awkwardness of outliving friends.

The essence of exploration (at least as it appears until now in our literature) is a man proving himself in a hostile environment, away from the social world and in particular away from the company of women. In this sense the 'other' or hostile environment is always likely to become a figure of sexual difference. In 'Malcolm Mooney's Land', the characters 'Elizabeth and the boy' are those left behind and they represent the social world. The 'furry queen' (a pun on the first Elizabeth, as Spenser's *Fairy Queen*) is someone else, the muse, present at the time of writing in the imagination of the narrator.

> Elizabeth, my furry
> Pelted queen of Malcolm
> Mooney's Land

The 'furry pelt' is of course an image of female sexuality that has long been in the domain of the advertising industry. The powerful connection of animal fur and hairless skin derives its power from the reversal and variation of what is revealed and what concealed.

Deeper in our store of imagery is Andersen's *Snow Queen*, which because it is all about the awakening of adolescent sexuality *and* journeying to the far north, has a special relevance here.[4] First a mirror distorts reality, making beautiful things appear small and ugly things grow large. A fragment of this mirror lodges next to the boy's heart (it has entered through his eye) and accounts for his cruel change of character and his running away from the girl. If the mirror is a rather fearful way of representing the coming of sexuality, through ugly things (genitalia when not yet understood) growing large, becoming erect, then it follows that the boy is altered by his awareness of this change (seeing it in a mirror) and is taken away by someone who better represents the adult sexual world than the girl. The Snow Queen invites the boy to sit with her in her fur coat as they travel far northwards together, leaving the girl behind. Fur as a badge of sex, standing for the pubic hair, is an important figure in the progress of the girl who follows to rescue the boy. On each stage of her journey she has to undress and re-clothe for the next stage of the journey. The boy is finally trapped in the far north beyond Lapland. In order to escape, he has to solve a puzzle, which is to spell the word 'eternity' from the splintered ice fragments littered about him. What better image could there be for making a poem?

> Tell him a story.
> Tell him I came across
> An old sulphur bear
> Sawing his log of sleep
> Loud beneath the snow.
> He puffed the powdered light
> Up on to this page
> And here his reek fell
> In splinters among
> These words. He snored well.
> Elizabeth, my furry
> Pelted queen of Malcolm
> Mooney's Land, (pp. 146–147)

The splintered word and the Queen with her furry pelt are there together – and earlier in the poem, we have the entry of the sexual theme:

> O benign creature with the small ear-hole,
> Submerger under silence, lead
> Me where the unblubbered monster goes
> Listening and makes his play (p. 143)

The 'benign creature' that skims under the ice may well be a seal or whale. What can the 'unblubbered monster' be? 'Unblubbered' just so that we do not confuse it with either of these – and we could not call a whale or a seal a 'monster'.

> I have reached the edge of earshot here
> And by the laws of distance
> My words go through the smoking air
> Changing their tune on silence. (p. 144)

> At least I speak on the edge of earshot here
> Where the voice travels far in strict air
> To the last distortion, to its furthest home.
> This north is too much all my own for comfort.
> In the vice of an icy whore.
> (Worksheets for 'Malcolm Mooney's Land', p. 9)

The first passage is from the published poem, and it shows where the second manuscript passage, fits in the scheme of the finished work. It is obvious that even at this early stage in the making of the poem, Graham was quite clear about the sexual nature of exploration into the frozen north.

> Elizabeth, you and the boy
> Have been with me often
> Especially on those last
> Stages. Tell him a story. (p. 146)

We have here the heroic male, the explorer, leaving instructions for the female, to domesticate the idea of danger. The social world is represented by that phrase 'Tell him a story' – a story is not quite the truth. What is suppressed or altered through being represented by beasts and monsters is sexuality, which is connected through the larger image of the snow with death. Knowledge of sexuality is held back because it brings with it knowledge of death and that is hard to bear. The speaker of this passage imagines that he will be dead by the time his message is read. Freud made the link between freezing, sexuality and death in *The Psychopathology of Everyday Life*:

> From a dream of P's it appears that ice is in fact a symbol by antithesis for an erection: it is something that becomes hard in the cold instead of – like the penis – in heat (excitation). The two antithetical concepts of sexuality and death are frequently linked through the idea that death makes things stiff.[5]

Graham uses the link to construct the voice that leaves us this record, the written document, with the right trace of emotion to stand like the blank eloquent pages at the end of Scott's diary. The fondness of 'Tell him a story' allows a statement of heroism without self-pity. The poem strongly suggests the fear of final isolation and extinction, by sexualising and then domesticating a figurative isolation in the text:

> I have made myself alone now.
> Outside the tent endless
> Drifting hummock crests.
> Words drifting on words.
> The real unabstract snow. (p. 147)

This particular isolation is self-imposed, at least from the point of view of the writer. In Malcolm Mooney's Land, the writer says to his beasts (lice):

> Come bonny friendly beasts, brother
> To the grammarsow and the word-louse,
> Bite me your presence, keep me awake

> In the cold with work to do, to remember
> To put down something to take back. (p. 144)

Writing, clearly, is what keeps him 'awake / In the cold'. Writing is the work that keeps him up and alone when most people go to bed, make love, sleep. He has traded domestic comforts for the isolation through which he comes to confront his 'furry queen' or muse. This would not be so clear but for the other poems in the volume which expand on the theme: 'Five Visitors to Madron' and 'Clusters Travelling Out'.

The circumstances of the narrator of 'Clusters Travelling Out' are an inversion of those in 'Malcolm Mooney's Land'. Instead of the boundless arctic waste we have the claustrophobic containment of a place which might be a prison, a mental hospital, a slaughterhouse, or a concentration camp. The *poem* is deliberately unclear about its setting because the uncertainty is one way in which we gain insight into the speaker's mental state. Again there is the overlay of theme right from the beginning which makes the voice quite indeterminate:

> Clearly I tap to you clearly
> Along the plumbing of the world
> I do not know enough, not
> Knowing where it ends. I tap
> And tap to interrupt silence into
> Manmade durations making for this
> Moment a dialect for our purpose.
> TAPTAP. Are you reading that taptap

It is like the voice in a Beckett novel, where we know very little about the person behind it except that he is continuing to speak or write. We know his circumstances are diminshed. In *How It Is*, with its broken form, offering us no chapters or other apparent order but the impulses of breath and speech, we get exactly the sense of silence that we get from this passage of Graham. 'I tap / And tap to interrupt silence into / Manmade durations' could be a Beckett protagonist, writing out of fear of silence and extinction. In Beckett, with the change of names and confusion of names, comes the sense of an unsteady mental state, perhaps illness, perhaps senility.

In Graham's poem we have the patient-prisoner attempting to communicate with fellow inmates of the institution by tapping on the pipes, but we must also imagine the poet tapping on his typewriter in the same room late at night, that we know from 'Malcolm Mooney's Land' ('awake / In the cold with work to do'). The shift in 'Malcolm Mooney's Land' was metered through the pun on 'print'; here it is the ambiguity in that phrase 'Are you reading' which is radio-ham slang for 'Can you hear me?' and thus suggests a message tapped out in morse, as well as us the readers looking at the printed words. Then, in part 2, the poet-as-himself takes over:

> Here in our concrete
> Soundbox we slide the jargon across
> The watching air, a lipless language
> Necessarily squashed from the side
> To make its point against the rules.
> It is our poetry such as it is.

This has the same effect as naming Nansen in 'Malcolm Mooney's Land': we cannot any longer accept the narrator as simply a patient-prisoner, since he is speaking as the poet (or *a* poet) so that the idea we have of a narrator or a persona is broken down. The speaking self is compound and unsteady.

'Burn this. I do not dislike this place. I like/ Being here. They are very kind. It's doing me good.' These lines, with their echo of Auden's *Orators*, describe a shift in the mental state of the narrator of 'Clusters Travelling Out'.[6] We will not find out what has happened to the narrator to make him change his tune. It might be that he is mentally ill and being kept in a hospital, it might be that he has been captured and is undergoing a more sinister kind of treatment, say brainwashing, sensual deprivation, or electric shock therapy. In the poem he has been talking about various methods of communication: a tapped message, radio, something spoken from the side of the mouth (so it could not be heard by a guard), semaphore, a signal from a distant star cluster. We turn each development in the prison-hospital world back to poetry. The deeper fiction is of some kind of damage which gives the poet access to the muse (called 'Brigit' in 'Clusters Travelling Out').

> History's
> Princes with canisters of gas
> Crystals to tip and snuff me out
> Strangled and knotted with my kind
> Under the terrible benevolent roof. (p. 184)

> But first I must empty my shit-bucket
> And hope my case (if it can be found)
> Will come up soon. (p. 188)

One might locate the first quotation with the Nazi regime, somewhere else in the past, but the reference to garotting which follows will not allow us to distance it that far. The second quotation immediately suggests Kafka's *The Trial*, but it might just as well be an internment camp in Northern Ireland, a prisoner-of-war camp in Vietnam.[16] As usual with Graham, there is no political placing of the activity, no ideology. 'Corridors have their character. I know well/ The ring of government boots on our concrete.' The fear is of somehow slipping onto the wrong side of a threatening State. The poem comes from the age of terrorism, but also from a time when its aged and infirm members can be terrified by intimidating institutions and the incomprehensible documents they produce. 'The Slaughterhouse' is a place in Madron. 'The Poorhouse' is where Alfred Wallis died a pauper's death in 1942; now they go into geriatric and mental hospitals, which fits with the place that Graham describes. The poem does not attack our society, but it is shaped by the way we deal with those that do not fit in.

> In the small hours on the other side
> Of language with my chair drawn
> Up to the frightening abstract
> Table of silence, taps. A face
> Of white feathers turns my head
> To suddenly see between the mad
> Night astragals her looking in
> Or wanted this to happen. She
> Monster muse old bag or. Something
> Dreamed is yes you're welcome always
> Desired to drop in.

In this first section of 'Five Visitors to Madron' the scene of the writer sitting at his table late at night is presented yet again, this time directly. As it progresses, the pauses and stops in the passage become stranger, and they seem to work against our understanding of what is 'going on'. The first four line-end pauses hold us back from completing phrases, rather than adding a new one at a natural break. The verse is uneasy. Then we get a half-rhymed couplet, stitched with 'head-mad,' but the rhyme is not end-stopped so that the next pause, between 'mad' and 'night', is worse for the sense because the pause is stretched by the rhyme. The end of line 7 is also worse because the poet has tacked on a phrase that will not do; we have to go back and look at the sentence to see what is going on. Then lines 8 and 9 contain a broken-off sentence, a suppressed ending. The cut-off signals a change of voice, the poet is now speaking in another way. The last sentence is hurriedly polite, eager to please, full of fear. The pauses and stops work against our easy reading because they perform another function, to enforce a meaning that is at first a supplement and eventually at odds with what is being said by the words.

After 'Monster muse old bag or' the poet stalls and changes because the muse is there and he is scared to offend her. She has appeared in a frightening form, so that even if he is able to summon her with the late night tapping noise as his ritual, he is not in command.

The fiction that is developed across these three poems – 'Malcolm Mooney's Land', 'Clusters Travelling Out' and 'Five Visitors to Madron' – is that of a narrator who sees his surroundings altered into a separate reality by the visitations of the muse, or through madness from some unnamed cause. The madness is that he imagines he is in the presence of the muse. It is not possible to choose between these two options from what is offered here. Either way the poet is located at some distance from the modern materialistic work that talks about its processes and is in that way self-generating, even though Graham is employing the surface of that kind of writing. Here he crosses over into another world, the 'other / Side' – that is, the other side of language. Once the poem is set up and printed, we can imagine the page and its writing as a barrier, and beyond that (out of sight, hidden by the page) is trapped Graham's writing persona, with his beasts, perhaps indistinguishable from them. 'O dear night / Cover up my beastly head'. From there he sends out these messages. It is a mythic world where the gods live. It is important also that they are written in just that way. 'God' or 'The Gods' would not be quite right for the inhabitants of this other reality that depends on ours and is given its expression by the human world and its literature. It is the world that Heidegger finds in the poetry of Holderlin:

> Poetry is primarily the naming of the gods, but the poetic word acquires this power only when the gods have provoked us into speech. How do the gods speak? Holderlin says: ' . . . and hints have forever been the language of the gods.' The speech of the poet captures these hints and sends them on to the people . . .
>
> The essence of poetry is fitted into two sets of laws, which strive to unite, but also to separate: the hints of the gods and voice of the people. The poet himself stands between both, the gods and the people. He is thrown into an in-between, the realm that lies between men and gods.[7]

Graham's idea of the muse, though developed into something quite his own, is partly derived from Robert Graves's book *The White Goddess*, which Graham had read by 1949.[8] Graves there defines 'true poetry' according to whether or not it expresses some aspect of what he calls the 'great theme'. Graves devotes most of his space to the Celtic versions of this story, but he does connect it with the transmission of a tradition in a westward movement from Africa and India across the Middle East and Europe. The prominence of Celtic material would no doubt have appealed to Graham, given his interest in that area of Britain and its languages: Scottish, Cornish and Irish in *Malcolm Mooney's Land*. Brigit is the Irish name for the moon goddess-muse in Graves's book, and 'Brigit' appears in Graham's work

('Clusters Travelling Out', 'Implements in Their Places') as an invocation of Aphrodite-Venus.

Shape-shifting from Graves's stories of Amergin and Taliesin would seem to be relevant to Graham's poem 'Five Visitors to Madron'. The first passage of that poem (lines 1 to 10, quoted above) seems to refer to Graves's note about the superstition that it is unlucky to see the goddess through glass (Graves, p. 108), and the horrific feathered aspect of the muse is mentioned by Graves: 'witches disguised as formidable night-birds who snatched children from their cradles and sucked their blood ... the White Goddess who destroyed children after disguising herself in bird or beast form' (p. 67).

Compare the following two passages from Graves and Graham:

> You reading over my shoulder, peering beneath
> My writing arm – I suddenly feel your breath
> Hot on my hand or on my nape,
> So interrupt my theme, scratching these few
> Words on the margin for you, namely you,
> Too-human shape fixed in that shape:-
>   'The Reader Over My Shoulder'

> And left these words at a loss to know
> What form stood watching behind me
> Reading us over my shoulder. I said
> Now that you have come to stand
> There rank-breathed at my elbow I will
> Not be put off. This message must
> Reach the others without your help.
>   'Five Visitors to Madron'

There really is a surprising similarity between Graves's and Graham's work here. Graham has adapted both the manner and theme, making them his own. There is fear in the Graves piece, but it is fear which has been made quite conventional. 'So interrupt my theme' is an annoyance, 'this message must / Reach the others' is an urgent personal concern. 'Hot on my hand or on my nape' has not the power of 'There rank-breathed at my elbow', since the Graham passage does not consider a choice ('hand or nape' in Graves) but records one present moment of fear. The speaker is at risk in the Graham poem. It is the difference between a poetic fancy and a terrifying hallucination.

Edward Lucie-Smith has said of Robert Graves that: 'The Movement poets found the way in which he wrote more acceptable than what he was saying ... Graves's worship of the Muse – the central doctrine of his work – was tactfully ignored.'[9] It is clear that what Lucie-Smith recognised was an understandable embarrassment on the part of the Movement poets, to Graves's *explicit worship*. In

Graham's work we find the muse (and it seems, almost the same one) presented in quite another way. She is either invoked by means of a discreet hint ('my musing love') or by an uncouth persona ('I slip / The muse a length') or as an indication of terror and madness ('She / Monster muse old bag or').

Graham's 'Brigit' figures much more prominently in the work-sheets for 'Clusters Travelling Out' than she does in the finished poem. There is also an unpublished poem 'Loch Long' which features 'Brigit'.[10] Graham compressed the material so that Brigit remains a figure about whom we know little. The passage used in the final version serves to link 'Clusters Travelling Out' and 'Five Visitors to Madron' with 'Malcolm Mooney's Land' because it names the days 'Tuesday' and 'Wednesday' and because it describes Brigit in the same position: 'at my elbow listening'. Brigit is a name with a Celtic history. Apart from Graves's use of her in *The White Goddess*, she may be found in *The Oxford Dictionary of Saints* as patron of poets, black-smiths and healers. This Irish saint is also identified with the heathen fire goddess 'Brig', meaning 'valour or might'. For the community with Celtic origins, then, the name has a resonance, and this is a further aspect of Graham's use of her.

One of Graham's major successes in *Malcolm Mooney's Land* is a poem which perfectly illustrates how his work, while it remains on the surface talking about language, writer and reader, is able to engage the deepest emotions concerning ordinary family life. 'The Dark Dialogues' is one of Graham's finest poems and one of his most difficult, though it admirably repays the expense of attention which it demands. It never moves far away from talking about itself, and the whole poem seems folded inward in the way that a sentence is in, say, 'The Nightfishing'. The combination of mythic material (Europa and Jupiter) with personal and family history (Greenock tenement life) makes it a poem about origins as they bear on the family and the person, which is constructed from memory and from belonging to the family group.

The poem is divided into four sections, and in each of them there is an approach to a specific speaking voice. In the first it is the poet, in the second it is his mother, in the third it is his father and in the fourth it is the poet again, reformed through making the poem. The approach to the subject in each section is through a kind of general voice that is made to float by the suspension of attribution in pronouns and the kind of reflexive formulation of sentences that reverses the expected agency in the verbs:

> I always meant to only
> Language swings away
> Further before me.

> Language swings away
> Before me as I go
> With again the night rising
> Up to accompany me
> And that other fond
> Metaphor, the sea
> And the sea changing
> Should know me well enough.

The voice is suspended even more than usual and it is difficult at first to see what Graham is up to. 'I always meant to' looks like a particular intention that has been interfered with by 'Language'. We lose sight of the original purpose and we learn that the speaker is in doubt and difficulty. Language, getting its capital from the line-beginning, and having activity and perhaps motive attributed to it, becomes a character in the poem. In the next stanza we have the kind of reflexive statement that is common in *The Nightfishing*: 'night / And the sea changing / Should know me well enough'. We do not normally think of the night or the sea knowing anything, any more than we think of language, in the normal state of things, actively resisting us.

The line is Graham's standard three-stressed pattern and the structure is built up with some repeats, but mostly by means of internalised rhyme: 'Before me / accompany / phor, the sea / Should know me'. The poet sets a scene of the night sky figured with Europa and the bull seen in the stars, falling. Someone is imagined walking a lonely road: 'striking / Your hobnail in the dark' (lines 23–24) and the same person appears in line 43: 'And you, whoever you are'. We cannot be sure if the person (the 'you') is the reader or the poet, and we cannot be sure if the voice that addresses the 'you' is supposed to be the poet or something more general like 'the sea' or 'night'. The strongest claim for the 'you' is the poet, since the reader probably does not go about striking hobnails, whereas Graham does, his poet's voice does (see 'Since All My Steps Taken', p. 47).

In the second section the mother is at home sitting by the fire and her children are asleep. At the opening of the section she hears her husband's step on the stair. The only hesitation is line 19 'whoever else I am'.

> I sit with the gas turned
> Down and time knocking
> Somewhere through the wall.
> Wheesht, children, and sleep
> As I break the raker up,
> It is only the stranger
> Hissing in the grate.

The 'stranger' in this passage that echoes Coleridge's 'Frost at Midnight' intimates the presence of another person, but in Graham's poem the other person is the reader invited in.[11] His or her presence is recognised, figured there as breath (the stranger hissing) and prefigured in the 'mantle-roar' and 'wheesht', which means 'be quiet' and draws our attention to the breath.

Section three begins 'Now in the third voice', and it is that mention of the word 'voice' that gets in the way of us hearing the father speak. It is line 9 before we get genuine 'father' perceptions, since before then we have the poem telling us about itself. The voice doesn't stabilise, however, since by the time we get to line 35 of section 3 'Or the way where, as a boy' it is clear that the voice has for some time been the poet. We can be quite certain of that when he speaks of 'the fathering tenement'.

> Otherwise I go
> Only as a shell
> Of my former self.

The young self is contained in the present one, so the present self is seen as a shell:

> The big wind blows
> Over the shore of my child
> Hood in the off-season.
> The small wind remurmurs
> The fathering tenement
> And a boy I knew running
> The hide and seeking streets.

The child's 'hood' is a duffel-coat or anorak 'hood' as well as the period of time, both of them holding and surrounding the child like the 'fathering tenement'. The poet's present adult self looks back and recognises, in his tenderness for his younger self, the feeling that his father had for him as a child. All the containers: 'hood', 'tenement', and the matched emotions of father and son, rhyme with the idea of a shell held to the ear, and Time is the territory they inhabit when they are brought together in the poem.

> Or I am always only
> Thinking is this the time
> To look elsewhere to turn
> Towards what was it
> I put myself out
> Away from home to meet?
> Was it this only? Surely

> It is more than these words
> See on my side
> I went halfway to meet.

Here, in the fourth section of the poem, there is nothing but the speaking voice looking at the words and describing his relation to them. This fills up time in the metre and makes a place for the reader. The words are put out in trust that the reader will come 'halfway to meet' the poet's effort of talking for some time to complete strangers he can't see. There is nothing here but 'home' and 'elsewhere' – and we have seen into 'home'.

> I stop and listen over
> My shoulder and listen back
> On language for that step
> That seems to fall after
> My own step in the dark.

Here the self that was, a few feet back down the road, is imagined co-existent with this speaking self which is drawn together out of this awareness in speaking, in language.

The mother voice in section 2 has been likewise drawn into being by the awareness of the step on the stair and the children breathing in the dark in their sleep. We are in touch with the children and their story (their dreams and their future) through the trace of breath in the dark: 'wheest' and 'the stranger'. The mother-voice and the father-voice are not separate from the poet, he holds his consciousness as part of the family group:

> I am the shell held
> To Time's ear and you
> May hear the lonely leagues
> Of the kittiwake and the fulmar.

The sense of spaciousness in this is wonderful. We have the identity between the shape of the ear and the inside of a shell, then the cliff edges and huge sea expanses that the birds inhabit. The 'shell' as the present self becomes an eggshell with its promise of birth.

> Maybe I should expect
> To find myself only
> Saying that again
> Here now at the end.
> Yet over the great
> Gantries and cantilevers
> Of love, a sky, real and

>   Particular is slowly
>   Startled into light.

The word 'startled' is used because it contains 'star'. It is a hint back to the Europa and bull theme that has been going on overhead of the perceptions and recognitions in the intimate darkness to which the reader is drawn in.

Europa, seduced by Jupiter disguised as a bull, is carried away from Phoenicia to Crete, where their descendants become the ruling dynasty. The story links a change in the economic priorities of agriculture with a sexual encounter and the establishment of a particular clan or tribe to whom the bull is – because of its economic importance – a totem for the group. The importance of the myth for Graham's purposes is the coincidence of sexual desire with the long time lapse and scale that makes the figures come regularly from the deep past into the night sky. The lovers drift timelessly through the heavens and see their story re-enacted in each generation, each season, each night. They are remote figures and their gaze down is equivalent to that of the reader looking down on Graham's text.

Graham's idea of community as developed throughout his work is never far from the family, and his political consciousness is closely allied to the Celtic communities of Britain as members of Europe. His language, by holding on to shards of Scottish, Irish, and Cornish speech, connects with his use of the European tradition of thought which finds its origins here in Greek myth, and elsewhere in Greek thinkers such as Heraclitus and Parmenides. He may well have been influenced in his choice of myth by Peter Lanyon's paintings on the same theme; also by his own visit to Crete, which registers in his poems 'Implements In Their Places' (nos 68, 70 and 71, pp. 253–54), 'A Dream of Crete' and 'Street of Knives'.[12]

Implements In Their Places

Implements In Their Places was published in 1977 and collected unchanged into *Collected Poems 1942–1977*. Like *Malcolm Mooney's Land*, the work is lucid and apparently simple in construction when compared to *The Nightfishing* and earlier work. The principal characteristics of *Malcolm Mooney's Land* are also present in *Implements In Their Places*: the examination of the reader-writer relationship, poems explicitly about language, the special vocabulary and the creation of a separate territory outside of normal experience (a domain inhabited by monsters, beasts and gods). In fact the striking thing about *Implements In Their Places* as a volume is how many of the poems are a development (in some cases quite radical) of pieces in *Malcolm Mooney's Land*. Given a certain familiarity with Graham's work, the reader will find that these later poems all seem to refer to their place in Graham's career. 'Johann Joachim Quantz's Five Lessons' extends 'Johann Joachim Quantiz's First Lesson', 'Implements In Their Places' extends 'Approaches To How They Behave', 'What is the Language Using us For?' extends 'Malcolm Mooney's Land' and so on. The autobiographical theme is highly developed in this work, which has poems on Graham's past in Greenock, London and Cornwall, and in which Graham becomes more firmly the poet of the St Ives community and Cape Cornwall, with his tributes and imaginative use of place.

The new note in *Implements In Their Places* which, though present in *Malcolm Mooney's Land* is more developed here, is the elegiac tone of many of the poems. There are elegies for Bryan Wynter, Roger Hilton and Alexander Graham, as well as two short poems that mourn Wynter while appearing at first to be simply nature poems. 'Loch Thom' mentions dead parents and goes back to childhood scenes. 'Imagine a Forest' is a poem about facing death as a simple personal fact and all three of the incident poems ('The Gobbled Child', 'The Lost Miss Conn', and 'The Murdered Drinker') deal with sudden death. 'Ten Shots of Mister Simpson' is about a man facing death by a firing squad and Johann Joachim Quantz's Five Lessons' is a poem about a pupil-teacher relationship where the driving force is the old man's failing powers and his wish to pass on his skill before he dies. Almost all the poems are about death in one way or another. The title poem, longest by far, is dealt with below; an important part of its shape is the urgency of getting things written up and put into a form with not much time left. Its autobiographical theme and the aphoristic compression of many of its sections make it a memorial to its author: 'It is only when the tenant is gone / The shell speaks of the sea' (p. 248).

The kind of linking across the book that was evident in *Malcolm Mooney's Land* is present throughout *Implements In Their Places*. For example, the magic wood of 'Implements In Their Places' places the poems 'The Secret Name', 'The Found Picture', 'Language Ah Now You Have Me' and 'Imagine a Forest'. The book is also consistent in its natural history of beasts and its invocations of the gods and the muse.

The poem 'Implements In Their Places' is modelled on *The Fragments of Heraclitus*; moreover it takes up and develops certain theoretical ideas embodied in Heidegger's *Being and Time*, which themselves refer back to Heraclitus.[1] Graham's purpose, in this essentially metaphysical poem, is to create a sense of language as inhabited space. The material he uses is that which is most private and personal in his life, and it is assembled to at once realise and prove the formula which Heidegger developed in his writings on Holderlin, that 'poetically man dwells on this earth'. The poem is a series of seventy-four separate verse fragments, each of from one to nineteen lines long, numbers one and seventy-four being the same. Like the Heraclitan *Fragments*, the work at first glance appears to be a scatter of content, but on closer examination a number of main themes emerge: Scottish location and past, Greek location and past, words and communication, Graham's personal past and loves, ships and the sea, and what I shall call the poetry domain.

When the poems are tabulated under these headings a kind of balance is obvious – that is there seems to be a deliberate symmetry between Scotland and Greece, between the wood and the sea. The verses are not arranged in thematic order, but there are runs on a particular subject, for instance, 20, 22, 24, 26, 27, 28, 29, 30, 31, 34, 35, 36, and 37 all deal with words and communication.

This first impression of a scattering is important to the logic of the sequence, for it is primarily a structure in which one piece echoes another across a considerable space. That space is separation in time and subject, and one imagines considerable pauses in a spoken performance of the poem. The repetition of the first and last sections is an indication against linear progress: the sequence is closed, circular, it speaks of itself. The prime relationship in the poem is that between the writer and his readers, and the writer continually compares this relationship with his own regard for his past. His past is seen as a series of previous selves, reinhabited in the process of writing – and this process is repeated for us as we read.

The previous Graham poem that is most like this one is 'Approaches to how they Behave' in *Malcolm Mooney's Land*. Those 'Implements' that are about words and communication would, on the whole, work perfectly well transferred to that poem. Number 26 is a good example. There is much more in 'Implements In Their Places' that is personal, or looks personal, and it is located in time and space more firmly. Within itself, 'Implements In Their Places' has the kind of coherence that occurs in the volume *Malcolm Mooney's Land*, and some of the 'Implements' are really very close to being complete poems, all they lack are titles to set them apart. Number 9 could work in this way.

'Malcolm Mooney's Land' is a poem that presents itself as the diary of an explorer, though it is a very strange self-conscious diary. 'Implements In Their Places' looks like a tidied-up poet's notebook, made of bits of past life, aphorisms, thoughts about writing. It is in fact no more a common-place boiok than 'Malcolm Mooney's Land' is a diary; like that poem it is a kind of semi-fictional document which very soon passes from narrative into a kind of meta-narrative, of thoughts about the status of the text and the relation between the writer and his readers.

> Out into across
> The morning loch burnished
> Between us goes the flat
> Thrown poem and lands
> Takes off and skips One
> 2,3,4,5,6,7,8,9,
> And ends and sinks under.   (no.10)

> There is no fifty-seven.
> It is not here. Only
> Freshwater Loch Thom
> To paddle your feet in,
> And the long cry of the curlew.   (no.57)

> Kind me (O never never).
> I leave you this space
> To use as your own.
> I think you will find
> That using it is more
> Impossible than making it.
> Here is the space now.
> Write an Implement in it.
> You ....
> You ....
> You ....

Implements In Their Places

> You ....
>   Do it with your pen.
>   I will return in a moment
>   To see what you have done.
>   Try. Try. No offence meant.   (no. 40)

These three sections speak to us in a playful and untrustworthy way about their own construction and place in the poem. Each of them pretends to measure an empty space: in 10 it is the extent of a stone skip, in 40 a space for us to fill, in 57 the blank before the poem-idea occurs. Each presents objects to us across the author's declared purpose. Is he inviting us into the process of creating a poem, or is he making that process ever more mysterious? Both at once.

The stone in 10 is not actually mentioned, 40 is not a blank space but printed all over, 'Implement' 57 is just as present as any of the others. It is full of landscape and wildlife. Our distance from the real 'Loch Thom' is made acute by the reference to the reader's body, the pun on 'feet'. It is this dimension of paradox that makes the poem so funny and so awe-inspiring at the same time. The poem about writing poems is full of strange objects, places and animals – whereas the expectation that we might have of this kind of writing would be artificial, discrete-seeming language bits.

We cannot forget for an instant that these pieces are made, that there is an author managing the words about. The writing seems unusually direct about its processes, but the author is acutely absent from the print. He takes the idea of reader participation and shows it up for what it is. Our notions of re-constructing a fragmented self from the dislocated narrative bits (the kind of argument that turns up in Pound/Eliot criticism) is given an old-fashioned look. The distance between the reader and the writer is not reduced but increased. *Things* seem to have been hauled into the poem while we were not looking, irreducible and actual, there inside the poem. This cannot be so, things in the poem are never more than their names. Graham's devices of keeping us attentive to the printed surface and crafted noise of the poem create a kind of inverted realism, whereby the subject of the poem is not precluded but relocated. To make the poem explicit about its creation, and repeatedly so, makes us rather trusting and unfinical. There is a fiction that the subject has been removed from fictional space, that this inversion of realism is somehow 'true'.

In Graham's work the process is carried out locally through a kind of punning and word substitution that he developed quite early in his career. Here he typically substitutes 'word' or 'poem' for something else: 'my barrier of propped words' (4), 'the flat/Thrown poem' (10), 'Commuting by arterial words' (28), 'the poem's horned head' (38), 'I want out of this underword' (42), 'She lifts my words' (51) – so that we read, respectively, books, stone, roads, beast, underworld, shell. Always when we read a pun in a poem we begin to fill in another meaning-surface in the imagination. We speak of a literary work having 'layers' of meaning. Graham is likely to extend the secondary layer or transfer to it:

> When I was a buoy it seemed
> Craft of rare tonnage
> Moored to me. Now
> Occasionally a skiff
> Is tied to me and tugs
> At the end of its tether. (no. 5)

Now 'When I was a buoy' is a sort of pun the wrong way round. The only way the phrase makes sense is if we see the 'hidden' meaning 'boy'. Graham, however, carries on with the movement of sense we read out of 'buoy' but is also talking about something else. 'Craft', that is ships and boats, are always referred to as feminine, and 'mooring' has a sexual meaning in this passage. Yet the familiar phrase 'At the end of its tether' is used, not as a metaphor in itself (as it usually is in our speech) but with its original meaning in order to complete a larger metaphor. 'Craft' can be read also as writing, especially for Graham perhaps since Dylan Thomas has the title 'In My Sullen Art or Craft', and 'tugs' is not quite steady as a verb, because with all this punning one is made to think of 'tug' as a separate noun, signifying the kind of boat.

> Member of Topside Jack's trades,
> I tie my verse in a true reef
> Fast for the purpose of joining. (no. 32)

Here is another ships/sea 'Implement' that is more directly about writing. The link is more explicit because 'verse' is there substituting the metaphor 'line' or 'rope'. We know it is one or the other from the context, which all belongs to the suppressed metaphor and not to 'verse'. Almost every word has another meaning, and since the statement is with a metaphor (at one remove from a simple surface) which is itself suppressed, they show up more: 'Member' becomes sexual (cf. 'our cock members', p. 251), 'Topside' is beef, 'Jack' is 'Jack of all trades' – but 'trades' are also winds, 'verse' conceals 'rope', 'reef' is a reef knot as well as a coastal hazard, 'Fast' suggests speed and wit, 'joining' suggests joining the 'trade', or becoming a 'Member', and joinery is a trade itself. The whole thing refers to a lover's knot, a true reef knot, like the bow in valentine verses and mottoes.

The play between surfaces that comes about through these substitutions, puns, and metaphors that are extended until they become primary, seems to be a quite important part of Graham's purpose. It says much about the reader he assumes, and about the way in which he wishes to present himself, as generous, amusing, an inventor of games.

The title 'Implements In Their Places' suggests that each of these stanzas has a specific use – that they are arranged, as on a rack, ready to be employed. There is a static but ready-for-action quality in the phrase. The word 'Implement' is derived from medical Latin (1454) *Implementa*, but taken as a verb (1 To complete, perform: to fulfil 1806; 2 To complete, supplement 1843; 3 To provide with Implements 1886) the word is described as 'chiefly Scottish' (*O.E.D.*). The sense is quite specific and general at the same time, since to have a use, the Implement must be specialised but the meanings: '1 Things that serve as equipment or outfit as household furniture, ecclesiastical vestments, etc – 2 The apparatus, instruments, etc employed in any trade or executing any piece of work; as agricultural Implements, flint Implements, etc' allow all possible uses, all kinds of work. (*O.E.D.*). It is the special status of such equipment, midway between the things of nature and completed work, that is of interest to readers of Graham's poem.

In Heidegger's work *Being and Time*, there is an extensive examination of what we mean by being-in-the-world, of how we know the world, and how our being is revealed to us. Heidegger claims that:

> Being-in-the-world shall first be made visible with regard to that item of its structure which is the 'world' itself ... to give a phenomenological description of the 'world' will mean to exhibit the being of those entities which are present present-at-hand within the world, and to fix it in concepts which are categorical. 'World' may stand for the 'public' we-world, or one's 'own' closest (domestic) environment. (p. 93)

He discriminates between the things of nature (stone, trees, earth, etc.) and things which are ready-to-hand, by considering the Greek term for 'Things':

> The Greeks had an appropriate term for 'Things': *pragmata* – that is to say, that which one has to do with in one's concernful dealings (*praxis*). But ontologically, the specifically 'pragmatic' character of the *pragmata* is just what the Greeks left in obscurity; they thought of these 'proximally' as 'mere Things'. We shall call those entities which we encounter in concern '*equipment*'. (Heidegger, pp. 96–97, my emphasis)

His translator and editor provides the following note on the term 'equipment':

> 'das *Zeug*'. The word 'Zeug' has no precise English equivalent.

> While it may mean any Implement, instrument, or tool. Heidegger uses it for the most part as a collective noun which is analogous to our relatively specific 'gear' (as in 'gear for fishing') or the more elaborate 'paraphernalia', or the still more general 'equipment', which we shall employ throughout this translation. (Heidegger, p. 97)

Heidegger's examination of 'Being-in-the-world' relies entirely on 'Implements', because it is through their use that we know the world: through hammering, for example, we know the specific 'manipulability' (*Handlichkeit*) of the hammer. We thus also know things from nature: wood and metal.

> What we encounter as closest to us (though not as something taken as a theme) is the room; and we encounter it not as something 'between four walls' in a geometrical spacial sense, but as equipment for residing. Out of this the 'arrangement' emerges, and it is in this that any 'individual' item of equipment shows itself. (Heidegger, p. 98)

> The region itself becomes visible in a conspicuous manner only when one discovers the ready-to-hand circumspectively and does so in the deficient modes of concern. Often the region of a place does not become accessible explicitly as such a region until one fails to find something *in its place*. The space which is discovered in circumspective Being-in-the-world as the spatiality of the totality of equipment, always belongs to entities themselves as the place of that totality. The bare space itself is still veiled over. *Space has been split up into places.* (Heidegger, pp. 137–138, my emphasis)

Now Heidegger's entire project, the strategies of his composition, the examples that he uses to explain himself, and the extreme reflexive mode of expression, are all very relevant to Graham's work, and nowhere is this more true than in 'Implements In Their Places'. Graham's 'Implements' depicted in the work, the use of material from early Greek philosophy, the idea of language actively participating in the fullness of creation; that is, the whole matter of the poem, is most likely derived from Heidegger. That Graham was considering this material before the composition of 'Implements In Their Places' is quite clear from a philosophy reading list, in Graham's hand, in a note-book of the Skelton manuscript collection.[2] The reading list mentions Heidegger's *Being and Time*, as well as Magda King's *Heidegger's Philosophy* (1964). Though we cannot be sure that Graham *actually* read these books, he does seem to have worked up the ideas in his poem. Either Graham had access to the books, or discussed their content with a friend who provided the reading list, which

Graham copied out. Either way, Heidegger is clearly a source of certain key ideas in the poem. It would have been possible, in any case, to gain access to Heidegger's theory of Being through a relatively easy to obtain work: H. J. Blackburn's *Six Existential Thinkers* which summarises Heidegger's discussion of equipment and being. This work had been available since 1952.

One of the main features of Heidegger's work is his continual attention to specific key words and their origins. The difference between modern German, Old German, Latin, and Greek versions of a word are discussed for the quite different understandings of the world that are implied in the various kinds of language use. The arguments tend to go back to the pre-Socratics, in particular Heraclitus of Ephesus, who for Heidegger is the early philosopher most misrepresented in the transmission through to the language of modern thought.

Eliot, Graham's editor and one of the most important influences on his work, prefaces 'Burnt Norton' with two of the fragments of Heraclitus – and one of these: 'The way up and down is one and the same' is rendered in 'Implement' 68:

The earth was never flat, Always
The mind or earth wanderers' choice
Was up or down, a lonely vertical.

where 'the way', typically for Graham, is included in the word 'Always'. The other clear allusion to Heraclitus comes in 'Implement' 70:

(Is where you listen from becoming
Numb by the strike of the same key?)
It is our hazard, Heraklion, listen.

In the John Fowles volume, *The Aristos* (1965), which is a personal philosophy that claims to be derived from Heraclitus, and is in fact for the most part a re-ordering and rephrasing of the fragments, Fowles has one section labelled 'The Necessity of Hazard' and one headed simply 'Hazard'. The titles come from Fowles's understanding of the fragment 'Thunderbolt pilots all things' which Fowles translates: 'The Keraunos (the thunderbolt, chaos, hazard) steers all things.' (Fowles p. 214)

Though he obviously diminishes the meaning of 'thunderbolt' (the presence of fire as an immanent ruling natural force and as an invocation by synechdoche for Zeus) by this translation, Fowles makes 'Hazard' one of the major terms in his philosophy. It is the medium in which man lives and grows, the condition which allows both pleasure and responsibility. So the linking 'Hazard, Heraklion' in the Graham piece ('Implement' 70) would seem to be an invocation of Heraclitus – the name Heraklion (the provincial capital of Crete) quite close enough in sound for Graham's allusive word use in this poem.

> (Is where you listen from becoming
> Numb by the strike of the same key?)
> It is our hazard. Heraklion, listen.   (no. 70, p. 253)

A simple paraphrase of this 'Implement' is not easy. As it relates to the writer-reader theme, it would be something like: 'Is the poem beginning to sound monotonous, that is always a risk.' For this reading the words 'Heraklion, listen' are out of place, irrelevant. The 'strike of the same key' refers perhaps to a typewriter, recognising the previous 'Implement's' alliteration on the letter 'l' – but all typewriter keys sound the same – so this aside to an imaginary typist or the reader does not make much sense. It *could* be that 'key' refers to a piano, used as a metaphor to bring forward the meaning 'monotone' – but again, this is unsatisfactory. If we think of someone calling Heraklion (say the airport) by telegraph or radio telegraph, then the idea of a piano wire and the striking of a morse message is combined and the piano metaphor seems to be used more fully. If, as I think here, Graham is using the word 'strike' to signify the thunderbolt through 'lightning strike', and the 'key' is that of Benjamin Franklin's experiment, the taut wire has yet another use – to invoke the presence of Zeus. 'Becoming' is a term used by Heidegger to discriminate 'Being', and it comes from the same pre-Socratic world, though it suggests Parmenides, whom Heidegger considers along with Heraclitus.[3] A simple paraphrase of the 'Implement' is not possible because it is written to indicate several areas of interest at once, and because its elements pick up threads from the 'Implements' surrounding it. Numbers 65 (Crete), 67 (numbness), 68 (pre-Socratics), 69 (flight, undercarriage), 71 (Greece/Scotland, also 'buzzing plucked wires'), and 73 (invocation) all make more sense through their connection with number 70. It is important, furthermore, that we can nowhere be quite secure about what Graham is doing, and that the invocations as such should merely hint:

> ... And at
> The meeting, dusk-filled end I see
> (I wish I saw.) the shy move
> Of the wood's god approaching to greet me.   (no. 60)

> Of air he knows nor does he speak
> To earth. The day is sailing round
> His heavenly wings. Daisies and cups
> Of butter and dragonflies stop

Their meadow life to look up wondering
How out of what ridiculous season
The wingèd one descends. (no 73)

This is exactly in line with Heidegger's statements in his essay 'Holderlin and the Essence of Poetry', published in *Quarterly Review of Literature*, a journal in which Graham's poems also appeared.

> Poetry looks like a game, but it is not a game. Games it is true, bring men together, but in such a manner that each of them forgets himself. Poetry, however, gathers each man on the foundation of his existence. . . . Poetry is primarily the naming of the gods, but the poetic acquires this power only when the gods have provoked us into speech. How do the gods speak? Holderlin says: ' . . . and hints have forever been the language of the gods.' . . . The essence of poetry thus is fitted into two sets of laws which strive to unite, but also to separate: the hints of the gods and the voice of the people. The poet himself stands in between both, the gods and the people. He is thrown into an in-between, the realm that lies between men and gods. Who man is and where he chooses to dwell, this is decided primarily and even exclusively in this realm. 'Poetically man dwells on this earth.' (Heidegger pp. 90–91)

By creating the kind of language-games that he does by consistently representing language as animate and living, by setting up the hints that invoke the ancient Greek world and its gods, Graham is deliberately creating a poetic domain in the terms of Heidegger's metaphysics. The form of the work is based on Heraclitus's *Fragments*, not just in that the text is made up of bits, but because of the continual use of paradox and of the literary qualities that have been attributed to Heraclitus. In *The Art and Thought of Heraclitus*, C. H. Kahn isolates *linguistic density* and *resonance* as the main components of Heraclitus's style. By 'linguistic density' he means 'the phenomenon by which a multiplicity of ideas are expressed in a single word or phrase', by 'resonance': 'a relationship between fragments by which a single theme or image is echoed from one text to another in such a way that the meaning of each is enriched when they are understood together' (Kahn p. 89). Both of these qualities could be seen as no more than what we expect from good poetry – but taken together with paradox *and* the fragment form, the model holds.

Heidegger's claim for the function of poetry – 'Poetically man dwells on this earth' – locates the poet in 'the realm that lies between men and gods'. This place is the territory of 'Implements In Their Places'. If in *Malcolm Mooney's Land*, there was a kind of territory explored, it was notable that we were taken into a place of madness (see also 'Implement' 30) abstracted from a common reality shared or understood by the audience. The abstraction itself was the main feature, hence the setting of icy barren waste as the page in 'printed snow'. 'Approaches to How They Behave' (which looks like a dummy run for 'Implements In Their Places') holds up this abstraction, talking as it does about an animal language, showing it as wayward and almost out of control. It is hard to see how, at first, that 'Implements In Their Places' completely re-places this mode and creates another kind of territory. The general method is much the same but the place is much more *inhabited* than that of the 'Approaches'. It is, first of all, sticky with personal traces of the author, or pieces written to look like that, as if private guilt and obsession were trapped in the poem. Yet we do not know all the details of this material and there remains a kind of detachment, lack of self-pity, that keeps the work from making the audience simply voyeurs. In 'Implement' 15, for instance, we do not need to know anything about the author to realise we are reading about an affair:

> Raped by his colour slides her delighted
> Pupils fondled their life together.
> It was the fifty dirty milkbottles
> Standing like an army turned their love sour.

In the first place, the fact that we don't get all the information we need to place this little story, makes it seem guilty and private. 'Raped,' 'dirty', and 'sour' have the same effect. Here is another:

> Under his kilt his master
> Led him to play the fool
> Over the border and burn
> A lady in her tower
> In a loud lorry road
> In tulipless Holland Park.   (no. 47)

We guess it signals another escapade. There is a theme in the work of sexual deceit; numbers 3, 8, 9, set it up. In each case, however, the material is used for other ends. The male in number 15 is a lecturer who uses slide illustrations, since there is a pun on rapt 'pupils' that makes the woman a teacher too. The relationship between the watching eyes of the pupils and those of the readers is of course implicit here – and our voyeurism is equivalent to the writer's sense of guilt.

> He has been given a chair in that
> Timeless University.
> The Chair of Professor of Silence.

We have it from number 6, with its fun over the use of the word 'chair', that this teaching is a part of the poet's role. The teacher's voice addresses us in number 40 'Do it with your pen' and in number 66 'I caught young Kipling'. 'Raped by his colour slides', moreover links up with number 41: 'Smudged on a coloured, shining plate'. The second piece quoted (47: 'Under his kilt') reminds us of ' . . . the muse in the guise / Of jailbait pressed against / That cheeky part of me' (number 3) and the use of the border ballad 'The Bonny Earl of Murray' in number 53. This kind of linking, which I have called 'resonance', works throughout the poem. Any track which is followed will ultimately take in the whole work. It has an important effect on this 'private material', however, since without making the poet seem any less 'inside' the work, it renders what is 'private' as part of an intelligible system. Intelligible, that is, up to a point. We are being teased with glimpses of someone's private life because he is at risk there, that is what he cares about. The fears we hold in common, we can measure against our own jealousies and 'failures of love'. In examining the poet's place, his public persona, Graham is accepting that part of the reader's interest and curiosity will be directed there. He does it because it is a forbidden area. He is looking at that phenomenon. We all know how much favoured author's works are autobiographical, hence the market for journals, letters, and biographies. Some part of being an author is dealing with this kind of attention, whatever kind of audience the writer has. We find out, in 'Implements In Their Places', bits of the writer's life and world but it adds up to no more than the assurance that there is much more that remains truly private. As in the 'Implements' that appeared to talk about the process of writing, the final sense is of an author acutely *absent* from the text. The poetry domain, then, is in part the poet's past life and his privacy. Another part of it is the literary territory signalled by allusion to other works. The authors actually mentioned in 'Implements In Their Places' are: Montgomerie, Scopoli (11), Rimbaud, Nansen (28), Corbière, David Jones, Shelley, Crane, Melville, Eliot (49 and 50), Graham (58), and Kipling (66). This is the simplest way in which Graham stakes out a literary territory, though the names are not just listed in the poem. In each case they are introduced in a playful way, like the elements of the knotting 'Implement' (number 32)

>Mister Montgomerie. Mister Scop.
>You, follicles. You, the owl.
>Two famous men famous for far
>Apart images. POLEEP POLEEP
>The owl calls through the olive grove.
>I come to her in a set-in bed
>In a Greenock tenement. I see
>The little circle of brown moles
>Round her nipple. Good Montgomerie.   (no. 11)

Now the middle section of this piece suggests, with 'fame' and 'images' taken together with the line 'The owl calls through the olive grove', Ezra Pound who wrote:

> under the olives
> saeculorum Athenae
> γλαύξ, γλαυκῶπις
>   olivi
> that which gleams and then does not gleam
>   as the leaf turns in the air   (Canto 74)

Here Athene's gleaming eyes are seen in the turning of an olive leaf which is light-coloured on the underside. She is, for the same attribute of 'gleaming eyes', often depicted as an owl for its huge eyes and night vision. As goddess of wisdom she is associated with the owl's proverbial intelligence. The owl in the Graham piece is a Scops owl, *Otus Scops*, the only small European owl with ear tufts. Its call is described by Peterson as a persistent, repeated 'pew'.[4] It was named by Linnaeus after Giovanni Antonio Scopoli, author of *Deliciae Flora et Fauna Insubricae a Specimen Zoologicum* (Pavia, 1786). Hence 'Mister Scop' (though we should note that 'scop' also means 'an Old English poet or minstrel' – *O.E.D.*). The way in which Graham renders the scops owl: 'POLEEP POLEEP' is itself a reference to the other name in the poem 'Montgomerie'. The sixteenth century Scots poet Alexander Montgomerie, famous for his poem *The Cherrie and the Slae* (presumably these 'follicles' – ie capsular fruits – are his 'far apart images') has the following stanza in the poem 'Polwart and Montgomerie's Flyting'.

> Polwart, yee peip like a mouse amongst thornes;
> Na cunning yee keepe; Polwart, yee peip;
> Ye look like a sheipe and yee had twa hornes:
> Polwart, ye peipe like a mouse amongst thornes.

'Polwart, yee peipe' becomes 'POLEEP POLEEP' in the Graham version, and the 'horns' are there in owl's ear tufts. There is also 'The little circle of brown moles' to remind us of 'a mouse amongst thornes'. In 'Implement' 38 we find 'the poem's horned head'. The Scopoli title is in 'Implement' 41 'I found her listed under Flora . . . As for Fauna' and the setting of number 38 is a zoo.

From evidence elsewhere in Graham's work it seems that someone else is characterised by 'Mister Scop'. In 'Malcolm Mooney's Land' there is 'My friend who loves owls' who becomes blind, and the poem 'Heath-Stubbs the Poet as Hero' identifies Graham's owl-loving, blind poet friend.[5] 'Montgomerie' is the same, the phrase 'MONTGOMERIE'S FOLLICLES' appears on Graham's holograph cover for the magazine *Promenade*.⁶ This issue of the magazine is devoted to W. S. Graham and the cover, which has been printed on a stencil-duplicator, features Graham's handwritten doodles and lists of names, sketches, as a kind of background texture over which the title is printed in green. The names are those of friends. 'Montgomerie' appears in company with 'Llareggub' (standing for Dylan Thomas, his Llareggub Hill in *Under Milk Wood*) and 'Sydney Goodsir Smith'. 'Montgomerie' must therefore refer also to the 'Scottish Renaissance' poet William Montgomerie (born 1904) who wrote the introduction to Graham's volume *The Seven Journeys*.

> I come to her in a set-in-bed
> In a Greenock tenement. I see
> The little circle of brown moles
> Round her nipple. Good Montgomerie.

The rest of the 'Implement' deals with what his readers will know from elsewhere: the 'set-in-bed' and the 'Greenock tenement' are familiar references to Graham's childhood. 'I come to her' would seem to refer to his mother. The 'little circle of brown moles round her nipple' are Montgomerie's tubercles (to rhyme with 'follicles') – glands which become more prominent during pregnancy and breast feeding.⁷

Scottish literature of the sixteenth century is the strongest content of 'Implement' 11, because it names 'Montgomerie' and echoes his verse. There is also a typical link between Greece and Scotland that is developed in numbers 68 onwards, where the poet persona is in Greece thinking of Scotland, or somewhere else shifting between the two. Another 'Implement' which is based on Scottish writing is number 53:

> The word unblemished by the tongue
> Of History has still to be got.
> You see, Huntly, it is the way
> You put it. Said Moray's Earl,
> You've spoilt a bonnier face than your ain.
> That's what he said when Huntly struck
> The Scots iron into his face.

The incident is the killing of James Stewart of Doune, who became Earl of Moray (Murray) in 1581 and was a supporter of the rebel Bothwell. On 7 February 1592, the Earl of Huntly was commissioned to bring him in for trial but killed him and burnt his castle. 'The word unblemished by the tongue / Of History has still to be got' would seem to refer to Ballad history, how an oral tradition is changed in transcription and then altered again by later editors. Apart from authors like Burns rewriting the ballads, Graham may be thinking of the modern authors who followed MacDiarmid in writing a kind of synthetic Scots composed of several dialects and spoken by no one. 'You see, Huntly, it is the way / You put it. Said Moray's Earl.' 'Put it' refers to speaking and to striking with the sword. 'Moray's Earl' is written that way round because it looks like 'Moray eel' which is another 'tongue'-like thing, and a sea-creature (see numbers 39, 58, 65, 67), as well as something that would have to be attacked in the face, since it hides in a hole with just the face showing. In its hole it would be sheathed like a sword – and it has a sexual meaning, since what is at stake in the combat between Huntly and the Earl is the favours of the Queen.

There is a great deal of Shakespeare allusion in the 'Implements', Graham picks out incidentals to use for his own purposes:

> Officer myself, I had orders
> To stay put, not to advance
> On the enemy whose twigs of spring
> Waved on their helmets as they less
> Leadered than us deployed across
> The other side of the ravine of silence   (no. 54)

> I stand still and the wood marches
> Towards me and divides towards
> Me not to cover me up strangled
> Under its ancient live anchors.
> I stand in a ride now. And at
> The meeting, dusk-filled end I see
> (I wish I saw.) the shy move
> Of the wood's god approaching to greet me.   (no. 60)

> Macbeth shall never vanquished be until
> Great Birnam wood to high Dunsinane hill
> Shall come against him.   (*Macbeth*, IV. i. 92)

The wood in 'Implements In Their Places' is a magic place. 'Implements' 54, 59, 60 and 62 relate it to *Macbeth*. In 59 the wood talks, as it does in Shakespeare, 'Stones have been known to move and trees to speak' (III. iv. 23) and the rooks are common to both: 'the crow/Makes wing to the rooky wood' (III. ii. 50), 'By maggot-pies and choughs and rooks brought forth' (III. iv. 125). It seems right that Graham should choose the play with a Scottish theme, but the connection is worked closer than that. Macbeth, son of Findlaech, who reigned in Scotland 1040–57, on whom Shakespeare's play is based, was mormaer (earl) of Moray. So the violent death of Moray from the ballad 'The Bonny Earl of Murray' is a kind of underpinning to the magic wood adapted from *Macbeth*, and therefore recognisable (to the reader) as a pre-existing, conventional, literary place like Arcadia or Arden where the trials of love are staged, where magic and the gods are to be expected (hoped for).

> I see it has fluttered to your hand
> Drowned and singed. Can you read it?
> It kills me. Why do you persist
> In holding my message upsidedown?   (no. 22)

'It kills me' echoes II Corinthians 6: ' . . . our sufficiency is of God; who also hath made us ministers of the new testament; not of the letter but of the spirit; for the letter killeth but spirit giveth life.' 'Drowned and singed' appears to be an echo of a passage from *King Lear*.

> Blow, winds, and crack your cheeks! rage! blow!
> You cataracts and hurricanoes, spout
> Till you have drenched our steeples, drown'd the cocks!
> You sulph'rous and thought executing fires,
> Vaunt-couriers of oak-cleaving thunderbolts,
> Singe my white beard!   (*Lear*, III. ii. 1)

It is a letter that has been 'Drowned and singed' in the Graham passage, but the next 'Implement' begins: 'Ho Ho Big West Prevailer, / Your *beard* brushes the gable'. And a later 'Implement' also appears to connect with *Lear*:

> Language, constrictor of my soul,
> What are you snivelling at? Behave
> Better. Take care. It's only through me
> You live. Take care. Don't make me mad.   (no. 30)

> O! let me not be mad, not mad, sweet heaven;
> Keep me in temper; I would not be mad!   (*Lear*, I. v. 43)

> I prithee, daughter, do not make me mad:
> I will not trouble thee, my child; farewell.
> We'll no more meet, no more see one another;
> But yet thou art my flesh, my blood, my daughter:
>   (*Lear*, II. iv. 216)

> that she may feel
> How sharper than a serpent's tooth it is

To have a thankless child   (*Lear*, I. iv. 285)

In 'Implement' 30, the tone is that of a father addressing a child:

> 'What are you snivelling at? Behave
> Better. Take care. It's only through me
> You live.'

This passage is, on the surface, spoken to 'Language', which in Graham's typical manner is characterised as animate. 'Constrictor of my soul' is a snake, which is how Lear characterises his relations with his daughter. It is the daughter who makes Lear fear madness. In these 'Implements' that appear to deal principally with language and communication, there seems to be a buried theme about relations between a father and daughter. It begins with 'Implement' 15, though there are earlier ones about sexual deceit. It comes to the fore in number 18:

> Because I could not gracefully
> Get out of what I was doing, I made
> An inner task come to fruit
> Invisible to all spectators.   (no. 18)

As it refers to language and the writing of poetry, this passage fits as the poet working alone without recognition. 'Not grace', however, is close to sin, 'get' is sexual, and 'inner task come to fruit' is a pregnancy. In number 20, 'The tails the tales of love are calling' brings this hidden theme forward again:

> When you were younger and me hardly
> Anything but who is in me still
> I had a throat of loving for you
> That I can hardly bear can bear.

'Who is in me still' is a view of a younger self retained inside the older – and this is another idea of pregnancy, since 'hardly bear can bear' seems to refer to delivery. 'Throat of loving' seems to connect with 'constrictor of my soul' (number 30). If numbers 22 and 23 refer to King Lear and his relation to a daughter, then 24 'It is how one two three each word' may be a further reference to Regan, Goneril, Cordelia. Number 26 has 'Nouns are very devil' and 'The King noun took the huff' which is what Lear did in his relations with Cordelia. Moving from one daughter's home to another, he crossed his kingdom in winter, impotent (unable to rule):

> Only now a wordy ghost
> Of my once firmer self I go
> Floating across the frozen tundra
> Of the lexicon and the dictionary. (no. 27)

The 'very devil' of number 26 is the link with 29 and 30. Both of them continue the discussion of language and the poet's task. 30 is the 'Implement' with a snake and a fear of madness. Number 29 is about language and original sin.

> These words as I uttered them
> Spoke back at me out of spite,
> Pretended to not know me
> From Adam. Sad to have to infer
> Such graft and treachery in the name
> Of communication. O it's become
> A circus of mountebanks, promiscuous
> Highfliers, tantamount to wanting
> To be servant to the more interesting angels.

Adam it was who named the things in the world. 'Know me from Adam' is the kind of common phrase that Graham seems to delight in making us pause over and notice in its parts. 'Know' here is sexual knowledge, brought out by '*mounte*banks', 'promiscuous', 'tanta*mount*' (which also suggests Tantalus and tantalise, or temptation), 'interesting angels' (i.e. Lucifer, his *interest* in tempting souls and mounting on high, bargains made with the devil as in *Faust*). 'Graft' is used to mean corruption, which is not remarkable, but here it reminds us of the tree of knowledge of good and evil. If the spiteful reaction of the words is something like the way his daughters treat Lear, 'graft' is a familiar Shakespearean trope.

> How are we doing not very well?
> Perhaps the real message gets lost.
> Or is it tampered with on the way
> By the collective pain of Alive? (no. 31)

Here it would seem that the two themes, language and some hidden guilty story, come together. The 'real message' tells us to look for another meaning and 'tampered with' again suggests corruption. The 'collective pain of Alive' is both what all people have in common in their daily lives *and* the moment of birth.

> I found her listed under Flora
> Smudged on a coloured, shining plate
> Dogeared and dirty. As for Fauna
> We all are that, pelted with anarchy. (no. 41)

While this 'Implement' links with number 15, with the theme of deceit, it would also seem to connect with the 'graft and treachery' of number 29 through the mention of 'Flora'. 'Fauna' is the first name of the female goddess, sister to Faunus, the shepherds' god identified with Pan. And the name contains 'Faun' the image of Pan that has been taken over by Christianity as one of the guises of the devil, the shaggy legs and cloven hoof. 'Pelted' is reminiscent of Graham's 'furry pelted queen' (in 'Malcolm Mooney's Land'). The use of the word 'pelted' as a verb in 'Implements In Their Places' brings out another connection with the devil, since the Greek root is 'diabolos' or throw across. The sense is to throw mud or slander. 'Pelted with anarchy' is at once the revolt of the angels and humanity's shame, the fur standing for the parts that are covered up. Our animal nature: 'Fauna', 'Dogeared and dirty'.

> Of air he knows nor does he speak
> To earth. The day is sailing round
> His heavenly wings. Daisies and cups
> Of butter and dragonflies stop
> Their meadow life to look up wondering
> How out of what ridiculous season
> The wingèd one descends. (no. 73)

The density of this piece is very beautiful indeed because it also seems so light and easy in expression. 'Of air he knows' comes out of nowhere, looks like the end of a quotation, especially since it is an iambic pentameter line if followed to the full stop. There is time for 'cups of butter', sheer fun, and another turn, like the placing of 'day' in the sentence to enhance the giddy feeling *and* fit 'day is' with 'daisies' (day's eyes). We have a bee or a butterfly coming down 'where the bee sucks, there suck I' and as in *The Tempest* the flower name noticed: there it's Cowslip' Cows lip, Cows slip. The 'wingèd one' is Ariel, Icarus (sailing), and the *wicked one*, Satan the 'dragon' whose fall is from the Christian 'heaven'. 'Implement' 71 would also seem to echo *The Tempest*'s 'Sometimes a thousand twangling instruments' (III. ii. 135) with 'Taverna of buzzing plucked wires' as there is also 'pinching' and boozing (ouzo).

The poetry domain of 'Implements In Their Places' appears to be made out of a combination of many themes. Scottish and Celtic materials, ancient Greece, Montgomerie, the Earl of Moray, *Macbeth* (which is the link with the 'language-wood') and *Lear*. There is the invocation in number 51 of a specifically Celtic Goddess:

> Hello. It's a pleasure. Is that a knowledge
> You wear? You are dressed up today,

> Brigit of early shallows of all
> My early life wading in pools.
> She lifts my words as a shell to hear
> The Celtic wild waves learning English.

The tone of address comes from an introduction at a party and thus links up with the more sophisticated social world of 'Implements' 3, 8, 9, 13, 15. 'Knowledge' worn like a flower or a brooch, or a new dress, is sexual knowledge and 'wading in pools' extends this meaning, since the next image is clearly an adaptation of Aphrodite-Venus being born from the waves. In the famous Boticelli picture she is standing on a shell, here she picks up a shell which is the poet's language.

Macbeth locates for us 'the language wood' which also seems to take in Kipling's jungle beasts and has its invocation in number 60; 'the shy move / Of the wood's god'. The wood links up with the sea setting through 'ancient live anchors' as the 'Brigit' 'Implement' (51) connects that material with a Celtic theme.

Another set is the poems that invoke Orpheus and the underworld, or what Graham calls the 'underword'. In number 42 'underword' occurs, and the pot-holer or miner is stuck in a narrow passage, unable to turn back and free himself. This is an echo of Orpheus's predicament, the idea of turning adapted to link with constriction that is used for the serpent-language (29–30). Number 43 has the poet as a miner and the muse named 'Mineral'. We are still in a modern underworld. The theme is extended in number 44 'And the little bad shaft emerged'. Where 'shaft' sexually puns thorn, arrow, and mineshaft. This theme is lost at this point but we have an identity between 'thorn' and sea-urchin's spine. 'Coming back to earth' is clearly coming to, or coming round, after orgasm – but also Orpheus coming back to earth from the underworld/underword, which is suggested here by 'under dear'. If the muse is named 'mineral' then 'extracted' refers to the process of getting pure mineral from ore. The 'dead right arm' is 'dead' to represent Eurydice who has to be brought back to the living world, and it is dead because it has been trapped, like the miner/pot holer, only this time under a sleeping lover. 'Pins and needles' is the arm coming back to sensation, but with more prickings and penetrations. 'Urchin' gives us a sea-creature, a child as issue of the union, and an invocation of Cupid.

'Implements In Their Places' is a strange poem that retains its strangeness. On one hand it looks like writing that has been put together in an emergency, as if things that might have been made into complete separate poems (given time and energy) have been stowed here to clear the decks, or to stop them from being lost. On the other hand, the organisation that creates resonance *across* the pieces, speaks of deliberate and highly controlled writing. It is a poem that discloses a world in glimpses, sometimes highly personal and private, where literary allusion folds back into something we therefore cannot know.

'Implements In Their Places' has a special status in Graham's work because it remains in the form of fragments that are not developed into the kind of continuity that we normally associate with finished poems. This is not the case in the other poems in *Implements In Their Places* and the last poem, 'To My Wife at Midnight', included in *Collected Poems 1942–1977*.

The first publication of 'Implements In Their Places' had the following 'Implement' to end the sequence at number 72:

> At your signal I dress in my best
> Gear of language and stand to the post.
> I refuse absolution a cigarette
> And the dirty blindfold. Shoot.
> I die for words I don't agree with
> Which told me nothing. Now my blood
> Hums on the common ground. They topple
> Me into the pit where I am special.[8]

This 'Implement', which was removed from the final version as published in the Faber volume, is clearly a germ for the poem 'Ten Shots of Mister Simpson', but their differences are instructive. In the 'Implement' quoted above, it is the poet who is presented as a victim to the firing-squad, which is not located anywhere, as any particular enemy or power. In 'Mister Simpson' we are introduced to two characters: 'Mister Simpson' the victim, and a photographer who is also the executioner of an unnamed totalitarian state. 'Simpson' in some sense represents the poet, but the executioner-photographer also represents the poet, and the latter is the stronger case.[9] Though the poem seems to be talking about language, it is not finally about poetry or Graham's poetic career in any narrow sense.

The writing is highly self-referential and powerfully structured by Graham's long practice in making the maximum use of ambiguity by punning, substitution, and the reclaiming of cliché. Thus when Graham (as the photographer) says 'I want the line of the sea in', he is referring to a wish to include the sea as a backdrop, but the line also refers to itself as a 'line' in the poem which includes the sea. Using the well-worn phrase 'Don't run away with the idea' at this point (where 'Simpson' would clearly be considering escape) reclaims it for a very literal use.

Simpson, we learn, is not the real name of the man in front of the camera: 'Move and turn your unpronounceable / Name's head to look at where the horse'. He is a man with a 'number' and he is an

Implements In Their Places 121

ex-prisoner of 'Hut K' which reminds us of Kafka. In case we think of 'Simpson' as simply a victim of a Nazi concentration camp, he is seen in 'Kiev light' in 'an ikon' no doubt of Russian origin. The present setting is in Zennor, near St Ives (which is what makes 'Simpson' a refugee) and the idea of a political prisoner is therefore generalised as it has been in Graham's earlier poems. 'Simpson' could be a prisoner of any nation or any regime, and he could be the victim of the media exposing a scandal.

The photographer-executioner maintains power over 'Simpson' by the skilful manipulation of equipment, the concentration that makes the operator look with a cold intensity. The photograph freezes action, and the operator, going under his black cloth, suggests the black cap of a judge passing sentence. 'Simpson' is a complete victim because he is not 'understanding the language'.

Graham is putting himself out here in the poem. The poem is a masquerade of himself acting out the parts of victim and manipulator in the setting that is his own place. The photo is described:

> So I made that. I got in also
> A His Master's Voice gramophone,
> A jug of Sheepsbit Scabious and
> A white-rigged ship bottled sailing
> And the mantel-piece in focus with even
> A photograph of five young gassed
> Nephews and nieces fading brown.

What Graham includes are kinds of talisman, 'the mantle brass / Fairly a mirror of surrounding sorrows' that we know from 'The Children of Greenock' and the 'rigged ship in its walls of glass' from 'The Nightfishing'. 'Sheepsbit Scabious' is there because of its punning name which economically adds more creatures (sheep, scabies) with the name of a common wildflower. The photograph in the poem is full of Graham's signatures, things which represent his life and work. The poem, like its original in the early version of 'Implements', is about facing death, alone and vulnerable. But the later version is also about the miraculously rich natural world in which we live. Complicating the narrative with different personae, while signalling real totalitarian enemies (but allowing none of them to be finally and firmly identified) greatly enlarges the scope of the poem.

Delight in the creatures admitted into the poem is evident in most of Graham's later poems. 'Enter a Cloud' which is a modern version of Shelley's 'The Cloud' has a final section which tells us the ingredients that went into the poem. Note that among them are 'bees owned by my friend / Garfield' like Shelley's 'swarm of golden bees' and that Shelley's 'blue smile' is echoed in the 'long empty blue' and 'good blue sun' of Graham's poem. Shelley's cloud is 'dissolving' and has 'strips of the sky fallen through me', Graham's cloud says 'Gently disintegrate me / Said nothing at all'. In both poems it is the cloud itself that 'speaks'.

Similarly 'Language Ah Now You Have Me' creates a densely populated darkness 'In the rain forest beside the Madron River', 'Where pigmies hamstring jumbo and the pleasure / Monkey is plucked from the tree'. The beasts include the perhaps supernatural 'great and small breathers' as well as the domestic cat with its fleas and their eggs. There is also the archaic-poetic 'leo pard' with the Germanic-African 'wildebeest'. Again it is a version of another poem, this time a pygmy hunting song which begins 'On the weeping forest' and has 'elephants' and 'monkeys' and 'hunters' in 'the forest lashed by the great rain'.[10]

The three incident poems 'The Gobbled Child', 'The Lost Miss Conn' and 'The Murdered Drinker' are similar in that they relate a short narrative with one important and enigmatic event at their centre. Like the border ballads they rely on a firm narrative line without much comment, and the events they relate are 'supernatural', or open to supernatural interpretation. 'The Gobbled Child' is a traditional kelpie story where 'Five-year-old-Iain' is 'gobbled up' by a 'big beast'. The kelpie is there in 'kelp and bladders' (line 4). In 'The Lost Miss Conn' a young woman disappears in a wood of 'Hazel and Oak and Rowan' (the Rowan or Mountain Ash being associated with supernatural in many Scottish folk tales) which sounds like a spell. Her 'young skirt / Flashing' echoes Kipling's 'And the swish of a skirt in the dew'.[11] It also alerts us with 'budding gently' to the sexual dimension of the poem. 'The Murdered Drinker' has 'Old Rab' killed by a falling branch, also suggesting that the trees are capable of malevolence towards people. This gives us the possibility of Fate ruling behind the scenes, or another deity associated with the wood.

The issues in the first two poems are child abuse and rape. 'Bladders', 'peeping', 'fair head / Cocked', 'big beast' and 'gobbled' are all words that encourage us to imagine something quite awful but not at all supernatural happening to the child. A sexual assault is the most likely way we interpret 'The Lost Miss Conn', because of the 'flashing skirt' and 'budding'; there is also the relationship with the perhaps innocent 'McIvor'. If we are led to re-read the ballad world through out modern knowledge of what happens in newspaper and television news stories, we must also ask ourselves what were the original events that were so strange, ghastly or unthinkable that they required ballads to be written with monsters and other mythic material included in them to explain what could not be credited in any other way.

This strand of interest is drawn out in 'The Found Picture' where Adam and Eve are seen by 'a third creature' who is 'not a bad man or a caught / Tom peeping' but a 'hiding god'. Peeping Tom is suggested by negation and we are brought into relation with that character as we too are made voyeurs, looking at the picture of nakedness in the poem.

The reader is led on into a wood again in 'The Secret Name' and again 'under the poem's branches two people / Walk and even the words are shy'. The poem plays with the terms of Structuralism in its 'Sound and sign signifying you'. The wood in all these poems and in 'Implement' 60 is derived from Kipling's poem 'The Way through the Woods'.

The elegies for Bryan Wynter and Roger Hilton first of all humanise those painters for the readers who may know the names from large exhibitions. They are to be read along with 'The Thermal Stair' which is an elegy for Peter Lanyon, and 'The Voyages of Alfred Wallis' as a group which celebrate and in their way to help to create the identity of the St Ives artists' community. In both of these later poems we get a remarkable sense of closeness to those who are mourned. In 'Lines on Roger Hilton's Watch' a delightful game of taking the point of view of a watch, looking at the poet, punning on 'watch' and 'watched' is a way of framing the grief of losing a close friend. It also contains the edge of 'terrible times' which could well be hard drinking sessions; 'pours himself a Teachers'. But it might be something that really was 'terrible', we cannot know, though we might guess from Hilton's own writings.[12]

'Dear Bryan Wynter' is one of Graham's finest poems in his late assured manner. What is good about it is obvious in the opening:

> This is only a note
> To say how sorry I am
> You died. You will realise
> What a position it put
> Me in. I couldn't really
> Have died for you if so
> I were inclined.

The poem talks directly to Bryan Wynter in a voice which seems completely natural, completely unconcerned at being overheard. This apparent simplicity and sincerity is a hard won gift in modern poetry, which, as we are told time and again, has no confidence in its audience or its relevance to modern life. The opening of the poem is true to a homely, somewhat naïve character, unused to writing letters, who breaks the uneasiness of beginning to write with a comforting well-known beginning-phrase. It is writing that has a job to do, which speaks honestly and without fuss.

> I would like to think
> You were all right
> And not worried about

> Monica and the children
> And not unhappy or bored.

It is not only what is said that is moving, it is the assumption that there is someone there to hear it. Graham's audience will hear and carry on the fiction – and that is a fitting tribute to the two artists involved here.

> I am up. I've washed
> The front of my face
> And here I stand looking
> Out over the top
> Half of my bedroom window.
> There almost as far
> As I can see I see
> St Buryan's church tower.
> An inch to the left, behind
> That dark rise of woods
> Is where you used to lurk.

'The front of my face' works like 'this is only a note', it is a piece of domestic and private language-use that is out of register (and therefore funny) in a public elegy. 'St Buryan's Church' alters 'Bryan's' name by just one letter 'u' (you) to remind us of burial. The punning language-games that Graham has developed are here brought to their most moving use. Nowhere is there an overstated emotion or a slip into self-pity, though there is space for strong sentiment: grief, nostalgia and loss.

Conclusions

Graham's poetic career goes through a number of radical changes, and his early work is so different from his late poems as to almost seem written by someone else. I say 'almost' because the subject of the poems does not change greatly, and there are ideas that he uses repeatedly. The difficulty that the early poems present to the reader has its own value and it would be wrong to suggest that we should concern ourselves with only the later work.

Graham's experience of language is the main thing that seems to change. The early poems resist our processes of naturalisation *and* show a sophisticated handling of latent material, calling for both the suspension of some reading habits and the development of some others. The language becomes a kind of screen on which the patterns of its management are displayed. Figured with the conventional language of love and resisting personal or private meaning, there are some close similarities between this kind of language use and that of the Elizabethan lyric.

What is withheld in this kind of composition is the introspective and private self, the fully developed individual that we have come to associate with lyric performance since Donne. Though his early work is modernist in conception, and though it inherits from Eliot and Pound, Graham has none of the ventriloquist qualities we find in Pound's *Personae*. We do not find a theatrically conceived voice, be it that of Pound's 'Seafarer' or Eliot's 'J. Alfred Prufrock'. Graham's only attempt at this kind of thing is in 'The Narrator', and characteristically it is an unspecified narrator who is by no means separable from the voice behind any other of the early poems. An unspecified narrator, for the purposes of Eliot's and Pound's early work, would be a contradiction in terms. It is only when the narrator is defined as *someone else*, that these poets can create their pretence of impersonality. Graham is up to something quite different. He is concerned with the surface in the way that a painter is who has eschewed representation as such.

Graham had just one year of formal literary education after a schooling that was not extended. He seems to have made the most of it. His studies in Scottish and English literature provided him with a strong sense of tradition. His relation to his sources is peculiar, however. Pound and Eliot ransacked the literatures of the past to make their work. Graham's attitude is characterised I feel in 'Implement' 63: 'Feeding the dead is necessary' and in the roll-call of heroes (numbers 49 and 50). Like any writer, Graham used what he could find for the task in hand, driven by his own probably deeply emotional needs. But there is a kind of respect for what he re-uses and a doggedness about the way in which he follows through an idea that is quite remarkable.

His reading of Rimbaud seems to have freed him to record certain aspects of his own experience and to get his native docklands, with their industrial character, onto the page. The 'pulleys' and 'primitive machines' that David Punter finds in the early poems are not, as he suggests, imagery from the stage. They are rather the industrial landscape in which Graham grew up and worked. His seaming together of industrial and rural material is no more than a view of Greenock and its surrounding hills, recorded in a manner very like that of Rimbaud in the translations that Graham had read.

When Graham wrote anything more extended than occasional poems, his work had a metaphysical intention. He saw the concept of a coherent self (that which is bound up in consistent chronological narrative) as a problem requiring examination through performance in language. He studied philosophy at Newbattle, and his reading probably began there. He read the Pre-Socratics, the Existentialists, Sartre and Heidegger, and no doubt much more. His structure for working out these ideas was consistently and patiently developed, though seldom fully explicit or (perhaps) completely conscious. Whilst his language use changed, this pattern was constant from the outset, as he adapted his model of the voyage.

The voyage poem first appears in Graham's work in *The Seven Journeys* (1944). Though it was published later it precedes *Cage Without Grievance* (1942) in Graham's writing. He collected only 'The Narrator' from this sequence. In it he begins to try the twinned ideas of the journey and a specific northern identity. The identity is envisaged in linguistic terms as a residuum of charged language that holds traces of Norse mythology. Crude as they are in some respects, these poems held much of Graham's future performance in them, and he may well have suppressed them because they were so rich a source for what came after.

The single most important theme of Graham's work, the voyage of exploration and self-discovery, is developed right through his career. *The White Threshold* is a confrontation with the unknowable sea and the poem remains there at the edge, explaining nothing, reproducing the conflict of endurance and destruction in nature, translating it into human and linguistic terms. *The Nightfishing* is a voyage out into the sea which seeks to establish a view of the self as a shifting and retrospective construction out of experience and work. In *Malcolm Mooney's Land* the voyage on the sea is extended to the frozen polar wastes. The poem develops a sense of territory out of isolation and madness that sees language in a heightened physicality, though still largely isolated from an extended social world. The social presences it implies are more often drawn out of memory than from any sense of current community. *Implements In Their Places* is a deferred activity, a neurotic sorting of options and equipment for various enterprises; its landscape includes scattered floes, woods seen as the sea, personal and historical pasts shifting in and out of view. Language is examined and considered as equipment for being, a technology and a place of habitation.

Holding to this path as he does, Graham creates a narrative sense that is not contained by any one work. Poems that seem to be finished in one place are then radically extended and made into a new thing. The work refers to itself. Quite indivisble from the voyage theme, Graham's relation to and characterisation of language consolidates our sense of an area charted and marked out. From the poem which is an impenetrable screen, resisting paraphrase, Graham moves to another kind of abstraction where his *expression* is relatively simple but where that simplicity draws us into paradox.

By making us follow him on this voyage into 'language' and paradox, Graham takes us into a territory similar to that in which the abstract painters work. He deliberately strove to find parallels in literature for what was happening in painting. His friends among the St Ives painters included those who became Britain's most influential abstract painters, and Patrick Heron (among them) was also the first British art critic to review American Abstract Expressionism in positive terms.[1] Graham's poems 'The Constructed Space' and 'Hilton Abstract' are explicit treatments of language as an abstract matter, and also recognitions of writer and reader both joined and separated by the print on the page (as a surface like that which the painter uses). Like the later work of Wallace Stevens, Graham's poetry makes an abstract space in which his readers may meet him.

In such an account of Graham's middle and later work a great deal is left out, however, for it makes us think of him working through a large and theoretical project as a sort of remote and heroic figure. While this may well be an important facet of his poetic career, it will not do for many of the strong medium and shorter-length works which are among Graham's finest poems.

We get from some of Graham's work the feeling of belonging to a family, to lovers and friends. As in the work of Beckett, the sense of isolation serves also to focus our attention more acutely on small occasions of tenderness and sympathy that occur between people. When they decided to eliminate the middle ground of particulars that comprises the steady voice of Realism, Beckett and Graham were able to show more clearly the basis of tenderness in the confrontation of one character with another. This happens (for example) in Beckett's *Watt* and also in Graham's 'Dark Dialogues', 'Ten Shots of Mister Simpson', 'Dear Bryan Wynter' and 'To My Wife At Midnight'.

In Graham's work the family is the basis for the larger idea of community and he never strays far from that base. His sense of Scottishness is derived from a wish to render the life and speech of his parents as well as the streets and dockland community where he grew up. From *The Seven Journeys* onwards, Graham consistently attempted to map out a distinct northern identity that he derived from Scottish, Norse and Icelandic sources. All his work includes a certain amount of special vocabulary that he holds to and conserves against the standardising force of English. During his lifetime English was affected in a powerful way by the new wider access to higher education and by the institutions, such as the BBC, which controlled the new media.

Graham grew up as one of the second generation poets of the 'Scottish Renaissance' (1920–1945), though he did not consider himself in any way a member or associate of any movement. Whilst he had a good relationship with Hugh MacDiarmid and other Scottish poets of that time, he did not think much of synthetic Scots. Here it is worth noting that Graham's actual speech as a Greenock boy and man would not have been anything like the literary language that Mac-Diarmid and his associates grafted on Lowland Scots. MacDiarmid himself turned to English for extended works after making the Scots masterpiece *A Drunk Man Looks at the Thistle* (1926), and the less well received *To Circumjack Cencrastus* (1930). By the time that Graham was at college (and therefore beginning his writing career), MacDiarmid himself was writing in English.

For Scottish poets, language is a choice to be considered in a way that it need not be by the English. There are three languages, Gaelic, Scots and English that each have their cultural wealth and those languages make demands on any poet who is not blind to tradition. Graham chose to write in English and to communicate in that wider arena the speech of his community and his time. *The White Threshold* contains a remarkable recreation of that Clydeside community in its relation to the warring 'United Kingdom' ruled from Westminster.

With the later work, Graham began to reclaim a sense of Scottishness by drawing on more traditional subjects through his ballads and ballad-related poems. He also made poetic connections between Scotland, Ireland, Wales and Cornwall, placing a Celtic people in the context of Europe rather than Britain. Later still there were the poems that directly confronted his past and Scotland: 'Loch Thom', 'To Alexander Graham', 'Sgurr Na Gillean Macleod', 'The Gobbled Child', many of the 'Implements' and strongest of all 'To My Wife at Midnight', which goes to the heart of the matter by using Culloden as

Conclusions

a theme folded into a poem about growing old in love. Relations between a husband and wife are implicitly compared to the love-hate relations between the ageing nations.

The special territory which Graham charts out from *Malcolm Mooney's Land* onwards, is a kind of in-between realm that lies, in Heidegger's words, 'between men and gods'. In seeking to find a place to examine what we might call the inner life, Graham has established this territory by transposing the Romantic notion of organic form into language itself. Through his monsters, beasts, and gods, Graham characterised language as a given, living, and animate being. His word play of puns and substitutions, quite without the social display of verbal wit, helps to reinforce this sense of a pre-existing animate language which we inhabit (again, in the Heideggerian sense) as the basis of our being-in-time.

In creating a self-conscious poetry that seeks to examine language and the relations between reader and writer, Graham is an heir to Eliot, Pound, Joyce and Beckett. But Graham's writing-about-writing, unlike so much work that inherits from these writers, is not a poetry of reduction and exhaustion with no subject to speak of. Graham rather relocates his subject in another place. He develops a poetry which goes through loops of paradox and in which metaphor turns in upon itself. He discloses a place that is entered through privation, isolation and even madness. In this domain the gods are, or may be, present. In a post-religious time this step is irreverent in certain important ways. Since the application of the language model has been so influential in what we have come to call formalism and structuralism, Graham's language, wayward and uncontrollable as it is made to seem, actively resists this coding. The model is more complex and irrational than what it has been made to represent.

He develops a muse poetry which is quite unlike that of Robert Graves, yet it remains a muse poetry with a sense of the supernatural as seen in the border ballads. He adapted the work of Graves to his own purpose. Central to that purpose is the equivocal portrayal of a muse figure, about whom we remain quite uncertain. Graham's muse is something hypothetical, sometimes evidence of madness, we never get a steady view of her. Graham establishes a special domain in which the supernatural is possible, and because it is signalled as such through our common literary heritage (through *Macbeth*, for instance, or the border ballads) it is recognisable as a privileged place. Presented as a necessary fiction, supernatural events have a function for us that Graham re-establishes with a great intuitive command. In Graham's work the gods are identified, in all cases, with the sexual drive; his 'animate' language is a link, or at least a correspondence in this sense, between the two worlds.

They are (as in his enigmatic incident poems: 'The Gobbled Child', 'The Lost Miss Conn', 'The Murdered Drinker') ways of containing and representing extremes of violence and sexuality that remain in our society and therefore in all of us. The torture of political prisoners, concentration camps, rape, child abuse, all these are elements of Graham's domain. The mode of the monstrous (the fearful aspect of the muse) connects therefore with modern life in a way that disallows escapism or grandiose conceits.

There is a notion of healing in this re-staging of the unthinkable in another place, though the treatment is not at all that of Freudian unconscious imagery or therapeutically interpretable dream-work. A connection is made between the supernatural world (the kelpie, the mysterious wood) of the border ballads, and what we all read, day by day, in the news. It carries forward those basic animal drives that we attempt to harness in civilised behaviour. It shows us how they have figured in the literature of the past and how we retain a need for the irrational to keep that aspect of what we call human and social behaviour in check

Early in his career, Graham's work looked like that of his immediate predecessors and contemporaries. Later, however, he made a major poetry that was quite beyond the range of these Neo-Romantic writers and against the grain of what was to become dominant in British writing.

The hedging tone and restriction in subject which Donald Davie described as typical of the Movement is the context of the time from which Graham's work appears to arise. It does not arise from there, of course, because it is the fact of isolation from the cultural centre of British life that Graham harnessed in his extraordinary and original turning-inward on language and the self. Graham's working-context was isolation, coupled with a sustained interest in the metaphysics of experience, language and the self. His company was those painters (Hilton, Lanyon, Wynter and some others) who were exploring the visual media in the way that Graham explored language.

The Nightfishing in itself is the achievement of an important poet. It takes the kind of imagery that we might find in a Neo-Romantic poet (Dylan Thomas would be the best example) but completely remakes it in a far more ambitious mode as a serious and sustained metaphysical poem. It is a work of the order of *Four Quartets*, and therefore quite beyond anything else published in its time (the decade of the Movement).

Graham went on to write *Malcolm Mooney's Land* and *Implements In Their Places*, both of which contain poems that are of major importance in our literature because of the way in which they explore and use the resources of language, while carrying on (in a simplified and assured manner) Graham's interests in Pre-Socratic thought. The theme of the relationship between reader and writer becomes more and more

Conclusions

explicit in these books, and there are also some of the strongest shorter poems among them.

We have seen poetry marginalised in our society. The standard explanation of this would be phrased in terms of the power of the new media. When we encounter poetry of the stature of Graham's, however, this kind of explanation will not do. It becomes clear that the place of poetry in our society may be a function of how seriously poets take themselves, whether, that is, they are willing or able to write about large and important issues that concern us all. Because Graham's work leads us to consider the experience that establishes the self, and because it is capable of taking us beyond those restricted social meanings that we associate with the mainstream, this poetry has a relevance and importance beyond the scope of that which has received much critical attention and acclaim in recent years.

It is the combination of two qualities that will best account for the power and originality of Graham's work. Firstly the will to engage with large metaphysical questions, to make a poetry that goes to the root of what it is that makes up identity, to show how it is that we are made by our experience of the world, recognising that experience is a matter of community, work and place. Secondly (and not lesser) it is to see this exploration of the resources and restrictions of identity and communication in strongly physical terms, in terms that is of the drives that operate in us beyond the control of the intellect.

For Graham the necessary connection was between his metaphysical interests and a passion deeply felt and strongly conveyed. The self is to be explored in language because it is firstly *perceived* as a function of communication, and then there are prime cases of communication in which the self is disclosed. They are the figures of the love-lyric which are a conventional notation of the privacies of love-talk. They are also the habits of phrasing learned in the closest of family relations (mother and child being Graham's most consistent interest) that become the basis of metre, generalised through children's rhymes that Graham takes up into his poetry, notably in *The Nightfishing*. They are also those extreme situations he examines through the figures of voyaging, exploration and isolation, through his heroes that venture beyond the comforts of the social world.

Through his use of the ballads and the traditions of European mythology (see for instance 'Imagine A Forest', 'The Dark Dialogues' and 'Implements In Their Places'), seen again in terms of the closest personal relations (the mixing of sexual passion and ambition in 'The Earl of Murray' and *Macbeth*, Europa's lust, Lear's mismanaged love for his daughter) he creates a historical dimension in his work. That dimension reinforces the importance of personal (and private) relations, that are lent the meanings of myth rather than being subsumed in it.

Like other post-modernists, Graham's mature work on the whole eschews the fragmentation of narrative line associated with modernist works such as *The Waste Land*, *Finnegans Wake*, and certain sections of *The Cantos* of Ezra Pound. He tackles his metaphysical problems from reduced social circumstances, holding on to the possibility of tenderness and comfort between individuals. This he makes into his subject and driving force, rather than experiment as such. Thus his narratives have a re-woven continuity, full of paradox-loops and inversions, but continuous nevertheless (see 'The Lost Other', 'The Dark Dialogues').

In a time in which the intellectual and emotional range of poetry has seemed restricted, Graham has enlarged it. Ignoring the reaction against Modernism that was made by the Movement writers, Graham's work carries forward the insights and achievements of Eliot, Joyce and Pound and develops them in a new way. When we take stock of writing in English from a position that fully values *Four Quartets*, *Ulysses* and Pound's *Cantos*, then like Beckett, W. S. Graham will be seen as central to the development of that tradition.

Notes

Chapter 1: Life and Contacts

1 Records of Newbattle Abbey College (now under threat of closure), supplied by the College Librarian, Mrs J. O. Kemp, in a letter to Tony Lopez, 30 November 1981.
2 Vivienne Koch, 'A Note on W. S. Graham', *Sewanee Review*, vol 56, no 4, Autumn 1948, pp. 665–70.
3 Mrs J. O. Kemp to Tony Lopez, 30 November 1981, also Newbattle Abbey College, *Prospectus*, session 1939–40, pp. 1–8.
4 Course outline at Newbattle Abbey College supplied by John Reid (ex-student) from his notes made in 1938–39.
5 From the official lecture schedule for the year 1938–39 at Newbattle Abbey College, supplied by Morley Jamieson (ex-student).
6 Morley Jamieson, letter to Tony Lopez 1981; Edwin Morgan, *Edinburgh Review* 75, p. 39; Tom Scott, *Edinburgh Review* 75, p. 58. Also Biographical note in Maurice Lindsay (ed), *Sailing To-Morrow's Seas*, p. 45.
7 Bulletin of Newbattle Abbey College, 1944, p. 8.
8 Rosalind Wade, 'The Parton Street Poets', *Poetry Review*, vol 54, Winter 1963–64, pp. 290–97.
9 George Barker, *Thirty Preliminary Poems*, 1933; Dylan Thomas, *18 Poems*, 1934; David Gascoyne, *Man's Life is this Meat*, 1936; W. S. Graham, *Cage Without Grievance*, 1942.
10 See Robert Frame, 'W. S. Graham at Sandyford Place', *Edinburgh Review* 75, pp. 60–65; Derek Stanford also mentions Graham's time in Glasgow when writing of Ian Hamilton Finlay, *Inside the Forties*, 1977, p. 113.
11 Hugh MacDiarmid, 'Preface', *The Collected Poems of Burns Singer*, 1970, p. xi.
12 David Wright, 'W. S. Graham in the Forties', *Edinburgh Review* 75, p. 50.
13 According to Dennis Wirth-Miller, painter, interviewed by Tony Lopez, Wivenhoe, Essex, February 1982.
14 W. S. Graham, letter to Bill Featherston, 19 July 1973.
15 See Mrs Graham (Nessie Dunsmuir) quoted in David Brown, 'Chronology', in *St Ives 1939–64*, 1985, p. 102.
16 David Wright, p. 52.
17 Interviews with Tony Lopez: John Heath-Stubbs, London 1982; Sue Wynter, Brightlingsea and Wivenhoe, Essex, 1982; Dennis Wirth-Miller, Wivenhoe, 1982.
18 W. S. Graham, Thirty Letters to Sven Berlin (1945–65), National Library of Scotland (Manuscripts), access nos 7389, 7581.
19 Julian MacLaren-Ross, *Memoirs of the Forties*, 1965, pp. 183–85.
20 According to John Heath-Stubbs, interviewed by Tony Lopez, London,

June 1982; see also David Wright, p. 54 about Julian Orde's role in obtaining employment for Graham. This work may well be a source for 'Implement' no 58.
21 Mrs Graham quoted in David Brown, 'Chronology', p. 102.
22 Mrs Sylvia Skelton, interviewed by Tony Lopez, Victoria, BC, Canada, August 1982.
23 Nancy Wynne-Jones, 'W. S. Graham in Cornwall', *Edinburgh Review* 75, pp. 66–9.
24 W. S. Graham, Skelton Collection, Letters folder no 2, 1958.
25 Nancy Wynne-Jones, p. 68.
26 W. S. Graham, 'Implement' nos 65 and 71 and 'The Street of Knives', *PN Review*, vol 6, no 6, 1980, p. 9.
27 W. S. Graham to Bill Featherston, 19 July 1973.
28 Sven Berlin, *The Dark Monarch: A Portrait from Within*, 1962. This book was published 7 September 1962 and withdrawn 17 September 1962 after four successful libel actions. 'Jamie Greenock' appears on pages 15–16, 74–6 and 110–14.
29 Michael Canney, Introduction, in Roger Hilton, *Night Letters and Selected Drawings*, 1980, pp. 7–12; Alan Bowness in *Bryan Wynter 1915–1975*, 1976, p. 4.
30 Oliver Watson, 'The St Ives Pottery' in *St Ives 1939–64*, pp. 220–27. See also Tom Cross, *Painting the Warmth of the Sun*, 1984, for an account of the St Ives community.
31 Graham's fishing experience 'at long-lining and pilchard driving' is mentioned in Frank Ruhrmund, 'Literary World Mourns W. S. Graham', *The Cornishman*, 16 January 1986, p. 1.
32 David Lewis, 'St Ives: A Personal Memoir 1947–55' in *St Ives 1939–64*, p. 18.
33 W. S. Graham, *Collected Poems 1942–77*; W. S. Graham, 'The Song of the Tower', National Library of Scotland, Edinburgh Collection, access no 7847; W. S. Graham, 'For Alan and Valerie', *Alan Lowndes: Paintings 1948–72*, 1972, p. 12.
34 Penelope Mortimer, 'A Poet's Interview With Himself', *Observer Magazine*, 19 November 1978, pp. 61–2; the photo is reproduced in black and white on the dustjacket of Graham's *Collected Poems 1942–1977*.
35 Michael Schmidt, *A Reader's Guide to Fifty Modern British Poets*, 1979, p. 297.
36 Alan Bold, *Modern Scottish Literature*, 1983, pp. 71–5.
37 Roderick Watson, 'Internationalising Scottish Poetry' in Cairns Craig (ed), *The History of Scottish Literature: Volume 4, Twentieth Century*, 1987, pp. 311–30; also Roderick Watson, *The Literature of Scotland*, 1984, p. 431.
38 Hugh MacDiarmid, Review of Cage Without Grievance, *The Free Man*, circa 1942.
39 W. S. Graham, Letters to Moncrieff Williamson, Skelton Collection, Letters folder 1, 1949–50.
40 W. S. Graham, 'A Page about my Country', *Aquarius*, no 11, 1979, pp. 37–8; Hugh MacDiarmid, 'For W. S. Graham', *Edinburgh Review*, 75, p. 104.
41 Blake Morrison, *The Movement: English Poetry and Fiction of the 1950s*, 1980.
42 D. J. Enright (ed), *Poets of the 1950s*, 1955; Robert Conquest (ed), *New Lines*, 1956.

Notes

43 Andrew Crozier, 'Thrills and Frills', in Alan Sinfield (ed), *Society and Literature 1945–70*, 1983, pp. 199–233.
44 Andrew Crozier, p. 207.
45 Philip Larkin, 'A Great Parade of Single Poems: Interview with Anthony Thwaite', *The Listener*, 12 April 1973, p. 473.
46 Donald Davie, *Purity of Diction in English Verse*, 1952, pp. 27–8.
47 Donald Davie, *Articulate Energy: An Enquiry into the Syntax of English Poetry*, 1955, pp. 128–9.
48 T. S. Eliot, 'Ulysses, Order, and Myth', *The Dial*, vol 75, no 5, November 1923, pp. 480–83; for the Movement view of Joyce see: Kingsley Amis, 'Editor's Notes', *Spectator*, 7 October 1955, p. 459; *What Became of Jane Austen*, 1970, p. 95; Donald Davie, *Ezra Pound: Poet as Sculptor*, 1965, p. 31; *Articulate Energy*, p. 19; *The Poet in the Imaginary Museum*, 1977, pp. 60–61 and p. 246; D. J. Enright, *Academic Year*, 1955, p. 44; John Wain, 'Lost Horizons', *Encounter*, January 1961, pp. 69–70.
49 Donald Davie, *The Poet in the Imaginary Museum*, pp. 60–65 and p. 105.
50 Blake Morrison, pp. 145–53.
51 Linda M. Shires, *British Poetry of the Second World War*, 1985, pp. 24–5.
52 Donald Davie, 'Three Poets' (Review of George Barker, *A Vision of Beasts and Gods*; W. S. Graham, *The Nightfishing*; Sheila Wingfield, *A Kite's Dinner*), *Dublin Magazine*, vol 30, no 4, Oct–Dec 1955, pp. 38–40.
53 Donald Davie, 'Remembering the Movement', in *Prospect*, edited by Elaine Feinstein, Cambridge, Summer 1959 (no issue number), pp. 15–16.
54 D. H. Lawrence, *Apocalypse*, 1931; J. F. Hendry and Henry Treece (eds), *The White Horseman*, 1941, p.v.
55 J. F. Hendry, Introduction, in Hendry (ed), *The New Apocalypse: an anthology of criticism, poems and stories*, [1940], pp. 10–12.
56 Henry Treece, 'Gerard Manley Hopkins and Dylan Thomas', *How I See Apocalypse*, 1946, pp. 129–39.
57 See Dawn Ades, *Dada and Surrealism Reviewed*, 1978, pp. 346–73, for an account of the Surrealist movement in London in the 1930s.
58 John Heath-Stubbs, as quoted in Shires, p. 28, from an interview with Shires, 8 November 1979.
59 Henry Treece, 'An Apocalyptic Writer and the Surrealists', in Hendry (ed), *The New Apocalypse*, pp. 49–58.
60 Dylan Thomas, letter to Henry Treece, 3 December 1938, in *Selected Letters of Dylan Thomas*, edited by Constantine FitzGibbon, 1965, pp. 290–91.
61 Dylan Thomas, 'How to be a Poet', *A Prospect of the Sea and other Stories and prose writings*, 1955, p. 112.
62 T. H. Helmstadter, The Apocalyptic Movement in British Poetry (dissertation), University of Pennsylvania, 1963.
63 John Goodland, letter to Henry Treece, now in private hands, quoted in Helmstadter, p. 18 and Shires, p. 30.
64 Maurice Lindsay (ed), *Modern Scottish Poetry: An Anthology of the Scottish Renaissance 1920–45*, 1946.
65 Dylan Thomas, 'Author's Note', in *Collected Poems 1934–52*, 1952.
66 W. S. Graham, Letter to Tony Lopez, 30 March 1981.
67 W. S. Graham, interviewed by Tony Lopez, Madron, Cornwall, May 1981.

Chapter 2: The Early Poems
1 Calvin Bedient, *Eight Contemporary Poets*, 1974, pp. 150–80; Michael Schmidt, pp. 297–304.
2 W. S. Graham, an annotated copy of *The Seven Journeys*, the Buffalo collection, The State University of New York at Buffalo, NY, USA, quoted by permission.
3 Agnes MacLellan, Letter to Tony Lopez, 5 February 1982.
4 *The Poetic Edda*, translated by Henry Adams Bellows, 1923, pp. 102, 376.
5 Edinburgh Collection, folder no 2, access no 2793, 1943, p. 9.
6 Edinburgh Collection, folder no 2, access no 2793, 1943, p. 6.

Chapter 3: The White Threshold
1 Bedient, p. 163.
2 Nessie Dunsmuir, 'Raith Pit', *Life and Letters*, vol 48, no 103, March 1946, p. 210.
3 Elizabeth W. Schneider, *The Dragon in the Gate: Studies in the Poetry of Gerard Manley Hopkins*, 1968, p. 14.
4 *The Poems of Gerard Manley Hopkins*, edited by Gardner and Mackenzie, 1967, note p. 254.
5 'Biographical Notes' in *St Ives 1939–64*, p. 144.
6 Letters from Alfred Wallis to Jim (H.S.) Ede, 1929–39, now in the collection of Kettle's Yard, University of Cambridge. The letters document both the occasions when Ede was sent bundles of pictures from Cornwall, and the remarks made by Wallis in replies to questions sent about his past.

Chapter 4: The Nightfishing
1 I quote the fragment in the form that Graham most likely knew it, from a letter from Mrs Graham to Tony Lopez, 3 April 1986. She gives the source as Aristotle, *De Caelo*, edited by Weise, 3:1:18.
2 G. S. Fraser, Review of *The Nightfishing* (letter), *London Magazine*, vol 2, no 9, 1955, pp. 67–9.
3 Edwin Morgan, 'The Poetry of W. S. Graham', *Cencrastus*, no 5, Summer 1981, p. 9.
4 W. S. Graham, letter to Tony Lopez, 30 March 1981.
5 According to Graham himself; see Penelope Mortimer, 'A Poet's Interview with Himself', *Observer Colour Magazine*, 19 November 1978, p. 62; also Frank Ruhrmund, Obituary, *The Cornishman*, 16 January 1986, p. 1.
6 W. S. Graham, Notes to 'The Nightfishing', Buffalo Collection, access no Graham SLO 90960A, p. 1.
7 F. M. Cornford, 'The Theaetetus', *Plato's Theory of Knowledge*, 1955, p. 23.

Chapter 5: Malcolm Mooney's Land
1 David Punter, 'Constructing a White Space', *Malahat Review*, no 63, October 1982, pp. 220–44.
2 *Mooney's* (where Guinness was available despite wartime shortages) is mentioned by Graham's contemporary George Barker, in his poem 'Elegy'.
3 See Tony Lopez, 'On *Malcolm Mooney's Land* by W. S. Graham', *Ideas and Production*, no 4, December 1985, pp. 47–70, for some examples of Graham's working through of this material.

Notes

4   My interpretation was prompted by Nick Totton, 'The Snow Queen' in *A Vision Very Like Reality*, edited by Peter Ackroyd et al, no 1, December 1979, pp. 3–7.
5   Sigmund Freud, *The Psychopathology of Everyday Life*, edited and translated by J. Strachey, 1966, p. 49.
6   'Better burn this': W. H. Auden, 'Letter to a Wound', *The Orators*, 1932, p. 30.
7   Martin Heidegger, 'Holderlin and the Essence of Poetry', translated by Paul De Man, *Quarterly Review of Literature*, vol 10, nos 1 & 2, 1959, pp. 79–94.
8   Robert Graves, *The White Goddess*, 1948; Graham quotes two passages from *The White Goddess* and strongly recommends the book to his friend: W. S. Graham, Thirty letters to Sven Berlin, Edinburgh Collection, letter dated 10 February 1949.
9   Edward Lucie-Smith, *British Poetry since 1945*, 1970, p. 46.
10 Edinburgh Collection, folder 3, access no 4967, pp. 17–18.
11 A fluttering film (or here mantle) is called a *stranger* and is supposed to portend the arrival of some absent friend, Coleridge notes the word and superstition as known 'in all parts of the kingdom', *Poetical Register*, 1802.
12 Peter Lanyon, *Europa* (painting), oil on masonite, 1954, first exhibited at Plymouth, 1955, full details and history in *St Ives 1936–64*, p. 196; See Nancy Wynne-Jones, *Edinburgh Review* 75, p. 69; W. S. Graham, 'From a Poem in Progress: A Dream of Crete', *Aquarius*, no 6, 1973, pp. 5–6; 'The Street of Knives, *PN Review*, vol 6, no 6, 1980, pp. 19–20.

Chapter 6: Implements in their Places
1   See C. H. Kahn, *The Art and Thought of Heraclitus*, 1979, for a modern translation of the *Fragments*, together with a commentary; Martin Heidegger, *Being and Time*, translated by John Macquarrie and Edward Robinson, 1962.
2   W. S. Graham, Skelton Collection, Notebook no 3 (dated 1964).
3   Martin Heidegger, *Introduction to Metaphysics*, p. 125 and pp. 136–46.
4   R. Peterson, G. Mountfort, P. A. D. Hollom, *A Field Guide to the Birds of Britain and Europe*, 1954, p. 186.
5   W. S. Graham, 'Heath-Stubbs the Poet as Hero', *Aquarius*, no 10, 1978, pp. 8–9.
6   W. S. Graham (ed), *Promenade*, nos 65 & 66, Cheltenham, 1955.
7   Sheila Kitzinger, *Pregnancy and Childbirth*, 1980, p. 31.
8   W. S. Graham, 'Implements in their Places', *Malahat Review*, no 22, April 1972, pp. 9–24.
9   There is a precedent for this figure in 'The Don Brown Route', pp. 166–167: 'Through the lens of language' and, notably, '*Stopped* in the lens of language' (my emphasis).
10 C. M. Bowra, *Primitive Song*, 1962, pp. 44–5.
11 Rudyard Kipling, 'The Way through the Woods', *Rudyard Kipling's Verse: Definitive Edition*, 1940, p. 490.
12 Roger Hilton, *Night Letters*, 1980.

Chapter 7: Conclusions
1   Patrick Heron, 'Americans at the Tate', *Arts*, New York, March 1956.

Bibliography

Section A: *Books and Pamphlets by W. S. Graham*

A1 *Cage Without Grievance*, Glasgow, 1942.
Published in August 1942 by Parton Press and printed by Robert Maclehose Ltd, Glasgow. Issued in ordinary and limited editions (limited edition of 50 copies has hand-coloured illustrations and is printed on 'mould made' paper). Both editions are illustrated by Benjamin Creme and Robert Frame.

> *Contents*
> Over the apparatus of the Spring is drawn
> Of the resonant rumour of sun, impulse of summer
> O gentle queen of the afternoon
> As if in an instant parapets of plants
> 1st Letter
> Here next the chair I was when winter went
> There was when morning fell
> Say that in lovers with stones for family
> This fond event my origin knows well
> Let me measure my prayer with sleep
> Endure no conflict. Crosses are keepsakes
> To girls at the turn of night love goes on knocking
> No, listen, for this I tell
> 2nd Letter
> I no more real than evil in my roof

A2 *The Seven Journeys*, Glasgow, 1944.
Published in 1944 by William MacLellan Ltd, Glasgow, as part of the Poetry Scotland series. Frontispiece by Robert Frame.

> *Contents*
> The Narrator
> The First Journey
> The Second Journey
> The Third Journey
> The Fourth Journey

The Fifth Journey
The Sixth Journey
The Seventh Journey

A3   *2nd Poems*, London, 1945.
Published by Editions Poetry London and Nicholson & Watson in 1945.

Contents
Explanation of a Map
Soon to be Distances
The Serving Inhabiters
Next My Spade's Going
His Companions Buried Him
The Name Like a River
Allow Silk Birds That See
Many Without Elegy
The Bright Building
A Letter More Likely To Myself
My Glass Word Tells of Itself
The Dual Privilege
Continual Sea and Air
Warning Not Prayer Enough
The Narrator
The Crowd of Birds and Children
By Law of Exile
The Halftelling Sight
Except Nessie Dunsmuir
At Her Beck and Miracle
One Is One
Remarkable Report By Some Poetic Agents
The Day and Night Craftsmen

A4   *The Voyages of Alfred Wallis*, London and New York, 1948.
A limited edition pamphlet of the poem, published in September 1948 by Antony Froshaug, London and Wittenborn Ltd, New York. Printed by Anthony Froshaug, a total of 200 copies.

A5   *The White Threshold*, London, 1949.
Published by Faber and Faber Ltd in an edition of 1000 copies printed by the Bowering Press, Plymouth. The American edition published by Grove Press, New York.

Contents
Since All My Steps Taken
Listen. Put on Morning
Lying in Corn

My Final Bread
With All Many Men Laid Down In the Burial Heart
The Hill of Intrusion
The Search by a Town
The Children of Greenock
The Children of Lanarkshire
The Lost Other
To a Tear
Two Love Poems
Other Guilts as Far
The Birthright Twins Outrun
Shian Bay
Gigha
Men Sign the Sea
Night's Fall Unlocks the Dirge of the Sea
At Whose Sheltering shall the Day Sea
Three Poems of Drowning
Michael's Sea-Lamb before My Breath this Day
The Voyages of Alfred Wallis
The Bright Midnight
Definition of My House
Definition of My Brother
At that Bright Cry Set on the Heart's Headwaters
For the Inmost Lost
The White Threshold
To My Brother
To My Father
To My Mother

A6   *For The Castle Wall*, St Ives, Cornwall (circa 1950).
This broadsheet, bearing no author's name, is printed on a single sheet of handmade paper. It was printed by Guido Morris at the Latin Press, St Ives, Cornwall. Morris annotated one copy with the statement:
   By (my friend) W. S. Graham author of 'The White Threshold' etc. Ptd about 1950? (or 49?) G.M.
   Note: The text is three stanzas reprinted with slight variations as part of 'Letter IV' in *The Nightfishing*, 1955; see *Collected Poems 1942–1977*, inset stanzas on p. 118. This broadsheet is not mentioned by Philip Brown and Anthony Baker in their tentative checklist of the Latin Press in the Winter 1969 issue of *The Private Library*.

A7   *The Nightfishing*, Rome, 1951.
Published in 1951 by *Botteghe Oscure*, the poem *The Nightfishing* was issued as a separate pamphlet in an edition of 50 copies.

Bibliography

A8 *The Nightfishing*, London, 1955.
Published by Faber and Faber Ltd in an edition of 1250 copies printed by the Bowering Press, Plymouth. The American edition published by Grove Press, New York.

Contents
The Nightfishing
Seven Letters:
Welcome Then Anytime
Burned in This Element
As Mooney's Calls Time
Night Winked And Endeared
Lie Where You Fell
A Day The Wind Was Hardly
Blind Tide Emblazoning
Two Ballads:
The Broad Close
Baldy Bane

A9 *Malcolm Mooney's Land*, London, 1970.
Published by Faber and Faber Ltd in a first edition of 1500 copies printed by the Bowering Press, Plymouth. Subsequently reprinted in an edition of 1000 copies.

Contents
Malcolm Mooney's Land
The Beast in the Space
The Lying Dear
Yours Truly
Dear Who I Mean
The Constructed Space
Master Cat and Master Me
The Thermal Stair
I Leave This at Your Ear
The Dark Dialogues
The Don Brown Route
Press Button to Hold Desired Symbol
Hilton Abstract
Approaches to How They Behave
The Fifteen Devices
Wynter and the Grammarsow
Johann Joachim Quantz's First Lesson
Five Visitors to Madron
Clusters Travelling Out

A10 *Implements In Their Places*, London, 1977.
Published by Faber and Faber Ltd in a paperback edition of 2500 copies printed by Latimer Trend, Plymouth.

> *Contents*
> What Is The Language Using Us For?
> Imagine a Forest
> Untidy Dreadful Table
> A Note to the Difficult One
> Are You Still There?
> Language Ah Now You Have Me
> Two Poems on Zennor Hill
> Ten Shots of Mister Simpson
> The Night City
> Enter a Cloud
> Greenock at Night I Find You
> Loch Thom
> To Alexander Graham
> Sgurr Na Gillean Macleod
> Private Poem to Norman Macleod
> Johann Joachim Quantz's five lessons
> The Gobbled Child
> The Lost Miss Conn
> The Murdered Drinker
> How are the Children Robin
> The Stepping Stones
> Lines on Roger Hilton's Watch
> The Secret Name
> The Found Picture
> Implements in their Places
> Dear Bryan Wynter

A11 *Collected Poems 1942–1977*, London, 1979.
Published by Faber and Faber Ltd in an edition of 1500 copies (hardback) and 5000 copies (paper wrappers).

> *Contents*
> Over the Apparatus of the Spring is Drawn
> Of the Resonant Rumour of Sun, Impulse of Summer
> O Gentle Queen of the Afternoon
> As If in an Instant Parapets of Plants
> Here next the Chair I was when Winter Went
> There was when Morning Fell
> Say that in Lovers with Stones for Family
> This Fond Event my Origin Knows Well
> Let Me Measure My Prayer with Sleep
> No, Listen, for This I Tell
> I, No More Real than Evil in My Roof

Bibliography

Explanation of a Map
Soon to be Distances
The Serving Inhabiters
His Companions Buried Him
The Name Like a River
Allow Silk Birds that See
Many without Elegy
Continual Sea and Air
The Narrator
The Crowd of Birds and Children
By Law of Exile
The Halftelling Sight
Except Nessie Dunsmuir
Remarkable Report by Some Poetic Agents
Since All My Steps Taken
Listen. Put On Morning
The Hill of Intrusion
The Search by a Town
The Children of Greenock
The Children of Lanarkshire
The Lost Other
Two Love Poems
Other Guilts as Far
Shian Bay
Gigha
Men Sign the Sea
Night's Fall Unlocks the Dirge of the Sea
At Whose Sheltering Shall the Day Sea
Three Poems of Drowning
The Voyages of Alfred Wallis
The Bright Midnight
Definition of My Brother
The White Threshold
To My Brother
To My Father
To My Mother
The Nightfishing
Letter I: Welcome Then Anytime
Letter II: Burned in This Element
Letter III: As Mooney's Calls Time
Letter IV: Night Winked and Endeared
Letter V: Lie Where You Fell
Letter VI: A Day the Wind was Hardly
Letter VII: Blind Tide Emblazoning
The Broad Close
Baldy Bane

Malcolm Mooney's Land
The Beast in the Space
The Lying Dear
Yours Truly
Dear Who I Mean
The Constructed Space
Master Cat and Master Me
The Thermal Stair
I Leave This at Your Ear
The Dark Dialogues
The Don Browne Route
Press Button to Hold Desired Symbol
Hilton Abstract
Approaches to How They Behave
The Fifteen Devices
Wynter and the Grammarsow
Johann Joachim Quantz's First Lesson
Five Visitors to Madron
Clusters Travelling Out
What is the Language Using Us for?
Imagine a Forest
Untidy Dreadful Table
A Note to the Difficult One
Are You Still There?
Language Ah Now You Have Me
Two Poems on Zennor Hill
Ten Shots of Mister Simpson
The Night City
Enter a Cloud
Greenock at Night I Find You
Loch Thom
To Alexander Graham
Sgurr Na Gillean Macleod
Private Poem to Norman Macleod
Johann Joachim Quantz's Five Lessons
The Gobbled Child
The Lost Miss Conn
The Murdered Drinker
How are the Children Robin
The Stepping Stones
Lines on Roger Hilton's Watch
The Secret Name
The Found Picture
Implements in Their Places
Dear Bryan Wynter
To My Wife at Midnight

A11 *Selected Poems*, New York, 1979.
Published by the Ecco Press and printed in the USA.

> *Contents*
> What Is The Language Using Us For?
> The Constructed Space
> Ten Shots of Mister Simpson
> Five Visitors To Madron
> Malcolm Mooney's Land
> Listen. Put On Morning.
> Approaches To How They Behave
> The Thermal Stair
> The Beast In The Space
> The Found Picture
> Lines On Roger Hilton's Watch
> Dear Bryan Wynter
> Baldy Bane
> Men Sign The Sea
> The Nightfishing
> Greenock At Night I Find You
> To Alexander Graham
> Johann Joachim Quantz's First Lesson
> The Narrator
> Explanation Of A Map
> Here Next The Chair I Was When Winter Went
> The Lying Dear
> Dear Who I Mean
> Letter IV
> Yours Truly
> Language Ah Now You Have Me
> I Leave This At Your Ear
> The Night City
> A Note To The Difficult One
> To My Wife At Midnight
> Implements in Their Places

Section B: *Works edited and with contributions by W. S. Graham*

B1 *Promenade*, nos 65 and 66 (bound together), Cheltenham, 1955.
Note: No 65 is written by W. S. Graham and Nessie Dunsmuir
(Graham). It is reproduced from their holograph on a stencil
duplicator. Cover: lettering and drawing in Graham's hand, inside
cover verses in Graham's hand.

[1–2]: introduction. [3–8]: a letter to Robert [Colquhoun] and
Robert [MacBryde], dated 13 April 1955. [9]: Letter to 'Auntie

Wirren', [in Nessie Dunsmuir's hand]. [10]: 'Here Next the Chair I was when Winter Went'. [11]: 'O Gentle Queen of the Afternoon'. [12–13]: Drawings and writing (scraps) by Graham. [14]: 'The Dark Intention'. [15–24]: *Promenade*, no 66, May 1955, edited by Ben Howard (local gossip and reviews).

B2   *Nessie Dunsmuir's Seven Poems.* Published by Greville Press, Emscote Lawn, Warwick in 1985 in an edition of 150 copies. Printed by Peter Lloyd at The Gamecock Press, 11 Park Road, Rugby, Warwickshire. Graham contributed the frontispiece drawing.

Section C: *Contributions to Periodicals by W. S. Graham*

Misattributions
1   'Threnody for a Ruined Landscape', *Poetry Quarterly*, vol 10, no 1, Spring 1948, pp. 14–15. The poem is by G. A. Wagner.
2   'Writer' (from A Tent for April), *Poetry Quarterly*, vol 10, no 2, Summer 1948, p. 76. The poem is by Patrick Anderson.

List Proper
1942
C1   'Fourth Sonnet', *Poetry (London)*, vol 2, no 7, October 1942, p. 23.
C2   'The Third Journey', *Poetry (London)*, vol 2, no 7, October 1942, p. 24. Reprinted in *The Seven Journeys*, 1944.
C3   'O Gentle Queen', *Poetry (London)*, vol 2, no 7, October 1942, p. 25. Reprinted as 'O Gentle Queen of the Afternoon' in *Cage Without Grievance*, 1942.
C4   'Soon to be Distances', *Poetry (London)*, vol 2, no 7, October 1942, pp. 25–6. Reprinted in *2nd Poems*, 1945.
C5   'Here next the chair I was when', *Poetry (London)*, vol 2, no 8, November 1942, pp. 72–73. Reprinted in *Cage Without Gievance*, 1942.
C6   'I, No More Real Than Evil', *Poetry (London)*, vol 2, no 8, November 1942, p. 73. Reprinted in *Cage Without Grievance*, 1942.
C7   'Who, With a Pen', *Poetry (London)*, vol 2, no 8, November 1942, pp. 73–4. Reprinted as 'Of The Resonant Rumour of Sun, Impulse of Summer' in *Cage Without Grievance*, 1942.
C8   'My Class World Tells of Itself', *Poetry Quarterly*, vol 4, no 4, Winter 1942, pp. 144–5. Reprinted in *2nd Poems*, 1945.

1943
C9   'Except Nessie Dunsmuir', *Horizon*, vol 7, no 37, January 1943, p. 9. Reprinted in *2nd Poems*, 1945.

C10 'Next my Spade's Going', *Horizon*, vol 7, no 37, January 1943, p. 10. Reprinted in *2nd Poems*, 1945.
C11 'The Narrator', *Life and Letters*, vol 36, February 1943, pp. 106–7. Reprinted in *The Seven Journeys*, 1944.
C12 'The Serving Inhabiters', *Life and Letters*, vol 36, February 1943, pp. 107–8. Reprinted in *2nd Poems*, 1945.
C13 'By Law of Exile', *Poetry Quarterly*, vol 5, no 3, Autumn 1943, p. 96. Reprinted in *2nd Poems*, 1945.
C14 'The Second Journey', *Poetry Quarterly*, vol 5, no 3, Autumn 1943, pp. 96–7. Reprinted in *The Seven Journeys*, 1944.
C15 'The Bright Building', *Poetry Folios*, Autumn 1943, p. 11. Reprinted in *2nd Poems*, 1945.
C16 'A Letter to Norman' (prose), *Tempest*, series 1, October 1943, pp. 14–6.
C17 'Continual Sea and Air', *Life and Letters*, vol 39, December 1943, pp. 185–6. Reprinted in *2nd Poems*, 1945.
C18 'The First Journey', *Life and Letters*, vol 39, December 1943, pp. 186–7. Reprinted in *The Seven Journeys*, 1944.
C19 'The Fourth Journey', *Life and Letters*, vol 39, December 1943, pp. 187–9. Reprinted in *The Seven Journeys*, 1944.
C20 'The Crowd of Birds and Children', *Poetry Scotland*, no 1, 1943, pp. 24–5. Reprinted in *2nd Poems*, 1945.
C21 'His Companions Buried Him', *Poetry Scotland*, no 1, 1943, pp. 25–6. Reprinted in *2nd Poems*, 1945.

1944
C22 'Warning Not Prayer Enough', *Sailing To-Morrow's Seas* (anthology edited by Maurice Lindsay), London, 1944, p. 23. Reprinted in *2nd Poems*, 1945.
C23 'The Name like a River', *Sailing To-Morrow's Seas*, London, 1944, pp. 24–5. Reprinted in *2nd Poems*, 1945.
C24 'Explanation of Map', *Angry Penguins Broadsheet* (no date, circa 1944), p. 14. Reprinted as 'Explanation of a Map' in *2nd Poems*, 1945.
C25 'Allow Silk Birds That See', *Life and Letters*, vol 40, no 79, March 1944, p. 150. Reprinted in *2nd Poems*, 1945.

1945
C26 'The Seventh Journey', *Briarcliff Quarterly*, vol 1, no 4, January 1945, pp. 205–6. From *The Seven Journeys*, 1944.
C27 'The Bright Building', *Contemporary Poetry*, vol 4, no 2, Summer 1944, p. 9. Reprinted in *2nd Poems*, 1945.
C28 'Continual Sea and Air', *Briarcliff Quarterly*, vol 1, no 4, January 1945, p. 208. Reprinted in *2nd Poems*, 1945.
C29 'I, No More Real than Evil', *Atlantic Anthology*, 1945. From *Cage Without Grievance*, 1942.

C30 'The Children of Lanarkshire', *Poetry Scotland*, no 2, 1945, pp. 34–6. Reprinted in *The White Threshold*, 1949.
C31 'The Day and Night Craftsmen', *Poetry Quarterly*, vol 7, no 2, Summer 1945, pp. 61–2. Reprinted in *2nd Poems*, 1945.
C32 'Since All my Steps Taken', *Poetry Quarterly*, vol 7, no 4, Winter 1945, p. 133. Reprinted in *The White Threshold*, 1949.

1946
C33 'The Lost Other', *New Poetry*, no 2 [circa 1946], pp. 9–13. Reprinted in *The White Threshold*, 1949.
C34 'Lying in Corn', *Life and Letters*, vol 48, March 1946, p. 208. Reprinted in *The White Threshold*, 1949.
C35 'Shian Bay', *Life and Letters*, vol 48, March 1946, p. 208. Reprinted in *The White Threshold*, 1949.
C36 'The Voyages of Alfred Wallis', *Life and Letters*, vol 48, no 103, March 1946, p. 209. Reprinted in *The White Threshold*, 1949.
C37 'The Arriving Angel', *Experiment*, vol 2, no 5, Spring 1946, p. 113.
C38 'Fourth Sonnet', *Contemporary Poetry*, vol 6, no 1, Spring 1946, p. 11.
C39 'The Common and Private River', *Briarcliff Quarterly*, vol 3, no 10, July 1946, pp. 97–8.
C40 'Apparatus', *Voices*, no 126, Summer 1946, p. 13.
C41 'The Hill of Intrusion', *Voices*, no 126, Summer 1946, pp. 16–17. Reprinted in *The White Threshold*, 1949.
C42 'Archipelago', *Voices*, no 126, Summer 1946, p. 13.
C43 'Lying in Corn', *Briarcliff Quarterly*, vol 3, no 10, July 1946, p. 99. Reprinted in *The White Threshold*, 1949.
C44 'Night Now Ties on the Ferret's Bell', *Briarcliff Quarterly*, vol 3, no 10, July 1946, pp. 99–100.
C45 'Definition of my Brother', *Poetry Scotland*, no 3, July 1946, p. 29. Reprinted in *The White Threshold*, 1949.
C46 'Notes on a Poetry of Release' (prose), *Poetry Scotland*, no 3, July 1946, pp. 56–8.
C47 'Definition of My House', *Poetry Scotland*, no 3, July 1946, p. 29. Reprinted in *The White Threshold*, 1949.
C48 'Explanation of a Map', *Counterpoint*, vol 1, no 1 (1946), p. 31. From *2nd Poems*, 1945.
C49 'Many Without Elegy', *Circle*, nos 7–8, 1946, pp. 114–15. From *2nd Poems*, 1945.
C50 'By Law of Exile', *Circle*, nos 7–8, 1946, p. 115. From *2nd Poems*, 1945.
C51 'The Serving Inhabiters', *Circle*, nos 7–8, 1946, p. 113. From *2nd Poems*, 1945.
C52 'With all Many Men Laid Down in the Burial Heart',

Windmill, vol 2, no 5, 1946, p. 63. Reprinted in *The White Threshold*, 1949.
C53   'Night's Fall Unlocks the Dirge of the Sea', *Windmill*, vol 2, no 5, 1946, p. 64. Reprinted in *The White Threshold*, 1949.
C54   'O Gentle Queen of the Afternoon', *Experiment*, vol 2, no 8, Fall 1946, p. 162. From *Cage Without Grievance*, 1942.
C55   'My Final Bread', *Jazz Forum*, no 2, September 1946, pp. 20–1. Reprinted in *The White Threshold*, 1949.

1947
C56   'The Day and Night Craftsmen', *Quarterly Review of Literature*, vol 3, no 4, 1947, pp. 339–40. From *2nd Poems*, 1945.
C57   'For the Inmost Lost', *Quarterly Review of Literature*, vol 3, no 4, 1947, p. 343. Reprinted in *The White Threshold*, 1949.
C58   'The Crowd of Birds and Children', *Quarterly Review of Literature*, vol 3, no 4, 1947, pp. 344–5. From *2nd Poems*, 1945.
C59   'Three Poems of Drowning', *Now*, no 7, February (1947), pp. 35–6. Reprinted in *The White Threshold*, 1949.
C60   'Other Guilts as Far', *Poetry (Chicago)*, vol 69, March 1947, p. 315. Reprinted in *The White Threshold*, 1949.
C61   'To a Tear', *Contemporary Poetry*, vol 7, no 3, Baltimore, Autumn 1947, p. 3. Reprinted in *The White Threshold*, 1949.
C62   'The Bright Midnight', *Poetry Quarterly*, vol 9, no 3, Autumn 1947, pp. 135–6. Reprinted in *The White Threshold*, 1949.
C63   'The Common and Private River', *Windmill*, vol 2, no 7, 1947, pp. 30–1.
C64   'The Halftelling Sight', *Quarterly Review of Literature*, vol 3, no 4, 1947, p. 337. From *2nd Poems*, 1945.
C65   from 'The Lost Other' (excerpt), *Quarterly Review of Literature*, vol 3, no 4, 1947, pp. 338–9. Reprinted in *The White Threshold*, 1949.
C66   'My Final Bread', *Quarterly Review of Literature*, vol 3, no 4, 1947, p. 341. Reprinted in *The White Threshold*, 1949.
C67   'Listen. Put on Morning', *Quarterly Review of Literature*, vol 3, no 4, 1947, p. 342–3. Reprinted in *The White Threshold*, 1949.
C68   'For the Inmost Lost', *Quarterly Review of Literature*, vol 3, no 4, 1947, p. 343. Reprinted in *The White Threshold*, 1949.
C69   'Notes On A Poetry of Release' (prose), *Quarterly Review of Literature*, vol 3, no 4, 1947, pp. 345–8.
C70   'To a Tear', *Contemporary Poetry*, vol 7, no 3, Autumn 1947, p. 3. Reprinted in *The White Threshold*, 1949.
C71   'The Search by a Town', *Chronos*, vol 1, no 3, Fall 1947, p. 13. Reprinted in *The White Threshold*, 1949.

1948
C72   from 'The Lost Other' (excerpt), *Interim*, vol 3, no 3, 1948, pp. 8–10. Reprinted in *The White Threshold*, 1949.

C73 'At that Bright City', *Wake*, no 7, 1948, p. 86. Reprinted in *The White Threshold*, 1949.
C74 'At Whose Sheltering Shall the Day Sea', *Poetry Quarterly*, vol 10, no 1, Spring 1948, p. 14. Reprinted in *The White Threshold*, 1949.
C75 'At Whose Sheltering Shall the Day Sea', *Poetry (Chicago)*, vol 71, no 6, March 1948, p. 308. Reprinted in *The White Threshold*, 1949.
C76 'The Children of Greenock', *Poetry Quarterly*, vol 10, no 2, Summer 1948, pp. 76–7. Reprinted in *The White Threshold*, 1949.
C77 'from 'The White Threshold'' (excerpt), *Poetry (London)*, vol 4, no 13, June 1948, pp. 15–16. Reprinted in *The White Threshold*, 1949.
C78 'It All Comes Back To Me Now' (prose), *Poetry (Chicago)*, vol 72, no 6, September 1948, pp. 302–7. (Review of Randal Jarrell's *Losses*).
C79 'The White Threshold', *Sewanee Review*, vol 56, no 4, Autumn 1948, pp. 658–64. Reprinted in *The White Threshold*, 1949.
C80 'The Voyages of Alfred Wallis', *Tiger's Eye*, vol 1, no 6, December 1948, p. 71. Reprinted in *The White Threshold*, 1949.
C81 'First Poem of Drowning', *Tiger's Eye*, vol 1, no 6, December 1948, p. 72. Reprinted in *The White Threshold*, 1949.

1949
C82 'Men Sign the Sea', *Accent*, vol 8, no 3, 1949, p. 169. Reprinted in *The White Threshold*, 1949.
C83 'Hymn', *The Cornish Review*, no 2, Summer 1949, p. 34.
C84 'To My Brother', *Hudson Review*, vol 1, no 4, Winter 1949, pp. 477–8. Reprinted in *The White Threshold*, 1949.
C85 'To My Father', *Hudson Review*, vol 1, no 4, Winter 1949, pp. 478–9. Reprinted in *The White Threshold*, 1949.
C86 'To My Mother', *Hudson Review*, vol 1, no 4, Winter 1949, pp. 479–80. Reprinted in *The White Threshold*, 1949.
C87 'The Bright Midnight', *Poetry Quarterly*, vol 9, no 3, Autumn 1949, pp. 135–6. Reprinted in *The White Threshold*, 1949.

1951
C88 'The Nightfishing', *Botteghe Oscure*, vol 8, November 1951, pp. 168–84. Reprinted in *The Nightfishing*, 1955.

1953
C89 'Letter II', *Merlin (Paris)*, no 3, (1953). Rewritten and extended version printed in *The Nightfishing*, 1955.
C90 'Letter II', *Lines Review*, no. 3, Summer 1953, p. 34. Rewritten and extended version printed in *The Nightfishing*, 1955.
C91 'As Brilliance Fell', *Poetry Book Magazine*, vol 6, no 3, Fall 1953.

1954

C92 'Letter III', *Hudson Review*, vol 7, no 2, Summer 1954, pp. 241–3. Reprinted in *The Nightfishing*, 1955.
C93 'Christopher Absolom Morris', *New Statesman and Nation*, 1222, 7th August 1954, p. 161.
C94 'The Dark Intention', *New Statesman and Nation*, 1228, 18th September 1954, p. 328.
C95 'The Ballad of Baldy Bane', *Nimbus*, vol 2, no 3, Autumn 1954, pp. 3–7. Reprinted as 'Baldy Bane' in *The Nightfishing*, 1955.
C96 'As Brilliance Fell', *Stand*, no 8, 1954, p. 3.
C97 'The Ballad of The Broad Close', *Botteghe Oscure*, vol 9, 1954, pp. 114–20. Reprinted as 'The Broad Close' in *The Nightfishing*, 1955.

1956

C98 'The Soldier Campion', *New Statesman and Nation*, 27th October 1956, p. 522. Reprinted in *Penguin Modern Poets*, no 17, Harmondsworth, 1970, p. 104.

1957

C99 'Hilton Abstract', *New Statesman and Nation*, 5th January 1957, p. 19. Reprinted in *Malcolm Mooney's Land*, 1970.

1958

C100 'Letter X: My Dear So Many Times', *Encounter*, vol 10, no 1, January 1958, p. 42.
C101 'The Constructed Space', *Poetry (Chicago)*, vol 93, no 1, October 1958, p. 30. Reprinted in *Malcolm Mooney's Land*, 1970

1959

C102 'The Dark Dialogues', *Botteghe Oscure*, vol 23, Spring 1959, pp. 79–86. Reprinted in *Malcolm Mooney's Land*, 1970.

1964

C103 'In Memoriam: Burns Singer', *The Times Literary Supplement*, 17th December 1964, p. 1142.

1965

C104 'In Memoriam – Burns Singer' (prose), *The Times Literary Supplement*, 21st January 1965, p. 54. A letter to the editor.

1966

C105 'Malcolm Mooney's Land', *Poetry (Chicago)*, vol 108, no 6, 1966, pp. 393–8. Reprinted in *Malcolm Mooney's Land*, 1970.

1967

C106 'The Beast in the Space', *Poetry (Chicago)*, vol 110, no 1, April 1967, pp. 1–2. Reprinted in *Malcolm Mooney's Land*, 1970.

C107 'Five Visitors To Madron', *Listener*, 22nd June 1967, p. 20. Reprinted in *Malcolm Mooney's Land*, 1970.

1968

C108 'Clusters Travelling Out', *Poetry (Chicago)*, vol 112, no 3, 1968, pp. 178–82. Reprinted in *Malcolm Mooney's Land*, 1970.

1969

C109 'Master Cat and Master Me', *Malahat Review*, no 10, April 1969, p. 16. Reprinted in *Malcolm Mooney's Land*, 1970.

C110 'Johann Joachim Quantz's First Lesson', *Malahat Review*, no 10, April 1969, p. 17. Reprinted in *Malcolm Mooney's Land*, 1970.

C111 'The Fifteen Devices', *Malahat Review*, no 10, April 1969, pp. 18–19. Reprinted in *Malcolm Mooney's Land*, 1970.

1971

C112 'Imagine a Forest', *Malahat Review*, no 17, January 1971 pp. 14–15. Reprinted in *Implements In Their Places*, 1977.

1972

C113 'Ten Shots of Mister Simpson', *London Magazine*, vol 11, no 6, February 1972, pp. 5–10. Reprinted in *Implements In Their Places*, 1977.

C114 'Implements in Their Places', *Malahat Review*, no 22, April 1972, pp. 9–24. Reprinted with substantial alterations in *Implements In Their Places*, 1977.

C115 'For Alan and Valerie', *Alan Lowndes: Paintings 1948–72*, Stockport Art Gallery, 1972, pp. 12.

1973

C116 'The Secret Name', *Malahat Review*, no 27, July 1973, pp. 8–9. Reprinted in *Implements In Their Places*, 1977.

C117 'From a Poem in Progress: A Dream of Crete', *Aquarius*, no 6, 1973, pp. 5–6.

C118 'Ten Shots of Mister Simpson', *New Poems 1972–73: A PEN Anthology of Contemporary Poetry* (edited by Douglas Dunn), 1973, pp. 65–9. Reprinted in *Implements In Their Places*, 1977.

C119 'A Note to the Difficult One', *Akros*, vol 9, no 27, April 1975, p. 72. Reprinted in *Implements In Their Places*, 1977.

C120 'What Age is Eliot Now?' *Akros*, vol 9, no 27, April 1975, p. 72.

1974

C121 'The Secret Name', *Poetry Nation*, no 3, 1974, pp. 33–4. Reprinted in *Implements In Their Places*, 1977.

C122 'Sgurr Na Gillean Macleod', *Poetry Nation*, no 3, 1974, pp. 34–5. Reprinted in *Implements In Their Places*, 1977.

C123 'Imagine a Forest', *Poetry Nation*, no 3, 1974, pp. 35–6. Reprinted in *Implements In Their Places*, 1977.

C124 'What Is The Language Using Us For?', *Malahat Review*, no 32, October 1974, pp. 51–5. Reprinted in *Implements In Their Places*, 1977.

C125 'The Gobbled Child', *Aquarius*, no 7, 1974, p. 3. Reprinted in *Implements In Their Places*, 1977.

C126 'The Murdered Drinker', *Aquarius*, no. 7, 1974, p. 4. Reprinted in *Implements In Their Places*, 1977.

C127 'Johann Joachim Quantz's Fourth Lesson', *The Times Literary Supplement*, 11 October 1974, p. 1123. Reprinted in *Implements in Their Places*, 1977.

1975

C128 'The Night City', *Listener*, 16 January 1975, p. 94. Reprinted in *Implements In Their Places*, 1977.

C129 'To Alexander Graham', *Malahat Review*, no 33, January 1975, pp. 108–9. Reprinted in *Implements In Their Places*, 1977.

C130 'Language Ah Now You Have Me', *Malahat Review*, no 33, January 1975, pp. 110–11. Reprinted in *Implements In Their Places*, 1977.

C131 'Enter a Cloud', *Malahat Review*, no 33, January 1975, pp. 112–5. Reprinted in *Implements In Their Places*, 1977.

C132 'What is the Language Using Us For?', *Poetry Nation*, no 4, 1975, pp. 40–4. Reprinted in *Implements In Their Places*, 1977.

C133 'Sgurr Na Gillean Macleod', *New Poems 1975: A PEN Anthology of Contemporary Poetry* (edited by Patricia Beer), 1975, pp. 20–1. Reprinted in *Implements In Their Places*, 1977.

C134 'To Alexander Graham', *Listener*, 17 July 1975, p. 91. Reprinted in *Implements In Their Places*, 1977

1976

C135 'Language Ah Now You Have Me', *Stand*, vol 17, no 1, 1976, p. 12. Reprinted in *Implements In Their Places*, 1977.

C136 'Are You Still There?', *Listener*, 8 January 1976, p. 30. Reprinted in *Implements In Their Places*, 1977.

C137 'Lines on Roger Hilton's Watch', *Malahat Review*, no 39, July 1976, pp. 90–1. Reprinted in *Implements In Their Places*, 1977.

C138 'Loch Thom', *Malahat Review*, no 39, July 1976, pp. 92–3. Reprinted with substantial alterations in *Implements In Their Places*, 1977.

1977
C139 'How Are the Children Robin?', *PN Review*, vol 4, no 2, 1977, p. 3. Reprinted in *Implements In Their Places*, 1977.
C140 'The Found Picture', *PN Review*, vol 4, no 2, 1977, p. 3. Reprinted in *Implements In Their Places*, 1977.
C141 'Johann Joachim Quantz's Five Lessons', *PN Review*, vol 4, no 4, 1977, pp. 10–11. Reprinted in *Implements In Their Places*, 1977.
C142 'To My Wife at Midnight', *PN Review*, vol 4, no 4, 1977, pp. 11–12. Reprinted in *Collected Poems 1942–1977*, 1979.
C143 'Falling Into the Sea', *Observer Magazine*, 20th November 1977, p. 17.

1978
C144 'Heath-Stubbs the Poet as Hero', *Aquarius*, no 10, 1978, pp. 8–9.

1979
C145 'A Page About my Country', *Aquarius*, no 11, 1979, pp. 37–8.
C146 'The Alligator Girls', *PN Review*, vol 6, no 2, 1979, p. 42.
C147 'The Visit', *PN Review*, vol 6, no 2, 1979, p. 42.
C148 'I will Lend You Malcolm', *PN Review*, vol 6, no 2, 1979, pp. 42–3.

1980
C149 'The Fifth of May', *PN Review*, vol 6, no 6, 1980, p. 19.
C150 'The Musical Farmer', *PN Review*, vol 6, no 6, 1980, p. 19.
C151 'The Street of Knives', *PN Review*, vol 6, no 6, 1980, p. 19.
C152 'Alice Where Art Thou?', *PN Review*, vol 6, no 6, 1980, pp. 19–20.
C153 'Beholding Thee', *PN Review*, vol 6, no 6, 1980, p. 20.
C154 'From Gigha Young', *Malahat Review*, no 55, July 1980, p. 46.
C155 'Look at the Children', *Malahat Review*, no 55, July 1980, p. 47.
C156 'Leonard in the Forest', *A Garland of Poems for Leonard Clark on his 75th Birthday*, 1980, p. 7.

Section D: *Manuscript Collections*

Austin
The collection of the Humanities Research Center, The University of Texas at Austin, USA.
D1 Graham, W.S. / Works 1 / Hanley II / B, The Broad Close, Holograph, 8 pages, not signed, no date, boxed.

Bibliography

D2 Graham, W.S./Works 2/Hanley II/B, The Dark Dialogues, Holograph, 12 pages, signed, no date, boxed.

D3 Graham, W.S./Works 1/Hanley II/B, The Nightfishing, Holograph with a few holograph emendations, 16 pages, not signed, no date, boxed.

D4 Graham, W.S./Works, The Nightfishing (poem), Typescript, holograph emendations, holograph printer's markings, 16 pages, signed, no date.

D5 Graham, W.S./Works 2/Hanley II/B, Notes on a notebook, Typescript with holograph corrections, 1 page, signed, no date, boxed.

D6 Graham, W.S./Works 2/Hanley II/B (Poetical Notebook) Holograph with typescript sections and numerous watercolour and ink sketches, 1956–1958, boxed.

D7 Graham, W.S./Works 2/Hanley II/B, Re-evaluation of 'The Nightfishing', Holograph with revisions, 13 pages, not signed, dated 5 January 1968. A Letter to Norman and Isobel.

D8 Gardiner, Wrey/Misc., Those Mermen in their Summer Saltings, Typescript, signed, dated 20 October 1955.

D9 Graham, W.S./Works 1/Hanley II/B, The White Threshold, Typescript, 6 pages, not signed, no date, attached to holograph signed letter to Rodgers, WR, 7 October 1947, boxed.

D10 Graham, W.S./Works 2/Hanley II/B, holograph signed letter Graham to unidentified recipient, about notebook, no date, boxed.

D11 Duncan, Ronald/Misc., holograph signed letter Graham to Ronald Duncan and Rosemary Duncan, no date.

D12 Duncan, Ronald/Misc., 4 holograph signed letters, 1 typed signed letter, 1 holograph signed postcard to Ronald Duncan from Graham, dated 1950–1951.

D13 Lehmann, John/Recip., 3 typed signed letters Graham to John Lehmann, 1 no date, 1941 October 7, 1942 December 10.

D14 PR/6013/R23/N5, Graham, W.S., *The Nightfishing*, with holograph Poem for Dr G. Schwarts.

D15 PR/6013/R23/WS/cop.1, Graham, W.S., *The White Threshold*, with tipped in review notice.

Buffalo

The poetry/rare books collection, the University Libraries, State University of New York at Buffalo, USA.

D16 Graham W. S., *The Seven Journeys*, with annotations in the poet's hand, signed, dated 1947.

D17 Graham W. S., An annotated typescript of four poems. [O Gentle Queen of the Afternoon, Here Next the Chair I was when Winter Went, His Companions Buried Him, The Serving Inhabiters.] Signed, dated, 1943.

D18   Graham W. S., A letter to Peter Russell.
D19   GRAHAM: SLO 90960A. Typescript of 'The Nightfishing' with a typescript introduction prepared for a poetry reading. Also Typescript with holograph notes of 6 stanzas of 'The Nightfishing', 2 pages, no date.

Rylands
The Archives of Carcanet Press, The John Rylands University Library of Manchester, UK.
D20   Graham W. S., 20 letters to Michael Schmidt written between 28 February 1974 and 25 January 1977.

Worksheets
D21   The Thermal Stair. Typescript with holograph emendations, 4pp. dated 13 October 1964.
D22   Ten Shots of Mister Simpson. Typescript with holograph emendations. 4pp. Variously dated between 16 March 1971 and 11 August 1971.
D23   The Don Brown Route. Typescript with holograph emendations, 2pp. Dated 20 April 1969.
D24   (A beginning of) A Dream of Crete. Typescript with holograph emendations. 1p. Dated 21 October 1972.
D21–24 above are all enclosed with the letter dated '10.7.10' (sic, for 1974).
D25   What is the Language Using Us For? Typescript with holograph emendations, 3pp. Dated 30 January 1973 and 7 June 1973. Enclosed with the letter dated 11 March 1975.
D26   How Are the Children Robin. Typescript. 1p. Dated 19 September 1976. Enclosed with the letter dated 19 September 1976.

Edinburgh
The Department of Manuscripts, The National Library of Scotland, Edinburgh, UK.
D27   Typescript of 'The Nightfishing', 1955, with a related letter: annotated typescript, 1943, of 'Nine Poems for a Poetry Reading'. Access nos 2792–2793.
D28   Manuscripts and Typescripts of five poems, 1960–1966. Access no 4967.
D29   Manuscript of 'The Song of the Tower'. Access no 7847.
D30   Thirty letters to Sven Berlin, 1945–1965. Access nos 7389, 7581.
D31   Six letters, 1955–1958, to Alan —. Access nos 107090, f.234, 4585. Alan — is Alan Hancox, Bookseller, Cheltenham.

Skelton
The private collection of Robin Skelton. Professor Skelton may be

contacted at The Department of Creative Writing, University of Victoria, Victoria, BC, Canada.

Letters

D32 Folder 1: W. S. Graham to Moncrieff Williamson. Photocopies of 17 letters, holograph and typescript, signed, dated, 1949–1950.

D33 Folder 2: W. S. Graham to Robin Skelton. 1 holograph dated 12 November 1955, signed. 10 holograph and typescript, signed 1958. 1 handmade Christmas card, no date.

D34 Folder 3: W. S. Graham to Robin Skelton. 8 holograph and typescript here with additions by Nessie [Dunsmuir] Graham, signed, dated, 1959.

D35 Folder 4: W. S. Graham to Robin Skelton. 2 holograph, signed, dated 1967. 1 holograph, signed, dated 1968. 1 typescript, signed, dated 1968. Last item includes typescripts of 'Master Cat and Master Me', 'Johann Joachim Quantz's First Lesson', 'Fifteen Devices'.

D36 Folder 5: W. S. Graham to Robin Skelton. 7 holograph and typescript, signed, dated 1970. 1 holograph signed 1971. 1 typescript, signed, dated 1971.

D37 Folder 6: W. S. Graham to Robin Skelton. 5 holograph signed, dated 1972. Five typescript, signed, dated 1972.

D38 Folder 7: W. S. Graham to Robin Skelton. 15 holograph and typescript, signed, dated 1973.

D39 Folder 8: W. S: Graham to Robin Skelton. 11 holograph and typescript, signed, dated 1974.

D40 Folder 9: W. S. Graham to Robin Skelton. 3 typescript, signed, dated 1975. 2 typescript, signed, dated 1976. 2 typescript dated 1977. 1 typescript dated 1978.

D41 Folder 10: Robin Skelton to W. S. Graham. 1 typescript, signed, dated 1968. 4 typescript, signed, dated 1970. 1 typescript dated 1972. 1 typescript dated 1973. Folder 10 includes Skelton's versions of 9 unpublished Graham poems which W. S. Graham considered unfinished and would not allow to be published. Summary: W. S. Graham to Moncrieff Williamson, 17 letters 1949–1950. W. S. Graham to Robin Skelton, 78 letters, 1955–1979. Robin Skelton to W. S. Graham, 7 letters 1968–1973.

Worksheets

D42 Folder 11: Worksheets for *The Nightfishing*. Ballads, holograph, 18 pages (9 sheets), signed, dated 1950–1954. 'The Ballad of Willie Peden', holograph, 1 page, not signed, no date [1950]. Excerpt from 'The Nightfishing', holograph and typescript, 1 page, signed, no date [1950].

D43 Folder 12: Worksheets for *Malcolm Mooney's Land*. item 1:

Malcolm Mooney's Land, holograph and typescript, 5 pages, not signed, no date. Holograph fair copy of the same, 7 pages, signed, dated 19 February 1968.

D44 Folder 12 item 2: The Beast in the Space. Typescript and holograph, 1 page, signed, dated 30 July 1966.

D45 Folder 12 item 3: Dear Who I Mean. Typescript and holograph, 2 pages, signed, dated 1968–1969.

D46 Folder 12 item 4: Master Cat and Master Me. Typescript and holograph, 1 page, signed, April 1968.

D47 Folder 12 item 5: The Dark Dialogues. Typescript and holograph, 6 pages, signed, dated 1956–1958.

D48 Folder 12 item 6: Press Button to Hold Desired Symbol. Typescript and holograph, 2 pages, signed, 13 March 1969.

D49 Folder 12 item 7: The Fifteen Devices. Typescript and holograph, 3 pages, signed, dated 15 April 1969.

D50 Folder 12 item 8: Five Visitors to Madron. Typescript, 1 page, not signed, no date.

D51 Folder 13: Clusters Travelling Out. Typescript and holograph, 44 pages, 3 signed, dated 1967–1968.

D52 Folder 14 item 1: What Is The Language Using Us For? Typescript and holograph, 3 pages, signed, dated 21 April 1974.

D53 Folder 14 item 2: Imagine a Forest. Typescript, 2 pages, signed, dated 18 May 1970.

D54 Folder 14 item 3: Language Ah Now You Have Me. Typescript and holograph, 7 pages, signed, dated 2 September 1974.

D55 Folder 14 item 4: The Night City. Typescript, 1 page, signed, dated 16 May 1974.

D56 Folder 14 item 5: Enter a Cloud. Typescript and holograph, 8 pages, signed, dated 1973–1974.

D57 Folder 14 item 6: Greenock At Night. Typescript and holograph, 1 page, signed, 30 March 1971.

D58 Folder 14 item 7: To Alexander Graham. Typescript and holograph, 1 page, signed 19 September 1974.

D59 Folder 14 item 8: Lines on Roger Hilton's Watch. Typescript and holograph, 1 page, signed, dated 1 October 1975.

D60 Folder 14 item 9: The Secret Name. Typescript, 2 pages, signed, dated 27 February 1973.

D61 Folder 14 item 10: The Found Picture. Typescript and holograph, 5 pages, signed, dated 1974–1975.

D62 Folder 14 item 11: To Bryan Wynter Dead. Typescript and holograph, 1 page, signed, dated 29 May 1975.

D63 Folder 15: Ten Shots of Mister Simpson. Typescript and holograph, 22 pages, signed, dated 1969–1971. Notebook, holograph, 22 pages, signed, dated 1971.

D64 Folder 16: Implements In Their Places. Typescript and holograph, 53 pages, signed, dated 1969–1970.

Unpublished Poems

D65 Folder 17 item 1: The Stone's Last Ripple, Prose Poem. Typescript, 2 pages, signed, no date. Addressed 13 Brisbane St, Greenock, therefore late 1930s.

D66 Folder 17 item 2: Frank Baker and the Years of Love. Typescript, 1 page, lined paper, signed, dated 1955.

D67 Folder 17 item 3: As Told to Davie Dunsmuir. Typescript, 1 page, not signed, dated 5 February 1966.

D68 Folder 17 item 4: Detain Detain or the Blue Tundra. Typescript, 1 page, signed, dated 14 March 1968.

D69 Folder 17 item 5: Lines for a Poster. Typescript, 1 page, signed 29 March 1968.

D70 Folder 17 item 6: About the Stuff. Typescript and holograph, not signed, dated 8 August 1968.

D71 Folder 17 item 7: The Greenock Dialogues. Typescript and holograph, 8 pages, signed, dated 25 August 1968.

D72 Folder 17 item 8: The Old Pornographer. Typescript and holograph, 1 page, not signed, dated 30 August 1968.

D73 Folder 17 item 9: About the Stuff. Typescript, 1 page, not signed, dated 26 October 1969.

D74 Folder 17 item 10: Myself the Day Desires. Typescript and holograph, 3 pages, lined paper, not signed, dated 26 October 1969.

D75 Folder 17 item 11: I Am Not As Good As Double You Es Graham. Typescript, 1 page, lined paper, not signed, dated 11 December 1969.

D76 Folder 17 item 12: Fill in this Form. Typescript, 1 page, signed, dated 5 May 1971.

D77 Folder 17 item 13: The Dredge. Typescript and holograph, 1 page, signed, dated 5 October 1971.

D78 Folder 17 item 14: The Particular Object. Typescript and holograph, 1 page, signed, dated 8 October 1971.

D79 Folder 17 item 15: Of Myself. Typescript and holograph, 1 page, signed, dated 7 March 1972.

D80 Folder 17 item 16: I Write as I Speak. Typescript and holograph. 1 page, lined paper, not signed, dated 14 May 1972.

D81 Folder 17 item 17: Is What We Call The World. Typescript and holograph, 1 page, signed, dated 13 May 1972.

D82 Folder 17 item 18: What Do Other People Do. Typescript and holograph, 1 page, signed, dated 8 April 1974.

D83 Folder 17 item 19: If It Is Only For You. Typescript and holograph, 3 versions, 3 pages, signed, dated 5 May 1975. Notes added and dated 20 November 1976.

D84   Folder 17 item 20: Surrealgraphs. Typescript and holograph, 1 page, signed, dated 11 November 1975. Notes added signed, dated 20 November 1976.
D85   Folder 17 item 21: So That I Fell Here. Typescript, 2 pages, not signed, no date.
D86   Folder 17 item 22: Letter VIII, Typescript, 1 page, not signed, no date.
D87   Folder 17 item 23: Beech Tree Carved When Young, Typescript, 1 page, torn, not signed, no date.
D88   Folder 17 item 24: The Real Sound. Typescript and holograph, 4 pages, not signed, no date.
D89   Folder 17 item 25: The Particular Pin. Typescript and holograph, 3 pages, not signed, no date.
D90   Folder 17 item 26: At Opening Time. Typescript, 1 page, not signed, dated 10 March 1966.
D91   Folder 17 item 27: The Words. Typescript, 1 page, not signed, no date.
D92   Folder 17 item 28: Chitterlings [Prose]. Typescript, 1 page, torn, not signed, no date.
D93   Folder 17 item 29: [14 pages of notes]. Typescript, 14 pages, not signed, no date.
Note: Items 1–20 (D66–D85) above may be considered finished or near finished poems. Items 21–29 (D86–D94) are notes and early versions.

Notebooks
D94   Item 1: Notes on the Making of Verse. W. S. Graham. Addressed, 2 Morley Road, Lewisham, London, SE 13. Signed October 1954.
Notebook and Sketchbook, 31.7 × 20 cms. Blue boards, lined paper. Cover: W. S. G. to SKELTON 1972. Ballpoint pen scratched into surface.
Writing: 18 pages. Drawing/painting: 42 pages. Blank: 28 pages. Inserts: The Old Mountaineer to His Son. Holograph on lined paper, torn, folded sheet, 2 pages, signed, dated 'about 1947'.
D95   Item 2: Artificial Limbs / W. S. Graham / F. G. ERNST / Book *Artificial Limbs* by F. G. Ernst, London, no date. 25 × 19 cms. Brown boards.
Graham's 98 pages of watercolour and ink paintings and drawings deface text and illustrations by F. G. Ernst, 1955. Inserts: Letter, W. S. Graham to Robin Skelton, dated 9 October 1974.
D96   Item 3: Places. Notebook. Page [5], watercolour title page reads: PLACES / Woodfield / 25 April 64 /
32 × 15 cms. Red Boards, lined paper. Cover: W. S. G. / for / Skelton / Ballpoint pen scratched into surface.
133 numbered pages of writing including notes for poems that are

included in *Malcolm Mooney's Land* and *Implements In Their Places*. Extensive notes for the poem 'Clusters Travelling Out'.

D97 Item 4: Toward The Well Being of Mankind. Defaced book. *Toward the Well Being of Mankind: fifty years of The Rockefeller Foundation*, text by Robert Shaplen, New York, 1964.
31 × 23 cms. White paper cover on brown boards. Cover: Addressed for posting to Robin Skelton from W. S. Graham, Madron, Penzance, Cornwall, England.
Defaced text and photographs with ink, watercolour and chalk sketches. Many inserted and pasted-in sheets of poems and early versions of poems. Notes by W. S. Graham, Typescript and holograph, many signed and dated 1967–1973.

Section E: *Items about W. S. Graham*

In Books:

E1 James Dickey, 'W. S. Graham', *Babel to Byzantium: Poets and Poetry Now*, New York, 1956; revised edition, New York 1981, pp. 41–5 and 'Afterword', pp. 293–4.

E2 Calvin Bedient, 'W. S. Graham', *Eight Contemporary Poets*, Oxford, 1974, pp. 159–80.

E3 Michael Schmidt, 'W. S. Graham', *A Reader's Guide to Fifty Modern British Poets*, London, 1979, pp. 297–304.

E4 Damian Grant, 'Walls of glass: the poetry of W. S. Graham', in Peter Jones and Michael Schmidt (eds), *British Poetry since 1970: a critical survey*, Manchester, 1980, pp. 22–38.

In Periodicals:

E5 Nicholas Moore, Review of *Cage Without Grievance*, *Poetry Quarterly*, vol 4, no 4, Winter 1942, p. 158.

E6 Anonymous, Review of *The Seven Journeys*, *The Times Literary Supplement*, 19 May 1945, p. 236.

E7 John Ormand Thomas, Review of *2nd Poems*, *Poetry Quarterly*, vol 7, no 4, Winter 1945, pp. 163–5.

E8 Derek Stanford, Review of *The Seven Journeys*, *Poetry Quarterly*, vol 8, no 1, Spring 1946, pp. 51–6.

E9 Vivienne Koch, Review of *Cage Without Grievance*, *Sewanee Review*, vol 54, no 4, Autumn 1946, pp. 699–716.

E10 Vivienne Koch, 'The Technique of Morality' (article), *Poetry Quarterly*, vol 9, no 4, Winter 1947, pp. 216–25.

E11 Hayden Carruth, 'Mr Graham and the Dead Cigar', (article) *Poetry (Chicago)*, vol 72, no 6, September 1948, pp. 307–11.

E12 Vivienne Koch, 'A Note on W. S. Graham' (article), *Sewanee Review*, vol 56, no 4, Autumn 1948, pp. 665–70.

E13 Anonymous, Review of *The White Threshold*, *The Times Literary Supplement*, 17 June 1949, p. 398.

E14 W. P. M., Review of *The White Threshold*, *Dublin Magazine*, vol (24), no 3, Jul–Sep 1949, pp. 68–70.

E15 Edwin Morgan, 'Graham's Threshold' (review), *Nine*, vol 2, no 2, May 1950, pp. 100–3.

E16 Frederick Morgan, Review of *The White Threshold*, *Hudson Review*, vol 3, no 3, Autumn 1950, pp 463–6.

E17 Vivienne Koch, Review of *The White Threshold*, *Sewanee Review*, vol 59, no 4, Oct–Dec 1950, pp. 664–77.

E18 Ray Short, 'W. S. Graham' (article), *Poetry Book Magazine*, vol 4, no 4, Summer 1952, pp. 1–3.

E19 Peter J. Stephens, 'Shelley and Mr Graham', *Poetry Book Magazine*, vol 6, no 1, Fall 1953, p. 103.

E20 Leonie Adams, Review of *The White Threshold*, *Poetry (Chicago)*, vol 82, no 5, August 1953, pp. 272–6.

E21 Austin Warren, Review of *Malcolm Mooney's Land*, *Partisan Review*, vol 21, no 1, Jan–Feb 1954, pp. 108–12.

E22 Anonymous, Review of *The Nightfishing*, *The Times Literary Supplement*, 8 July 1955, p. 379.

E23 Anonymous, 'The Scottish Literary Revival', *The Times Literary Supplement*, 5 August 1955 (special autumn no, p. x).

E24 Reed Whittemore, Review of *The Nightfishing*, *Poetry (Chicago)*, vol 86, no 5, August 1955, pp. 295–302.

E25 Walter Keir, Review of *The Nightfishing*, *Saltire Review*, vol 2, no 5, Autumn 1955, pp. 75–7.

E26 Donald Davie, Review of *The Nightfishing*, *Dublin Magazine*, vol (30), no 4, Oct–Dec 1955, pp. 38–40.

E27 G. S. Fraser, Review of *The Nightfishing* (letter), *London Magazine*, vol 2, no 9, 1955, pp. 67–9.

E28 Harri Webb, Review of *The Nightfishing*, *Promenade*, no 72, November 1955, pp. 15–17.

E29 James Dickey, Review of *The Nightfishing*, *Sewanee Review*, vol 64, no 2, Spring 1956, pp. 324–8.

E30 John Silkin, Review of *The Nightfishing*, *Stand*, no 11, Winter–Spring 1956, pp. 29–31.

E31 Robin Skelton, Review of *The Nightfishing*, *Poetry London–New York*, vol 1, no 2, Winter 1956, pp. 55–7.

E32 Edwin Honig, Review of *The Nightfishing*, *Partisan Review*, vol 23, no 1, Winter 1956, pp. 115–20.

E33 Anonymous, Review of *Malcolm Mooney's Land*, *The Times Literary Supplement*, 31 July 1970, p. 849.

E34 William Montgomerie, Review of *Malcolm Mooney's Land*, *Akros*, no 15, August 1970, pp. 97–100.

E35 John Saunders, Review of *Malcolm Mooney's Land*, *Stand*, vol 11, no 4, 1970, pp. 68–72.

E36 Calvin Bedient, 'Absentist Poetry: Kinsella, Hill, Graham, Hughes' (article), *PN Review*, vol 4, no 1, 1977, pp. 18–24.

Bibliography

E37 Michael Schmidt, Review of *Implements in their Places*, *The Times Literary Supplement*, 4 November 1977, p. 1298.

E38 C. Falck, Review of *Implements in their Places*, *New Review*, vol 4, nos 45 and 46, December 1977, pp. 70–3.

E39 Jascha Kessler, Review of *Implements in their Places*, *Parnassus*, vol 6, no 2, Spring 1978, pp. 205–12.

E40 Herbert Lomas, Review of *Implements in their Places*, *London Magazine*, vol 18, no 2, June 1978, p. 83.

E41 Anne Stevenson, *Review of Implements in their Places*, *Listener*, 13 July 1978, p. 62.

E42 Robert Duxbury, 'The Poetry of W. S. Graham', *Akros*, Vol 13, no 38, August 1978, pp. 62–71.

E43 Penelope Mortimer, 'A Poet's Interview with Himself', *Observer Magazine*, 19 November 1978, p. 62 (photograph by Sally Fear).

E44 Richard Burns, Review of *Malcolm Mooney's Land* and *Implements In Their Places*, *Perfect Bound*, no 5, 1978, pp. 68–72.

E45 Edna Longley, Review of *Collected Poems 1942–1977*, *The Times Literary Supplement*, 14 March 1980, p. 301.

E46 Hayden Carruth, Review of *Selected Poems*, *Harper's Magazine*, December 1980, pp. 74–6.

E47 Anne Cluysenaar, Review of *Collected Poems 1942–1977*, *Stand*, vol 21, no 4 (1980), p. 66.

E48 Jeffrey Wainwright, Review of *Selected Poems*, *Parnassus*, vol 9, no 1, Spring 1981, pp. 242–51.

E49 Edwin Morgan, 'The Poetry of W. S. Graham' (article), *Cencrastus*, no 5, Summer 1981, Edinburgh, pp. 8–10.

E50 Thom Gunn, Review of *Selected Poems*, *Threepenny Review*, no 6, Summer 1981, San Francisco, pp. 4–5.

E51 David Punter, 'Constructing a White Space' (article), *Malahat Review*, no 63, October 1982, pp. 220–44.

E52 Jeffrey Wainwright, Review of *Selected Poems*, *Virginia Quarterly Review*, vol 57, Winter 1981, p. 26.

E53 R. Watson, Review of *Collected Poems 1942–1977*, *Studies in Scottish Literature*, (Columbia), vol 17, 1983, p. 218.

E54 Tony Lopez, 'On *Malcolm Mooney's Land* by W. S. Graham' (article), *Ideas & Production*, no 4, December 1985, pp. 47–70.

E55 Anonymous, 'Obituary', *The Times*, 14 January 1986, p. 16.

E56 Michael Schmidt, 'Journey to truth' (obituary), *Guardian*, 14 January 1986, p. 11.

E57 Douglas Dunn, 'Poet's Affection for Clydeside' (obituary), *Glasgow Herald*, 15 January 1986.

E58 Frank Ruhrmund, 'Literary world mourns W. S. Graham' (obituary), *The Cornishman*, 16 January 1986, p. 1.

E59 Dennis O'Driscoll, Obituary for W. S. Graham, *Irish Times*, 20 January 1986.

E60 Hayden Murphy, 'W. S. Graham' (obituary), *Scotsman*, 25 January 1986.
E61 Tony Lopez, 'W. S. Graham: An Introduction' (article), *Edinburgh Review*, no 75, February 1987, pp. 7–23.
E62 Edwin Morgan, 'W. S. Graham: A Poet's Letters' (article including Graham's letters), *Edinburgh Review*, no 75, February 1987, pp. 38–48.
E63 David Wright, 'W. S. Graham in the forties' (memoir), *Edinburgh Review*, no 75, February 1987, pp. 49–56.
E64 Tom Scott, 'W. S. Graham in the forties and fifties' (memoir), *Edinburgh Review*, no 75, February 1987, pp. 57–9.
E65 Robert Frame, 'W. S. Graham at Sandyford Place' (memoir), *Edinburgh Review*, no 75, February 1987, pp. 60–5.
E66 Nancy Wynne-Jones, 'W. S. Graham in Cornwall' (memoir), *Edinburgh Review*, no 75, February 1987, pp. 66–9.
E67 Ronnie Duncan, 'W. S. Graham – A Memoir', *Edinburgh Review*, no 75, February 1987, pp. 70–4.
E68 Robert Calder, 'W. S. Graham's Poetry' (article), *Edinburgh Review*, no 75, February 1987, pp. 75–82.
E69 Tom Leonard, 'Journeys' (article), *Edinburgh Review*, no 75, February 1987, pp. 83–7.
E70 Sebastian Barker, 'Memoir of W. S. Graham', *Edinburgh Review*, no 75, February 1987, pp. 88–91.
E71 Matt Simpson, 'A Letter to W. S. Graham', *Edinburgh Review*, no 75, February 1987, pp. 92–3.
E72 Frank Kuppner, 'Marginalia to *Implements In Their Places*', *Edinburgh Review*, no 75, February 1987, pp. 94–100.
E73 W. N. Herbert, 'The breathing words' (article), *Edinburgh Review*, no 75, February 1987, pp. 101–2.

Secondary Bibliography

Ades, Dawn, *Dada and Surrealism Reviewed* (exhibition catalogue), London, 1978
Amis, Kingsley, 'Editor's Notes', *Spectator*, 7 October 1955, p. 459
  What Became of Jane Austen, London, 1970
Auden, W. H., *The Orators: An English Study*, London, 1932
  and Louis MacNeice, *Letters from Iceland*, London, 1937
Barker, George, *Thirty Preliminary Poems*, London, 1933
  Collected Poems, London, 1988
Bedient, Calvin, *Eight Contemporary Poets*, Oxford, 1974
Bellows, Henry Adams (ed and trans), *The Poetic Edda*, New York, 1923
Berlin, Sven, *Alfred Wallis – Primitive*, London, 1949

The Dark Monarch: A Portrait from Within, London, 1962
Blackburn, H. J., *Six Existential Thinkers*, London, 1952
Bold, Alan, *Modern Scottish Literature*, London, 1983
Bowness, Alan, 'Foreword' in *Bryan Winter 1915–1975* (exhibition catalogue), The Hayward Gallery, London, 1976, pp. 1–8
Bowra, C. M., *Primitive Song*, London, 1962
Breton, André, *What is Surrealism?*, translated by David Gascoyne, London, 1936
Brown, David, 'Chronology', *St Ives 1939–1964* (exhibition catalogue), The Tate Gallery, London, 1985, pp. 97–113
Burns Singer, (James), *The Collected Poems of Burns Singer*, edited by W. A. S. Keir, London, 1970
  Living Silver : An Impression of the British Fishing Industry, London, 1957
Canney, Michael, 'Introduction', Roger Hilton, *Night Letters and Selected Drawings*, selected by Rosemary Hilton, Newlyn (Orion Galleries), Cornwall, 1980, pp. 7–12.
Child, Frances James (ed), *English and Scottish Ballads* (8 vols), Boston, 1857–1859
Conquest, Robert (ed), *New Lines*, London, 1956
Cornford, F. M., *Plato's Theory of Knowledge*, London, 1955
Craig, Cairns (ed), *The History of Scottish Literature* (4 vols), Aberdeen, 1987–1988
Crane, Hart, *White Buildings*, New York, 1926
  Complete Poems, Newcastle, 1984
Cross, Tom, *Painting the Warmth of the Sun: St Ives Artists 1939–1975*, Penzance (Alison Hodge), Cornwall, 1984
Crozier, Andrew, 'Thrills and Frills: Poetry as figures of Empirical Lyricism', *Society and Literature 1945–1970*, edited by Alan Sinfield, London, 1983, pp. 199–233
Davie, Donald, *Purity of Diction in English Verse*, London, 1952
  Articulate Energy: An Enquiry into the Syntax of English Poetry, London 1955
  'Three Poets', *Dublin Magazine*, vol. 30, no 4, October–December 1955, pp. 38–40
  'Remembering the Movement', *Prospect* (edited by Elaine Feinstein), Cambridge, Summer 1959, pp. 15–16
  Ezra Pound: Poet as Sculptor, London, 1965
Dunsmuir, Nessie, 'Raith Pit', *Life and Letters*, vol 48, no 103, March, 1946, p. 210
Eliot, T. S., *Collected Poems*, London, 1963
  'Ulysses, Order, and Myth', *The Dial*, vol 75, no 5, November 1923, pp. 480–3
Eluard, George, *Thorns of Thunder: Selected Poems of George Eluard*, translated by Samuel Beckett, George Reavey and others, edited by George Reavey, London [1936]

Enright, D. J., *Poets of the 1950s* (ed), Tokyo, 1955
Academic Year, London, 1955
Farmer, David Hugh, *The Oxford Dictionary of Saints*, Oxford, 1978
Fowles, John, *The Aristos*, London, 1965
Freud, Sigmund, *The Psychopathology of Everyday Life*, edited and translated by J. Strachey, London, 1966
Fuller, Roy, *Collected Poems 1936–1961*, London, 1962
Gascoyne, David, *A Short Survey of Surrealism*, London, 1935
Man's Life is this Meat, London, 1936
Glen, Duncan, *Hugh MacDiarmid and the Scottish Renaissance*, Edinburgh and London, 1964
Graves, Robert, *The White Goddess*, London, 1948; third edition, London, 1952
Collected Poems 1914–1947, London, 1948
Helmstadter, T. H., The Apocalyptic Movement in British Poetry (dissertation), University of Pennsylvania, 1963
Hendry, J. F. (ed), *The New Apocalypse: an Anthology of Criticism, Poems and Stories*, London [1940]
Hendry, J. F., and Henry Treece (eds), *The White Horseman*, London, 1941
The Crown and The Sickle, London [1944]
Heidegger, Martin, *An Introduction to Metaphysics*, translated by R. Manheim, Yale, 1959
'Hölderlin and the Essence of Poetry', translated by Paul De Man, *Quarterly Review of Literature*, vol 10, nos 1 and 2, 1959, pp. 79–94
Being and Time, translated by John Macquarrie and Edward Robinson, London, 1962
See also King, Magda.
Heraclitus, *The Art and Thought of Heraclitus*, translation and commentary by C. H. Kahn, Cambridge, 1979
Hewison, Robert, *Under Siege: Literary Life in London 1939–1945*, London, 1977
Hilton, Roger, *Night Letters and Selected Drawings*, selected by Rosemary Hilton, Newlyn (Orion Galleries), Cornwall, 1980
Hopkins, Gerard Manley, *The Poems of Gerard Manley Hopkins*, edited by W. H. Gardner and N. H. Mackenzie, Oxford, 1967
Hugill, Stan, *Sea Shanties*, London, 1977
Hynes, Samuel, *The Auden Generation: Literature and Politics in the 1930s*, London, 1976, new edition 1979
Joyce, James, *Ulysses*, Paris, 1922
Finnegan's Wake, London, 1939
Kafka, Franz, *The Trial*, translated by Willa and Edwin Muir, London, 1950
Kahn, C. H., *The Art and Thought of Heraclitus*, Cambridge, 1974
King, Magda, *Heidegger's Philosophy*, Oxford, 1964

Kipling, Rudyard, *Rudyard Kipling's Verse: Definitive Edition*, London, 1940
Kitzinger, Sheila, *Pregnancy and Childbirth*, London, 1980
Koch, Vivienne, *W. B. Yeats: the Tragic Phase; a Study of the Last Poems*, London, 1951
Larkin, Philip, *Whitsun Weddings*, London, 1964
  The Oxford Book of Twentieth-Century Verse (ed), Oxford, 1973
  'A Great Parade of Single Poems: Interview with Anthony Thwaite', *The Listener*, 12 April 1973, p. 473
Lawrence, D. H., *Apocalypse*, Florence, 1931; London 1932
Lewis, David, 'St Ives: A Personal Memoir 1947–1955', *St Ives 1939–1964* (exhibition catalogue), The Tate Gallery, London, 1985, pp. 13–41
Lindsay, Maurice (ed), *Sailing To-Morrow's Seas*, London, 1944
  Modern Scottish Poetry: An Anthology of the Scottish Renaissance 1920–1945, London, 1946
Lowndes, Alan, *Alan Lowndes: Paintings 1948–1972* (exhibition catalogue), Stockport Art Gallery, 1972
Lucie-Smith, Edward (ed), *British Poetry since 1945*, Harmondsworth, 1970
MacDiarmid, Hugh, 'Preface', *The Collected Poems of Burns Singer*, edited by W. A. S. Keir, London, 1970, pp. xi–xviii
MacLaren-Ross, Julian, *Memoirs of the Forties*, London, 1965
Montgomerie, Alexander, *The Poems of Alexander Montgomerie*, edited by James Cranstoun, Edinburgh, 1887
Montgomerie, William, 'Introduction' in W. S. Graham, '*The Seven Journeys*, Glasgow, 1944, pp. [3–4]
Morrison, Blake, *The Movement: English Poetry and Fiction of the 1950s*, Oxford, 1980
  Seamus Heaney, London, 1982
Nansen, Fridjof, *Farthest North* (2 vols), Westminster, 1897
Peterson, Roger, Guy Mountford and P. A. D. Hollom, *A Field Guide to the Birds of Britain and Europe*, London, 1954; revised edition 1974
Rahner, Hugo, *Greek Myths and Christian Mystery*, translated by Brian Battershaw, London, 1963
Read, Herbert, *Surrealism*, London, 1936
Rimbaud, Arthur, *Prose Poems from Les Illuminations*, translated by Helen Rootham, London, 1932
Schneider, Elizabeth W., *The Dragon in the Gate: Studies in the Poetry of Gerard Manley Hopkins*, Los Angeles, 1968
Scopoli, Giovanni, *Deliciae Flora et Fauna Insubricae a Specimen Zoologicum*, Pavia, 1786
Scott, Captain R. P., *Scott's Last Expedition* (2 vols), arranged by Leonard Huxley, London, 1913

Shires, Linda M., *British Poetry of the Second World War*, London, 1985

Sinfield, Alan (ed), *Society and Literature 1945–1970*, London, 1983

Singer, Burns, see Burns Singer

Stanford, Derek, *Inside the Forties*, London, 1977

St Ives, Tom Cross, *Painting the Warmth of the Sun: St Ives Artists 1939–1975*, Penzance (Alison Hodge), Cornwall, 1984

St Ives 1939–1964 (exhibition catalogue), The Tate Gallery, London 1985

Thomas, Dylan, *18 Poems*, London, 1934

New Poems, Norfolk USA, 1943

Deaths and Entrances, London, 1946

Collected Poems 1934–1952, London, 1952

Under Milk Wood, London, 1954

A Prospect of the Sea and other Stories and Prose Writings, London, 1955

Selected Letters of Dylan Thomas, edited by Constantine FitzGibbon, Boston, 1965

Totton, Nick, 'The Snow Queen', *A Vision Very Like Reality*, edited by Peter Ackroyd et al, issue 1, December 1979, pp. 3–7

Treece, Henry, 'An Apocalyptic Writer and the Surrealists,' *The New Apocalypse*, edited by J. F. Hendry, London [1940]

How I see Apocalypse, London, 1946

See also Hendry, J. F.

Dylan Thomas: Dog Among the Fairies, London, 1949

Wade, Rosalind, 'The Parton Street Poets', *Poetry Review*, vol 54, Winter 1963–1964, pp. 290–7

Wain, John, 'Lost Horizons,' *Encounter*, January 1961, pp. 69–70

Watson, Oliver, 'The St Ives Pottery', *St Ives 1939–1964* (exhibition catalogue), The Tate Gallery, London, 1985, pp. 220–7

Watson, Roderick, *The Literature of Scotland*, London, 1984

'Internationalising Scottish Poetry' in Cairns Craig (ed), *The History of Scottish Literature: Volume 4 Twentieth Century*, Aberdeen 1987

Wynter, Bryan, *Bryan Wynter 1915–1975* (exhibition catalogue), The Hayward Gallery, London, 1976

Index

Amis, Kingsley 12, 14
Apocalyptics 19–21, 23, 24, 31
Archer, David 2–3, 11
Auden, W. H. 19, 37, 38, 91

ballads 79, 111, 113–15, 122, 129, 130, 131
Beckett, Samuel 14, 22, 90, 127–8, 129, 132
Bedient, Calvin 27, 44
Berlin, Sven 8, 9, 50
Blake, William 28, 31
Burns Singer, J. 3, 73

Coleridge, S. T. 63, 64, 67, 74, 97
Conquest, Robert 12, 13
Crane, Hart 30–1, 111
Creme, Benjamin 2, 26

Davie, Donald 12, 13–14, 15–18, 23
Dunsmuir, Agnes (Nessie) 2, 3, 5–6, 8, 78; poems 46, 56–7
Eliot, T. S. 5, 11, 13–14, 19, 22, 41, 126, 130, 132; Graham and 2, 5, 10, 11, 47–8, 66, 70, 72, 73, 78, 82–3, 85, 86, 107, 111, 125, 129
Enright, D. J. 12, 13, 14

Frame, Robert 2, 26
Fraser, G. S. 62

Gascoyne, David 19, 20, 35
Graham, Alexander 100
Graham, W. S.: beliefs 23–4; letters 7, 11; life 1–9, 11–12, 25, 40, 41, 50, 51, 125–6, 127, 128, 130; notes 37, 38; reputation and critical views of 9–11, 12, 15–18, 21, 23, 26, 62, 63; works: 'Allow Silk Birds That See' **38–9**; 'Approaches to How They Behave' **82–3**, 100, 102, 110; 'Baldy Bane' **78–9**; 'The Beast in the Space' 82; 'The Broad Close' **78–9**;

Cage Without Grievance 2, **26–31**; 'The Children of Greenock' 42, **44–6**, 60, 121; 'The Children of Lanarkshire' 43, **45**, 46, 60; 'Clusters Travelling out' 38, 56, 81, 82, **90–2**, **93–4**, **95**; *Collected Poems 1942–1977* 9, 10, 31–2, 100; 'The Constructed Space' 127; 'The Dark Dialogues' 25, 56, 83, **95–9**, 128, 131, 132; 'Dear Bryan Wynter' 9, **123–4**, 128; 'Dear Who I Mean' **81–2**; 'The Don Brown Route' 81, **120–9**; 'A Dream of Crete' 99; 'Enter a Cloud' **121–2**; 'Explanation of a Map' **37**, 38; 'Five Visitors to Madron' 81, 82, 90, **92–3**, **94**, **95**; 'For Valerie and Alan' 9; 'The Found Picture' 101, **122–3**; 'Gigha' 44, **51–2**, 80; 'The Gobbled Child' 79, 100, **122**, 128, 129–30; 'Heath-Stubbs the Poet as Hero' 112; 'Hilton Abstract' 9, 127; 'His Companions Buried Him' 38, **84–5**; 'I Leave This at Your Ear' 25; 'Imagine a Forest' **53–4**, 79, 100, 101, 131; *Implements In Their Places* 8, 9, **100–24**, 127, 130–1; 'Implements In Their Places' 3, 33, 56, 94, 99, **100–20**, 126, 127, 128, 131; 'Johann Joachim Quantz's First Lesson' 81, 100; 'Johann Joachim Quantz's Five Lessons' 100; 'Language Ah Now You Have Me' 101, **122**; 'Lines on Roger Hilton's Watch' 9, **123**; 'Listen. Put on Morning' 43; 'Loch Long' 95; 'Loch Thom' 100, 128; 'The Lost Miss Conn' 79, 100, **122**, 129–30; 'The Lost Other' **46–9**, 57, 60, 132; 'The Lying Dear' 82; *Malcolm Mooney's Land* 6, 8, 9, 38, **80–99**, 100, 101, 102, 109–10, 127,

Graham, W. S.—*contd*
130–1; 'Malcolm Mooney's Land' 33–4, 35, 52, 64, 80, 82, **83–90**, 91, **93**, **95**, 100, 102, 112, 118; 'Master Cat and Master Me' 9; 'The Murdered Drinker' 79, 100, **122**, 129–30; 'The Narrator' 31, 125, 126; *The Nightfishing* 4, 10, 56, 58, **61–79**, 96, 100, 126–7, 130, 131; 'The Nightfishing' 4, 5, 16–18, 23–4, 29, 33, 54, **61–75**, 95, 121; 'O Gentle Queen of the Afternoon' **29–31**, 38, 45; 'Of the Resonant Rumour of Sun, Impulse of Summer' **26–8**; 'Over the Apparatus of the Spring is Drawn' **26–7**; 'Press Button to Hold Desired Symbol' 81; 'Private Poem to Norman Macleod' 3; 'Remarkable Report by Some Poetic Agents' **37**, 38, 39; 'The Search by a Town' 43; *Second Poems* 3, 31–2, **36–40**; 'The Secret Name' 101, **123**; 'The Serving Inhabiters' **37–8**, 62; *The Seven Journeys* 3, 24, **31–6**, 41, 65, 84, 126; 'Seven Letters' **75–8**, 80, 84; 'Sgurr Na Gillean Macleod' 128; 'Shian Bay' 44, 51, **52**, 80; 'Since All My Steps Taken' **43–4**, 96; 'The Song of the Tower' 9; 'The Street of Knives' 99; 'Ten Shots of Mister Simpson' 100, **120–1**, 128; 'The Thermal Stair' 9, 81, 123; 'Three Letters' 44, 84; 'Three Poems of Drowning' 50; 'To Alexander Graham' 128; 'To My Wife at Midnight' 25, 47, 120, **128–9**; 'Two Ballads' **78–9**; 'The Voyages of Alfred Wallis' 9, **50–1**, 123; 'What is the Language Using Us For?' 83, 100; *The White Threshold* 4, 5, 25, 34, **41–60**, 65, 80, 126, 128; 'The White Threshold' 3, 29, 33, **41–2**, **49–50**, **52–60**, 65; 'Wynter and the Grammarsow' 9, 81; 'Yours Truly' 80
Graves, Robert 93–4, 129

Heidegger, Martin 93, 101, 105–7, 108, 109, 126, 129
Heraclitus 62, 101, 107–8, 109
Hilton, Roger 8, 9, 100, 123, 130
Hopkins, Gerard Manley 19, 23, 29, 31, 48–50, 53, 55, 64, 72

Jones, David 111
Joyce, James 13, 14, 19, 22, 67, 129, 132

Kipling, Rudyard 111, 123
Koch, Vivienne 3, 4, 5, 31, 41–2, 59

Lanyon, Peter 9, 99, 123, 130
Larkin, Philip 10, 12, 13, 14
Lawrence, D. H. 19, 22, 23
Lowndes, Alan 8, 9

MacDiarmid, Hugh 2, 10–11, 40, 114, 128
Melville, Herman 41, 51, 111
Montgomerie, Alexander 111, 112–13
Montgomerie, William 32, 111, 113
Morgan, Edwin 63, 69, 70
'Movement, the' 12–15, 18–19, 22–3, 130, 132

Nansen, F. 35, 63, 64, 84, 85–6, 111
Neo-Romanticism 19, 23, 24, 130

O'Malley, Tony 9, 81

Plato 62, 67–8, 73
politics 43, 45–6, 81, 91–2, 121, 130
Pound, Ezra 13, 14, 19, 126, 132; Graham and 10, 63, 64–5, 112, 125, 129

Rahner, Hugo 63–4, 72
religion and religious imagery 22, 23–4, 39, 48, 50, 58–9, 63–4, 71–3, 115, 117, 122
Rimbaud, J. N. Arthur 23, 28, 31, 34, 41, 111, 126

Schmidt, Michael 10, 27
'Scottish Renaissance' 11, 21–2, 24, 31, 128
Shakespeare, William 114–15, 116, 118, 119, 129, 131
Shelley, Percy Bysshe 111, 121–2
Skelton, Robin 6–7
Surrealism 19–20, 22, 24, 35

Tambimuttu 3, 11
Thomas, Dylan 5, 14, 15, 19, 20–2, 23; Graham and 23, 26, 27–8, 29, 31, 45, 54, 64, 104, 113, 130
Treece, Henry 19, 20–1, 29

Wain, John 12, 14
Wallis, Alfred 9, 50–1
Wynter, Bryan 8, 9, 100, 123, 130

Yeats, William Butler, 13–14, 19, 22